# Integrating Faith and Psychology

## Twelve Psychologists
## Tell Their Stories

Edited by **Glendon L. Moriarty**

Foreword by **Gary R. Collins**

## IVP Academic

An imprint of InterVarsity Press
Downers Grove, Illinois

*InterVarsity Press*
*P.O. Box 1400, Downers Grove, IL 60515-1426*
*World Wide Web: www.ivpress.com*
*E-mail: email@ivpress.com*

*InterVarsity Press* ® *is the book-publishing division of InterVarsity Christian Fellowship/USA* ® *, a movement of students and faculty active on campus at hundreds of universities, colleges and schools of nursing in the United States of America, and a member movement of the International Fellowship of Evangelical Students. For information about local and regional activities, write Public Relations Dept., InterVarsity Christian Fellowship/USA, 6400 Schroeder Rd., P.O. Box 7895, Madison, WI 53707-7895, or visit the IVCF website at <www.intervarsity.org>.*

*All Scripture quotations, unless otherwise indicated, are taken from the* Holy Bible, New International Version®. NIV®. *Copyright ©1973, 1978, 1984 by International Bible Society. Used by permission of Zondervan Publishing House. All rights reserved.*

*Design: Cindy Kiple*
*Images: Leontura/iStockphoto*

*ISBN 978-0-8308-3885-1*

*Printed in the United States of America* ∞

**Library of Congress Cataloging-in-Publication Data**

*Integrating faith and psychology: twelve psychologists tell their*
*stories/edited by Glendon L. Moriarty.*
      *p. cm.*
   *Includes bibliographical references and index.*
   *ISBN 978-0-8308-3885-1 (pbk.: alk. paper)*
   *1. Christian biography. 2. Psychologists—Biography. 3*
   *Christianity—Psychology. 4. Psychology and religion.  I. Moriarty,*
   *Glendon.*
      *BR1702.I55 2010*
      *261.5'15—dc22*

*2010014317*

| P | 19 | 18 | 17 | 16 | 15 | 14 | 13 | 12 | 11 | 10 | 9 | 8 | 7 | 6 | 5 | 4 | 3 | 2 | 1 |
|---|----|----|----|----|----|----|----|----|----|----|---|---|---|---|---|---|---|---|---|
| Y | 25 | 24 | 23 | 22 | 21 | 20 | 19 | 18 | 17 | 16 | 15 | 14 | 13 | 12 | 11 | 10 | | | | |

To Michael, Marcella, Michelle and Edith;

Thank you for being part of my journey.

And, in memory of Leonard Valliere:

A joyous, affirming and gracious man.

# Contents

# Foreword

More than fifty years have passed since I walked onto the campus of McMaster University in Canada and met for the first time with my advisor. I had never been in a professor's office before so I was more than a little overwhelmed. When he informed me that all freshmen were required to take either psychology or philosophy I didn't know the difference, so I chose psychology because I liked the class schedule better. I've been in psychology—the field of study, not that freshman class—ever since. It has been a great career ride.

This book is a collection of stories about the career rides of a dozen Christian psychologists. All took time from busy schedules to reflect on their life journeys. All have written as active professionals whose careers are still growing and evolving. These are contemporary perspectives on psychology and Christianity—perspectives that can inform, inspire and encourage new generations of Christian caregivers. Before we move into these mini-autobiographies, however, might there be value in considering some of the foundations on which this whole contemporary integration venture was built? At times an awareness of history can enlighten the present and give clearer insights for the future.

## LATE-TWENTIETH-CENTURY FOUNDATIONS OF INTEGRATION

In the years following World War II, psychology students like me learned a lot about Skinner and the many psychological studies of white rats and college students—the two most manageable and readily available sources of research subjects at the time. We didn't learn much about religion except that it was passé according to Freud, an illusion with a declining future. At times I wondered how psychology could be useful in the ministry of the church where I grew up, but nobody in psychology or in my church seemed interested in addressing questions like that. This was not exactly the dinosaur age, but at the time there were no computers, no organizations or conferences of Christian counselors, no Christian graduate schools of psychology, few courses in counseling for seminary students, and only one trained Christian psychologist that I knew about—a writer and radio speaker in California named Clyde Narramore.

After graduate school and a year or two working in a counseling center, I joined the world of academia. Before long I found myself being pulled into a mostly unnoticed war. This was not the *Saving Private Ryan* kind of war that my graduate school classmates and I knew about as kids. This was different from the cold war that occupied the attention of our political leaders and politicians. The war I met early in my career was more like an academic skirmish about psychology. When I heard about the fray I jumped in, and so did a few others with names that rarely or never get mentioned today in classrooms or in books like this one.

The psychology war was fought on two fronts. On one side were the academic psychologists and other mental health professionals at odds about the value and place of religion. William James, G. Stanley Hall (founder and first president of the APA) and other early pioneers in psychology saw value in religion. Later APA presidents like O. Hobart Mowrer, Gordon Allport and Paul Meehl also took a positive view. In contrast, B. F. Skinner and the behaviorists saw no need for religion in scientific psychology. Freud had viewed religion as evidence of pathology, and most psychologists agreed. Outspoken critics like Albert Ellis were articulate in their opposition, although Ellis modified his stance later in life. More common, perhaps, were people like one of my clinical supervisors who was highly critical of me (that is putting it mildly—she was livid) because I made the mistake of taking a patient's religious concerns seriously without acknowledging the supervisor's position that "talk about religion is always pathological." Nicholas Cummings, another former APA president, coedited a book that described much of this as *Psychology's War on Religion.*

In those days, Christian mental health professionals went to professional meetings, like we do now, and tried to do their work as competently as possible. My professors and non-Christian colleagues were gracious and willing to accept that I had religious beliefs. But sometimes I wondered if we Christians were perceived as part of a pre-scientific era that would pass as we all grew up and discovered the value of human progress without beliefs in a fictional god or the need for religious crutches. Today, of course, there is more openness to spirituality, loosely defined, and even a greater tolerance for the value of religion. But that is a relatively recent development for mainstream psychology.

If one side of the war was represented in a book titled *Psychology's War on Religion,* the other side might be characterized as *Religion's War on Psychology.* I don't know of any one book with that title, but there were a number of individual books written by fundamentalist or evangelical writers, most critical of psychology, and many willing to attack those of us who wanted to be both competent professionals and committed followers of Jesus Christ.

The attacks had been going on for years, but the battle lines were sharpened when Jay Adams wrote a book titled *Competent to Counsel* in the late 1960s. He argued that the only people competent to counsel are (male) pastors who have completed seminary. As part of the book, he condemned most psychological theories and principles, concluding that all problems (except those with a physical basis) come from sin in the counselee's life. Jay's directive approach was labeled *nouthetic* counseling. It involved confession of sin by the counselee and a commitment to change and to live in accordance with biblical principles. In response to the then-prevailing assumption that pastors should refer difficult cases to therapists, Dr. Adams proclaimed that pastors alone are competent to counsel. After reading the manuscript I was among those who urged Jay not to publish the book, but he chose to publish it anyway. The book became a bestseller and launched a movement that still is strong, especially in many conservative churches and seminaries around the world.

In the years that followed, Jay Adams wrote other books, some of which criticized psychologists by name. He became well known on the speaking circuit and, more than anybody else, galvanized thousands of Christians, especially pastors, against psychology and the work that many of us were doing. We were trying to bring psychology and the Bible together to improve counseling, help people and assist pastors in their ministries. Adams was arguing that by bringing psychology into the mix we were doing more harm than good, and replacing scriptural principles with the humanistic teachings of secular psychology. In time the nouthetic counselors took on the name *biblical counseling* and referred to the rest of us as integrationists. Presumably that would include most or all of those whose writings form the core of this book.

As Dr. Adams has grown older, he has left the leadership of his movement to well-informed, less militant but equally committed voices. When he stood alone, undoubtedly he felt the need to be strong in his assertions. Those of us who were criticized read his books and learned from his writings, even though we disagreed with much of what he wrote. But the anti-psychology war that swirled around in the seventies and early 1980s was more vehement than anything that came from psychologists attacking religion. The Christian psychological community was stirred to action. We fought for our cause in classrooms, lectures, Christian talk shows, churches and the pages of books and journals. The anti-psychology forces fought back.

Some of the book titles tell the story. David Hunt, for example, was a cult expert who coauthored strongly worded books about the New Age movement with its roots in Eastern mysticism and its embrace of psychology. He acknowledged that many Christian psychologists were "sincere and dedicated servants of the Lord whose lives and ministries influence millions." But he saw us as victims and maybe naive accomplices of the seductive sorceries that were sweeping the culture and bringing a Trojan horse of pagan psychological teachings into the church. Hunt was joined by Martin and Deidre Bobgan, who described

Christian therapy as *psychoheresy* and called this "the psychological seduction of Christianity." In *Prophets of Psychoheresy I,* they took on four
integrationists, including Lawrence Crabb, Paul Meier and Frank
Minirth. They began the book with several chapters about a guy named
Gary Collins.

I hesitate to continue the list lest it appear that many of us were on
the defensive—and may still be there today. But we felt as strongly
about the value of psychology and counseling as our critics believed in
the dangers. A book titled *Psychological Seduction: The Failure of Modern
Psychology* described two kinds of faith: faith in God and faith in psychology. The author sought to "disentangle Christianity from the psychological religion." A different writer described the world of psychology and the work of Christians in the field as *psychobabble.* Another
wrote *The Emperor's New Clothes: The Naked Truth About the New Psychology.* The author of a book titled *Christian Psychology: The Evil Within*
circulated a brochure proclaiming that Jim Dobson and other Christian
psychologists were "blaspheming the Holy Spirit." When I countered
with a book titled *Can You Trust Psychology?* a rebuttal book appeared
titled *Why Christians Can't Trust Psychology.*

Sometimes hanging in was tough, especially when fellow believers
felt called to undermine what we felt called to do. We agreed with a lot
of what the critics wrote about disturbing psychological conclusions
that were both critical of Christianity and growing in popularity. We
had read similar critiques in our own professional journals and even in
books by insightful psychologists and psychiatrists who challenged
their own professions. We tried to write in less bombastic ways, arguing that God, in his wisdom, may have given us psychological principles
that were consistent with Scripture and useful for bringing help and
healing. John White, a Christian psychiatrist in Western Canada,
wrote more balanced books about the debates. *The Integration of Psychology and Theology* by John Carter and Bruce Narramore rose to become a classic textbook that still is influential. I wrote a few books in
this area myself, including one that urged Christian psychologists to
rebuild their field and methodologies on biblical foundations.

Many counselors and pastors were involved in these discussions, and a few who were prominent include Paul Tournier, Lee Travis, Newton Maloney, Kirk Farnsworth and Dick Mohline. Some were more scholarly and academic, like Paul Vitz. Other Christians in psychology and pastoral counseling—David Seamands, Larry Crabb, John Townsend, Henry Cloud, Dan Allender, Siang-Yang Tan, Les Parrott, among others—were less involved in the battles but went on to more practical issues. The integration movement began the shift to a younger, more pragmatic, less theoretical generation.

## TWENTY-FIRST-CENTURY DIRECTIONS
## FOR INTEGRATION

From my perspective, this history provides the background and foundation for the chapters of this book. In the earlier days of integration there were a variety of leaders with different levels and types of training, different personalities, different callings. The same is true of the insightful men and women who tell their stories in the pages that follow. They embody a second generation of integrationists. They tell their stories, unencumbered by documentation and the parameters of APA writing styles. They know that in telling stories there may be no better way to communicate their experiences, struggles, concerns, hopes and perspectives.

Not all of the second-generation leaders could be included in this book, but the writers who are here give living examples of what others have done and are doing to bring their professions and their beliefs together. These writers walk alongside innumerable unrecognized psychological and counseling practitioners and pioneers who do their work away from the public spotlight. They rarely get noticed except by their students and by God. A few of these unseen integrationists may be assigning this book for their classes to read. All have stories that could be included in these pages. I hope many of these tell their own stories in classes so students can learn how their own professors have walked the integration journey.

In time, this picture of the present will be replaced by a new generation. Some of the coming leaders appear already on the horizon. Perhaps a few of these will share their own stories in some future book, years from now. Hopefully their numbers will include a greater number of emerging leaders, male and female, who are neither white nor American.

All of us have been called to bring together our faith and our professions in ways that honor God and impact lives. This book can be a guide as we ponder what has gone on in the past and rejoice in what God is doing in the present. Even more, I hope that the following pages stimulate and give enthusiastic encouragement to those who are emerging as caregivers who love Jesus and are learning to bring their insights and compassion to the world where we are privileged to live and serve. I am honored to write this foreword and to give my warm endorsement to this book.

*Gary R. Collins*
*Regent University*
*Richmont Graduate University*

# Acknowledgments

There are many people who helped this book become a reality. First, I want to thank the contributors. Many of them stated that writing their chapters was much more challenging than they initially expected. Thank you for pushing through and sharing your stories with us. I also want to thank Gary Collins. He is mentioned numerous times throughout this book. He is a mentor to many. Gary's fingerprints are all over the integration field. He may not like this term, but he is clearly one of the "grandfathers" of integration. Gary, thank you for your friendship and for graciously agreeing to write the foreword.

Second, I want to thank my colleagues at Regent University. I am delighted to be part of this team. Thank you for your support. Bill Hathaway and Judy Johnson, thank you for your ongoing leadership and for your efforts in helping me become a better leader.

Third, I am thankful to my students. Ward Davis, teaching assistant extraordinaire, has been very helpful in the copy editing process and also in providing feedback throughout this project. Elizabeth Anderson and the students in my practica classes have also been very helpful. Thank you for being my focus group as I refined the ideas behind this book.

Fourth and finally, I want to thank my lovely wife, Nicole. Thank you for making our home a garden that is bursting with life. I love seeing our children learn and grow. You are a tremendous gift. Thank you also to Colin, Madeleine and Avery. I love you guys!

**1**

# Introduction

## Catching Integration

*Glendon L. Moriarty, Regent University*

It was February 2005. I was at work and my wife, Nicole, called my cell. She was pregnant and had gone in for a doctor's appointment that morning. I picked up the phone. She was crying. I could not tell if they were happy or sad tears. Through the tears she said, "We are having twins." We both rejoiced. Her mother, Wendy, had boy twins, so we knew it was a possibility. However, Nicole's first ultrasound indicated just one child, so the idea that there was another one was a huge surprise.

Fast forward to April 2005; I'm at work and my wife calls me on my cell. She went in for a routine doctor's appointment, but it turned out that her water had partially broken. This was a crisis. If the twins came now, then they would likely not survive. It was much too early.

Nicole held on for six more weeks. She was on bed rest and in and out of the hospital, doing everything she could to give the twins more time. On our fifth trip to the hospital, the lead doctor decided there was no turning back. She had dilated too much and the twins were going to be delivered no matter what. They had to do a C-section and deliver the twins even though it was only week 29 of her 40-week pregnancy. On May 7 at 8:35 p.m., Colin and Madeleine were delivered. Colin was 3 pounds, 5 ounces, and Madeleine was 2 pounds, 10 ounces. They were extremely little, but they came out screaming and breathing on their own, which was a very good sign.

They were immediately transferred to the Level II nursery. They were placed in separate isolates, connected to monitors, and given oxygen to help them breathe. We were dumbfounded. Nicole was wheeled to her room to recover from the surgery. I went down and looked at the twins. I was in a complete state of shock. They did not look good. The picture I had in my head was nothing like what I was seeing. I went back to see Nicole to assure her that everything was okay. I did my best to look strong. I got back to the room, and Nicole said that despite what I was saying, I looked scared and worried. At that point, I made an uncon-scious switch. My denial mechanisms kicked in and I began to minimize the gravity of the situation. I needed to be strong. Nicole was barraged by post-pregnancy hormones, grief and pain from the surgery. She could not contain her initial feelings. The shock set in on both of us.

Weeks went by. Nicole would visit them several hours throughout the day. I would go see them before or after work. It was terrifying to see them. They had trouble getting enough oxygen at times; sometimes their heart rates would fall too low; Madeleine had a couple of infec-tions; and Colin could not seem to get enough juice to keep his system up without assistance. It was two steps forward, one step back. This went on for six weeks, but they were finally strong enough to leave the nursery and join us. This homecoming was cause for cautious celebra-tion. We were almost out of the woods.

Colin and Madeleine continued to struggle with typical premature birth issues for the first eighteen months of their lives. They would get sick easier and stay ill longer than other children. They had a harder time keeping food down. They were a bit delayed in meeting their milestones. They were significantly smaller than other children their age. However, by the time they went to see their developmental spe-cialist for their eighteen-month check up, they had covered lost ground and were fully caught up to their nonpremature peers. We were ecstatic. Our family had made it through the most challenging obstacle we had ever faced.

Facing and working through this entire time really affected me. I felt helpless and out of control. We reached out to God and petitioned him to protect and save our children. We asked him to guide the nurses and doctors; to put his hands on Colin and Madeleine and to strengthen their minds and bodies. We asked family and friends to pray for them. Prayer chains were called, pictures of the twins distributed, and God was asked by thousands to intervene. He did.

However, God does not always intervene in ways that I might hope or expect. I learned this lesson when I was sixteen years old. I lost my grandfather to a tragic neurological disorder—Huntington's Disease. At that point in my life, I was part of a nondenominational church that firmly believed in healing. My pastor preached that healing was absolutely the will of God and that if we just had faith, then healing would come about in the lives of those for whom we prayed. My grandfather was remarkably special to me. He helped raise me as an infant and was extremely close to me throughout my childhood. I had a close bond with him and was strongly attached to him. At that time, I believed with every fiber in my being that he could be healed.

When my grandfather continued to decline and eventually passed on, I grew very angry and frustrated with God. His untimely death was a tragic injustice. This loss shook my faith to its core. I believe that God could have reached out and saved my grandfather, but, for whatever reason, he did not. It seemed terribly unfair. This was devastating, but through this process I learned what Isaiah meant when he penned: "'For my thoughts are not your thoughts, neither are your ways my ways,' declares the LORD. 'As the heavens are higher than the earth, so are my ways higher than your ways and my thoughts than your thoughts'" (Isaiah 55:8-9). I came to deeply understand that God often works mysteriously and in ways that my finite mind cannot even begin to comprehend.

I went into the situation with the twins with this same mindset. I wanted desperately for God to intervene, but I recognized that he might not—he might allow them to suffer. I did not know what was going to happen. I urgently wanted them to be healthy and strong, just as I wanted my grandfather to be healthy and strong, but I was not sure what the outcome would be.

I prayed and poured all of my energy into everything that I could to insure their health. However, I recognized that my efforts were limited. Their resources were also limited. They were struggling and trying to make it, but their little bodies could only do so much. God, as always, was in full control. I didn't know which way it would break. On the one hand, death was a possibility. On the other hand, the twins could be healthy and fine—like "normal" kids. As you might imagine, this uncertainty was extraordinarily stressful for Nicole and me. We didn't know how the twins would be—they could fall anywhere along the spectrum of death and abundant life.

The beautiful thing was that I could trust. I know, as with my grandfather, that God would not leave us alone in this time of struggle. He would support us and give us the strength to courageously face whatever happened.

In the end, he gave us the strength to rise above the challenges that faced us. He protected our children and empowered them to overcome. For months following their birth, whenever the song by Chumba Wumba would come on the radio, with the chorus, "I get knocked down, but I get up again, you are never going to keep me down," I would think of the twins, their fighting spirit, and I would get choked up.

We also felt great support from our family and friends. Brennan Manning (2000) argued that the greatest sin is self-sufficiency, and that is certainly one of my chief sins. However, in the position that Nicole and I were in, we had no choice but to depend on others. We needed the prayers and support of our family and friends to make it through.

What did I learn from this process? I learned in a deep and implicit way that no matter the situation, no matter my negative feelings and anger, God will never abandon me. In my heart, I concurred with St. Paul:

> For I am convinced that neither death nor life, neither angels nor demons, neither the present nor the future, nor any powers, neither height nor depth, nor anything else in all creation, will be able to separate us from the love of God that is in Christ Jesus our Lord. (Romans 8:38-39)

I also learned that my family and colleagues deeply love me and support my family. They cooked, prayed, emailed, visited and called us regularly. They were Christ's hands and feet to us. This trying situation enabled me to gain faith in God and God's children. I am convinced that I would not have learned this without this trying experience.

These events also impacted my understanding of the integration of psychology and Christianity, particularly the way that I look at pain and suffering. I feel that God can remove hardships from our lives, but often he does not. He allows us to experience suffering in order to help us grow and become more like him. This assumption colors how I relate with clients, students and colleagues. I agree with M. Scott Peck (2003) that psychological and spiritual difficulties arise when we try to avoid, ignore or minimize the genuine struggles we face in life. Counterintuitively, growth occurs through facing and successfully working through difficulties. I believe that God is with us in our suffering. He does not remove our trials; instead, he walks alongside us as we face them—together. Through this process, we grow psychologically and spiritually. In other words, we become sanctified.

Why did I share this story and these thoughts with you? I shared them because I believe that hearing them allows you to learn something about the integration of psychology and Christianity that you cannot learn from a class or a book that describes the theoretical or technical aspects of integration. The late Randall Sorenson captured this approach when he said, "The integration of psychology and Christianity is *caught*, not *taught*." My narrative makes it personal. The raw story communicates in an intimate manner—in a way that theological discussion cannot. Here, my stories facilitate a personal exploration of the problem of evil and the role of suffering in faith and psychology.

I could write about these concepts from an in-depth psychological or theological perspective. For example, I could talk about different ways to resolve the problem of evil: a good, but limited God; a God that is both good and evil; a good and loving God that operates above human understanding. However, I have found that often what affects us the most is hearing other people's stories. There is something so powerful and profound about someone sharing personal narratives with you. For this reason, I have asked several key figures in the field of Christian integration to share with us about their "integration journey." I believe that you can better understand and explore issues of Christian integration by hearing about where these individuals are, have come from and are going in their journey as Christians and as Christian integrationists. Hopefully as you are finding your own way you will be able to both identify with aspects of their journey and respond to their advice and exhortation.

There is a fair amount of research that supports this narrative approach (Epstein & Pacini, 2000; Kirkpatrick & Epstein, 1992; Bucci, 2000). I'm not going to delve too deeply into that here, but will include a few quick anecdotes to further underline my point. I teach in the School of Psychology and Counseling at Regent University. I thoroughly enjoy my job and like to believe that what I teach gets internalized and implemented in the lives of my students. I thoughtfully craft my PowerPoint presentations and carefully pick my texts and course readings. I'm mildly obsessive, so I put a fair amount of thought into this process. My main concepts, or course objectives, are clearly spelled out in the syllabus and carefully measured and achieved by the end of the semester. I reiterate salient ideas relentlessly over the course of the semester, and by the end of our time together, typically the students have a strong grasp of at least these basic concepts.

Often I will ask my students about these main concepts about six to twelve months after the class has ended. Do they remember them? Unfortunately, no, they do not remember them. They act like they do, and they may even throw in a few key words, but it is clear that the cobwebs have spread. The concepts that were once crystal clear are now covered in dust and pushed into the back of their minds.

This discovery used to really surprise me. I used all kinds of fancy pedagogical techniques to make the information more "sticky." This strategy has tended to increase students' ability to remember the knowledge, but has not been nearly as effective as their ability to remember a personal story, movie, myth or parable.

In short, we are simply wired to learn through stories (McAdams, 1993). Our ancestors passed on knowledge through the oral tradition, and I do not think it is any accident that the Bible is a rich and detailed narrative. Personal stories are easy to identify with. We do not have to try to remember them. Unfortunately, students have to deliberately learn my course information. I wish it would naturally be internalized, but we just do not work that way.

This bias of mine—this preference for personal narrative—has led me to structure this book in a way that I think will naturally teach integration. The field of Christian integration is already quite rich. For example, there are a number of stellar texts that describe the theoretical, philosophical, technical and theological foundations of integration (Carter & Narramore, 1979; Jones & Butman, 1991; McMinn & Campbell, 2007). Similarly, there are more and more books that focus on techniques and interventions (Moriarty, 2006; Moriarty & Hoffman, 2007). However, to my knowledge there is nothing currently available that illustrates integration in the kind of personal, intimate manner that characterizes this book.

Toward this end, I asked twelve leading scholars in the integration field to write about their own spiritual journeys, personally and professionally speaking. I deliberately sought out authors with different perspectives and experiences, reflecting gender and ethnic diversity. These authors are considered to be the foremost clinicians and academics in the field of Christian integration. Each of these contributors was asked to share their thoughts on the following components of their spiritual journey.

## DEVELOPMENT

In this section, contributors discuss significant psychological and spiritual experiences they had in childhood, adolescence and early adulthood. In addition, they share their thoughts on having a sense of calling, along with any early career insights they achieved.

## MENTORING

Here contributors explore how significant relationships have impacted their understanding of Christian integration. Psychology and Christianity are both fundamentally relational, so particular attention is focused on influential mentoring relationships.

## STRUGGLES

Another key part of coming to a solid and tested view of integration is overcoming personal and philosophical struggles. Thus, in this section, contributors openly discuss their struggles and doubts, in order to provide encouragement to others who are working through similar issues.

## SPIRITUAL DISCIPLINES

Many Christian psychologists have experienced significant spiritual encounters with God. These numinous experiences are often powerful and influential in their lives. Similarly, on a more day-to-day basis, Christian psychologists practice spiritual disciplines, such as Bible reading, church attendance and contemplative prayer. Here contributors share how these felt experiences of God and spiritual disciplines shaped, and continue to shape, their understanding of integration.

## THERAPY

Integration occurs in the relationship between client and therapist. It gets worked out in the mind of the therapist, but it gets tested and refined through the therapeutic alliance with the client. In this section, contributors share insights they have gleaned therapeutically, both as clients and as therapists.

## LETTER

The final section of each chapter, and perhaps the most potentially influential, is a letter. Contributors wrote personal letters to readers, sharing lessons learned and wise advice. They considered the following questions: What do you wish your mentors/professors would have told you when you started this career? What recommendations do you have for Christian counselors engaged in clinical practice? In other words, this letter is meant to wrap up each contributor's spiritual autobiography and provide the reader with a warm and relevant note they can reference as they walk on their own integration journey.

My main goal in using this chapter template is to provide you with an opportunity to compare how different people have passed through these stations in life. I want you to benefit from the candid thoughts of each contributor, so that you can better understand hurdles you have already overcome and can manage obstacles that you might face in the future.

Many of you have had the benefit of mentors who have shared their wisdom and lives with you. Many of you have not. This book is meant to be a companion or a guide—a close friend that you can reference as you work through a difficult personal situation or try to resolve a theological puzzle, particularly as it relates to your work as a Christian clinician.

Thank you for taking the time to walk down this path with me. It is my sincere prayer that you will find wisdom, guidance, comfort and peace in the stories that follow. I would also love for you to share stories from your integration journey with us at www.psychologycrossroads.ning.com. At this website, you can share your stories, experiences and insights. You can also ask questions and support others in their integration journey.

## REFERENCES

Bucci, W. (2000). The need for a "psychoanalytic psychology" in the cognitive science field. *Psychoanalytic Psychology, 17,* 203-24.

Carter, J. D., & Narramore, S. B. (1979). *The integration of psychology and theology.* Grand Rapids, MI: Zondervan.

Epstein, S., & Pacini, R. (2000). The influence of visualization on intuitive and analytical information processing. *Imagination, Cognition and Personality, 20,* 195-216.

Jones, S. L., & Butman, R. E. (1991). *Modern psychotherapies.* Downers Grove, IL: InterVarsity Press.

Kirkpatrick, L. A., & Epstein, S. (1992). Cognitive-experiential self-theory and subjective probability: Further evidence for two conceptual systems. *Journal of Personality and Social Psychology, 63,* 534-44.

Manning, B. (2000). *The ragamuffin gospel.* Sisters, OR: Multnomah Press.

McAdams, D. P. (1993). *The stories we live by: Personal myths and the making of the self.* New York: Guilford Press.

McMinn, M. R., & Campbell, C. D. (2007). *Integrative psychotherapy: Toward a comprehensive Christian approach.* Downers Grove, IL: InterVarsity Press.

Moriarty, G. (2006). *Pastoral care of depression: Helping clients heal their emotional experience of God.* New York: Haworth.

Moriarty, G. L., & Hoffman, L. (Eds.). (2007). *God image handbook for spiritual counseling and psychotherapy: Research, theory, and practice.* Binghamton, NY: Haworth/Routledge.

Peck, M. S. (2003). *The road less traveled.* New York: Touchstone Books.

# 2

# Surprised by Grace

## God's Faithfulness in Developing a Christian Psychologist

*Everett L. Worthington Jr.*
*Virginia Commonwealth University*

In the 1970s, Kirby (my wife) and I got lost on Mt. Rainier at dusk. We were picking fresh blueberries. When we realized we had been following a deer trail instead of a marked trail, we tried to compensate by bushwhacking across country. We missed the way home. I remember the panic of wandering over a mountain and through thick brush. Eventually, we made our way to the top of a mountain. From there we could look back and see where we had deviated from the path and where we had chosen wisely to climb the hill for a better view.

That experience on the mountain is similar to other experiences in our spiritual life. Going through life, we often feel as though we are whacking through impenetrable underbrush. But from a spiritual vantage point, looking back, we often can see the surprising hand of God—how it led us in ways that now seem clear, but then were anything but clear. We are truly surprised by God.

## DEVELOPMENT

We were poor, but not dirt-floor poor. Daddy and Mama both came from coal-mining towns in East Tennessee. I was the oldest of three children. When I was six years old, my mother, a stay-at-home mother, disappeared.

"Your mama's in the state mental hospital," my aunt said. "You'll be staying with us until she gets out. She's feeling sad." As a psychologist, I later figured out that my mother was hospitalized for unipolar depression—the first of three hospitalizations, each requiring electroconvulsive therapy.

My father was perhaps one of the brightest people I have ever known, yet he felt trapped because he had he failed to use his intellect. A railroad man who was on the road three of every four days, he started drinking. By the time I was in the seventh grade, he had become a full-blown alcoholic. He became sarcastic, often mean and unpredictable. Even when he was not drinking, he had a deep-seated disappointment in himself.

With an often-depressed mother and alcoholic father, my childhood was often sad, but there were beautiful moments. I can still remember my mother washing dishes or making beds and singing Southern Baptist songs: "What a Friend We Have in Jesus," "I Come to the Garden Alone," "The Old Rugged Cross." Those songs got into my heart and created a longing for God. When I was about eight, I started walking (about three miles) to church with my younger brother. I was searching for the way home through some thick family underbrush.

As a psychologist, looking back, I see that I had little sense of attachment to any adults. The role of eldest son in my family meant that, on the one hand, I spent a lot of time being a peacemaker. On the other hand, I felt unofficially deputized to redeem the family. My parents must have said 10,000 times, "Education is the way out of poverty." My goal became to get a master's degree in engineering from MIT and then an M.B.A. from Harvard Business School. Then I could (as my parents said), "write my own ticket." But it felt more like writing someone else's ticket—being a redemptive banner for the family.

I pursued that plan. I got a B.S. in nuclear engineering at the University of Tennessee, Knoxville, and an M.S. in nuclear engineering from MIT, and was admitted with a fellowship to Harvard Business School. But Vietnam interceded, and I was commissioned as a naval officer in February 1970. I planned to gather technical management experience in the Naval Nuclear Reactors program. God had other plans. He surprised me by sending me to teach nuclear physics at the Naval Nuclear Power program in Vallejo, California.

I was married soon thereafter (August 1970) to Kirby, which was a crucial event and relationship in my spiritual journey. Kirby was a Christian. Although I knew God the Father, I did not understand the importance of Jesus. But God was merciful, and he permitted me (in my unbelief) to marry a beautiful Christian woman. I believe that God had miraculously blinded her to the verse about not being unequally yoked to non-Christians (2 Corinthians 6:14). I was extremely blessed to marry Kirby. Because I had few emotional bonds with my parents, and those I had were unreliable, Kirby became my first strong and enduring adult attachment figure. She was a way that Jesus was calling me through the tangled underbrush of external achievement toward a higher place.

At the same time that God was using Kirby to draw me to him, my Senior Division Officer during my first year in the Navy invited Kirby and me to a marriage enrichment course at St. Paul's Lutheran Church. Although I didn't know it at the time, that experience of marriage enrichment in a Christian context took me toward Christianity, set our marriage on a positive course, directed me further toward Jesus, and sowed the seeds of my later desire to develop Hope-Focused Marriage Enrichment (to help others similarly).

*Three conversions.* Near Christmas in 1970, I asked Pastor Tom Allport, a loving exemplar of Christianity, how I might become a Christian. He suggested I pray Mark 9:24, "I do believe; help me overcome my unbelief!" I prayed it often. By Christmas 1970, I yielded my will to Jesus. I had little understanding of what I had done, but I believe that my will was converted.

I was baptized and quickly became involved in the church activities. One night, Pastor Tom handed me a book to read and summarize for him, Dr. D. James Kennedy's *Evangelism Explosion*. That night I read Kennedy's method. He asked people, "If you were to die tonight and God asked why you should be admitted to heaven, what would you say?" He said that many people answer that they tried to live a virtuous life. I silently nodded assent. Then Kennedy said, "Of course, this is absolutely wrong."

I snapped alert. Kennedy then explained how Jesus' death redeems us. For the first time I really heard the gospel. Although I had attended a Southern Baptist church growing up, my ears had been closed. Until the Holy Spirit opens our eyes to see and ears to hear, we truly are blind and deaf. Lying in bed, I understood that Jesus died for all (me included), and that faith applied his death to the believer. My mind was converted.

Kirby and I co-led the youth group at St. Paul's. In the spring of 1971, we took them to a conference in Southern California. During that week, I was a leader of break-out sessions, and youths were randomly assigned to break-out groups. When my group convened, the "youths" I was supposed to mentor were (1) a Lutheran pastor, (2) a head elder, (3) a missionary and (4) a Christian college student—a strange collection of "youths." On the last night of the conference, I brought up something that had puzzled me. "The speaker kept talking about having a personal relationship with Jesus," I said, "but I don't understand what that means."

There was silence in the group. I could feel the pastor's head turn in my direction. "Would you like to understand?" he said. "Why don't we go to one of the conference rooms upstairs?" We wound our way through the crowd of teens, and by the time we arrived at the room, there must have been twenty-five people with us. We sat in a circle, and the Pastor explained his understanding of having a personal relationship with Jesus. He asked whether we could pray that I would experience such a personal relationship with Jesus. We held hands, closed our eyes and prayed silently.

Such is the depth of my spiritual maturity that my thought processes were as follows: *These people seem sincere, but I am skeptical about their sincerity. So I am going to do a test. I am going to open my eyes and look around. If any of them are peeking, I will know that they are not sincere.* I snapped my head up, opened my eyes and looked quickly around the circle. Every person was fervently praying for me. I started laughing. I couldn't seem to stop. I felt joy enter my life that I had never really known. I felt that I really understood who Jesus was and that I was experiencing his joy. I must have laughed for ten minutes. My emotions had been converted.

*The charismatic renewal and a fourth conversion.* Around 1970, the charismatic movement exploded in California. It was an exciting time even though I was not fully enthralled by some of the charismatic elements. Healing, miracles and signs seemed to be everywhere.

At a New Years Eve party in 1971, a tall, middle-aged man introduced himself to me. "My name is Nick," he said. "I am dead." As an opening conversational gambit, that won the prize for the night—maybe for my life. I asked him to explain.

Nick had been a Navy Warrant Officer. He contracted an aggressive form of cancer. The Navy doctors knew that his end was near, so they discharged him and declared him officially dead. His wife and children began to receive survivor's benefits. They moved to Ashland, Oregon, to spend Nick's last days. One night, Nick was in his car reading his Bible, and he came upon James 5:14-16. He immediately went into the house and phoned his pastor. His pastor answered groggily.

Nick said, "Do you know what it says in the Bible?"

"Can you be a little more specific than that, Nick?"

"In James, it says, If anyone among you is sick let him call for the elders of the church. They will anoint him with oil in the name of the Lord and pray the prayer of faith, and he will be healed."

The pastor told Nick that in modern day, that is referred to as "last unction." "That means that, when someone is dying, we pray this prayer."

Nick said, "That's not what it says. Read the verse aloud." A few minutes later, the pastor said he would round up some elders. That night, Nick was healed.

During those days of the charismatic renewal, amazing healings and miracles were occurring, and occasionally I was blessed to be present as God healed or worked a miracle. In our small congregation at St. Paul's, we had five documented healings. I believe that those signs and wonders that accompanied the charismatic renewal were ways that Christ strengthened that entire generation for some of the political and public battles of the 1980s and 1990s. God was showing that he worked in the world today. Those experiences converted my sense of Jesus' miracle-working presence.

As I reflect on my conversion to Christianity and my process of trying to understand Jesus, I see it as a series of surprises. As I wandered through the forest, the way home was opened to me not all at once, but step by step. It was exactly what I needed. By personality, I like to stay in control as much as possible. But my conversion of the will came through the surprise of simple faith. My conversions of mind, emotion and spirit were just as sudden, just as unexpected.

## MENTORING

God had begun to bring stable Christian role models into my life, but I had no mentor who helped me integrate psychology, psychotherapy, theology and faith in my studies. My graduate school advisor encouraged my scientific pursuits, but I mostly learned to integrate psychology and theology through reading. Authors were my mentors.

In 1974, the University of Missouri, Columbia (UMC) was hostile to the public expression of religious beliefs and values. When training at its militantly secular university counseling center, I was trying to formulate my approach to psychology and therapy, but with no Christian psychologists available to talk to during those four years, my development in integration depended on "conversations" with authors. I pulled together ideas from Christian existential philosophy (e.g., psychiatrist Paul Tournier), from Reformed (e.g., Francis Schaeffer) and Augustinian (e.g., C. S. Lewis) theology, and from those psychologists I read in my training—family systems (e.g., Salvador Minuchin) and cognitive-behavioral self-control (e.g., Donald Meichenbaum). Few books were available on Christian counseling, but Jay Adams's *The Christian Counselor's Manual* was the most influential on my thinking.

Near my graduation in 1978, I began to write a book on Christian lay counseling. In the process, I discovered Larry Crabb's writing on biblical counseling. I completed the manuscript of my book in the summer of 1978, and because Francis Schaeffer had published with InterVarsity Press, I sent my manuscript to IVP. They liked the manuscript, and it eventually became two books: *When Someone Asks for Help* (1982) and *How to Help the Hurting* (1985).

I took an assistant professor teaching position at Virginia Commonwealth University (VCU—now Virginia's largest state university) in 1978. In 1983, I went up successfully for promotion to associate professor with tenure on the basis of research on self-control of pain. I changed research areas in 1983 to study marriage and family. For the first time in my academic career, I was anxious. I knew that 1989 would mark my first eligibility to be considered for promotion to professor. Developing expertise with marriage and family issues in six years seemed to be an impossible challenge. I continued to write books and papers on integration at a modest pace, but I had no confidence that such work would matter in my academic life at VCU. However, God had another surprise up the sleeve.

In 1980, Allen Bergin had written an article in *Journal of Consulting and Clinical Psychology* that brought religious therapy out of the closet. In 1986, I published a review paper in the *Journal of Counseling and Development*, which provided a basis for researchers doing studies in religious psychology. I followed that with a 1988 paper in the *Journal of Counseling Psychology* putting forth a theory of religious values in therapy and other interpersonal relationships. In 1989, I wrote the major contribution for *The Counseling Psychologist* on religious counseling across the lifespan and also published *Marriage Counseling: A Christian Approach to Counseling Couples*. This book integrated Christianity with behavioral couples counseling, Minuchin's structural family therapy, Haley's strategic family therapy and some cognitive couple therapy. In 1990, I was awarded promotion to professor. As another surprise from God, my writing on religious values made the persuasive case.

## SPIRITUAL DISCIPLINES:
## GOD IS ALWAYS AT WORK IN OUR LIVES

In much of my research between tenure and promotion to professor, I studied marriage and family dynamics and counseling. Whereas that research did not see me through to academic promotion, it had some unexpected effects in the kingdom of God.

In 1985, Dick Simmons, a long-time leader in the charismatic renewal movement, visited "Christ Prez," our small Presbyterian church. Dick led a Saturday workshop on revival. He challenged men of the church to come together and pray for two hours a day from Monday through Friday the next week. Monday at 5:00 a.m. over one hundred men of mixed ethnicities and denominational backgrounds met for prayer.

We prayed for two hours. This was not sequential prayer like most group prayer. Rather, each person prayed silently for the full two hours. By the end of the week, I had found out two things about myself. First, I was probably never going to be a prayer warrior. It was hard for me to pray for any extended period. My thoughts of the day kept intruding. I made lists in my head. I got distracted. I would fight to snap myself back into prayer only to find myself wandering away. Second, I knew for a fact that God wanted me to conduct research on parental involvement in adolescent pregnancy decision-making. I am one hundred percent aware that this was not my idea. In 1985, the abortion issue was extremely politically charged. I was a new associate professor. No way was I going to stick my head into that political lion's mouth. I spent most of the week arguing with God silently about whether I was hearing his voice. But by the end of the week, I yielded in my fight with God. I began to collect research articles on adolescent pregnancy. However, I insisted to God that I would not publish that research. To do so would be professional suicide. I abstracted over two hundred articles over the next two years.

In the spring of 1987, Beth York, one of the owners of the Logos Bookstore that is located near my office at VCU, phoned, "Ev, I am involved with trying to get a bill before the houses of the Virginia General Assembly. It requires parental notification prior to an adolescent making a decision to abort. We want to find a psychologist to give expert testimony. You are one of the few psychologists I know. Do you know any pro-life psychologists who are doing research in this area who might come to Virginia and testify?"

I muttered, "Beth, you're not going to believe this. I have been collecting studies on that very topic." I started to offer her a list of psychologists she could conveniently choose among.

But Beth was quick on the uptake. "That's great, Ev! Why don't *you* testify?" I was too surprised to say no. But as I hung up, I was hitting my head and muttering, *Boy, what were you thinking!*

I organized the testimony into a brief research summary and delivered it at committee meetings for the House of Delegates and later the Senate. Soon after that, I received a call from Jerry Regier, then president of the Family Research Council in Washington, D.C. "I understand that you testified on parental notification at the Virginia General Assembly. I'm organizing a little conference for people concerned with this issue in Washington, D.C. Would you present your findings to that conference?"

I agreed reluctantly. In Washington, I found that Jerry Regier's and my ideas of a "little" conference did not coincide. I expected twenty people. There were more like four hundred. Many of those were government policy makers. Soon afterward, Jerry Regier published an edited book in which two chapters described my research.

You will recall that this was the research I had insisted to God that I would do but *not publish*. But God's plan had been different. I had by then testified publicly, presented to policy makers, and published two chapters, but the work had not been submitted to scientific scrutiny. In the 1980s, the American Psychological Association had published an amicus curiae brief taking a position against parental involvement in adolescent pregnancy decision-making. I wrote a brief article against that position based on my research. At the last minute, before sending it off to the *American Psychologist*, I thought that our case might be improved by involving a psychiatrist on the paper in a coauthorship. So I phoned a friend, David Larson, who worked for the federal government. To our surprise, the *American Psychologist* published the article in 1989, which was eventually reprinted in controversial readings books. We then wrote another article on physicians' roles in adolescent pregnancy decision-making. The *Journal of Adolescent Health Care Research* published it in a point-and-counterpoint format. Again, books of readings on controversial issues reprinted it. Numerous state legislatures and judicial decision makers eventually cited this research.

These articles and chapters were not something I set out to publish. In fact, I was adamantly opposed to going public, and I fought God over it. But God had another idea. Remember, this began at a prayer meeting during which I concluded that I was an abysmal failure at prayer. Yet I entered into this research out of obedience. That research may possibly end up influencing more lives than any other research I ever do. And, as we will see, the connection with Dave Larson turned out also to be crucial.

## THERAPY AND RESEARCH IN FORGIVENESS

Although I did not have any mentors except the authors I read, I have learned from many people—from therapists I supervised to students who worked with me on research.

In 1989, I wrote my first journal article on forgiveness. In the early 1980s, Don Danser (a graduate student in VCU's program) and I together created an intervention to help couples confess wrongdoings to and forgive each other. At the same time, I served as clinical supervisor for a Christian counseling agency directed by Fred DiBlasio, another close friend who was on the faculty at VCU. I told him about the forgiveness intervention, and he began to use it. By 1989, we had seen amazing changes in couples as they confessed their wrongs and forgave each other. So I wrote an article describing the intervention. Fred added a case study, and we sent it off. It came out in August 1990, in *Psychotherapy*. I had written about forgiveness in couples in my 1989 book, *Marriage Counseling: A Christian Approach to Counseling Couples*. Now I had an article in the scientific literature, though it was mostly aimed at clinical practice.

A few weeks after the article came out, Mike McCullough showed up as a new graduate student in counseling psychology to work with me, and he chose forgiveness as the area he wanted to pursue. At that time, I knew little about the scientific study of forgiveness. Mike found articles on forgiveness and would summarize them in our weekly meeting. I would nod and stroke my beard wisely, but basically every article that Mike read was absolutely new to me. So immediately after Mike would leave, I would run to the library, photocopy the article, and read it. Mike basically dragged me into the forgiveness literature. A couple of years later, Steve Sandage became a student in the program. He also wanted to study forgiveness. Steve was more psychoanalytically inclined, whereas Mike was more interested in social psychology. This kept me moving to the library twice a week to read different literatures about forgiveness.

In 1994, I attended a colloquium on forgiveness presented by Mike and Steve for our developmental psychology program. They did such an amazing job at presenting the research on forgiveness that I proposed that we write a book together, which became *To Forgive Is Human* (McCullough, Sandage & Worthington, 1997).

Mike graduated in 1995, and in 1996 I connected him with David Larson, who then owned a religion-and-health think tank in Washington, D.C. David was a trustee for the John Templeton Foundation (JTF), and he suggested my name as a potential member of their board of advisors. I was appointed to the board, and I applied for a grant to the JTF to study forgiveness in couples. At the end of 1995, I was poised to make a major shift in my research focus toward the study of forgiveness. God must have been preparing the way through the desert, because my life was about to change.

## SURPRISING GRACE THROUGH STRUGGLES

I sent that book to InterVarsity Press in December 1995, and that New Year's Eve my mother was murdered. On New Year's Day, I received the phone call, and my sister, her husband and I drove to Knoxville. The police walked us through the trashed house to see whether we knew what might have been stolen. We tried to avoid looking at the blood-spattered walls and the two puddles of blood on the carpet where my mother's head and hips had rested. I consoled myself by thinking that at least she must have died quickly, until they pulled back the rug to reveal an ocean of blood beneath it.

That night was emotionally dark. My brother, sister and I reconstructed the crime. As we talked, we got furious. At one point, I pointed to a baseball bat and said, "I wish the murderer were in front of me. I would beat his brains out." Later I was unable to sleep, filled with rage. At three a.m., I realized that I, a Christian researcher of forgiveness, had gone through about twenty-four hours without allowing myself to think the word *forgiveness*. But in the next hour, I received the surprising grace to decide to forgive the murderer, and I have experienced full, lasting emotional forgiveness. What an undeserved gift of grace God gave to me that long night in 1996!

I received another gift in June of 1996. I was invited by Mervin Van der Spuy to come to South Africa to speak at three conferences for Christian counselors at Cape Town, Durban and Pretoria. I eagerly agreed. Because I try to minister to both Christian and secular communities and to both counselors and researchers when I travel, I asked Mervin whether he might arrange for me to speak to universities in South Africa. Due to his effort, I was appointed by the South African government as a visiting research scholar. Their requirements: I had to speak to as many universities as possible and to write a report.

When I was appearing on national television in South Africa, the interviewer suggested that I talk to the South African Truth and Reconciliation Commission (TRC) in Johannesburg. He gave me contact information for Piet Meiering. Mervin and I met with Piet on a Friday. He arranged for me to talk with the TRC. But the only time possible for the TRC was the following Friday at nine o'clock—my last of twenty-three days in South Africa.

That Sunday, I was scheduled to speak at two services at a church in Randburg (near Johannesburg), then hurry to Soweto, the township where the uprisings began, to preach a third sermon. At the early Randburg service, the worship was superb and was even better at the second. I began to feel like God was telling me to insert into the sermon a description of worship at the 1975 International Charismatic Conference in Kansas City. I was having a heated debate with God over this, saying things like, *Lord, don't you realize that* we *(you and me) are supposed to be in Soweto?* We *are going to be late. I don't have time to add this story.* I was "winning" the argument with God until the middle of my sermon, when I yielded and described my experience at the conference.

During the following week, Mervin and I wrapped up my commitments in South Africa. When we returned to Mervin's home Thursday night, I began to plan what to say to the members of the TRC in Johannesburg the next morning. Mervin came into my room and said, "I just got a fax. I think you will want to read this." The fax was from a member of the Supreme Court of South Africa. He said, "I was at the service when you described attending the International Charismatic Conference in Kansas City in 1975. I was at that conference, too, and I heard a prophecy that I think you should share with the TRC tomorrow. I photocopied the pages from the Proceedings of that conference so that there would not be any mistakes." The Proceedings recounted how a woman had prophesied, "I see a map of Africa. A spotlight fell on the southern part of Africa, and there was great violence and bloodshed. Out of the bloodshed, there arose a black man and a white man who extended their arms to each other and were reconciled."

I was in a quandary. The TRC had few Christian members, and most who were, were traditional Dutch Reformed Christians. They almost certainly would not understand charismatic prophecies. Of course, I started arguing with God—again—telling God that I should not read this prophecy to the TRC. I was firm. I would *not*.

The next morning, in my talk, I described my mother's death, my forgiveness of the murderer and my research. I did *not* mention the prophecy. We ended the meeting. *Ha. This proves that I can win an argument with God,* I thought. As we were picking up our things, a commissioner said, "I somehow cannot help but feel that someone was supposed to say something today, and that person didn't say it. Does anyone have something to say before we go our separate ways?"

I yielded. When I finished reading the prophecy, the Commissioners and staff basically looked at me with blank stares. We had a brief reception afterward. I said to the person who was chairing the commission, "I head home this afternoon. I have no literature about the TRC. Can you supply some?"

"Do we ever have literature!" he said. They brought me a packet. There was the logo of the TRC. It was a black man and a white man extending their arms toward each other. Beneath the picture it said, Truth and Reconciliation. I pointed at the picture, and I said to the chair, "Look! *You* are the fulfillment of that prophecy that was given in 1975 before the Truth and Reconciliation was even a thought in anybody's mind."

## THE DAVID LARSON CONNECTION, REDUX

In 1996 and 1997, David Larson organized three John Templeton

Foundation (JTF)–funded conferences on science and religion. Dave asked me to direct the mental health panel. At the first one of the conferences, I arrived at the banquet late. Because the tables were full, I sat by myself. Soon a man arrived and introduced himself as Charles Harper, who had been appointed as the new executive director of the JTF. Chuck said to me, "I wanted to find out what research each participant thought the John Templeton Foundation should fund."

I must have smiled to myself, but I said, "Have you ever thought of funding forgiveness research?" Within a couple of months I received a call from the JTF. They had decided to fund a $2M research competition to study forgiveness scientifically and asked whether I would co-chair that competition. We received a plethora of excellent proposals, and the JTF funded twenty (at about $3M instead of $2M) and the Fetzer Institute funded another two.

Dr. Jack Templeton and Chuck Harper set up a nonprofit corporation called A Campaign for Forgiveness Research (www.forgiving.org) to raise money to support additional research in forgiveness. They asked whether I would serve as executive director. The Campaign raised an additional $3.25M from donations and grants, to fund research projects in forgiveness, organize two national conferences and disseminate the research widely.

As I've taken you through the wilderness of God's adventures with me, it seems appropriate to stop and look back. Remember, this work began with my "unsuccessful" prayer yet my obedience to God back in 1985, which led to collaborating with David Larson, which led in turn to the conference Dave organized that Chuck Harper attended. God works in surprising ways.

### LETTER

As we look back over this tale of my experiences, we can discern three major themes. First, God is surprising, rarely working the way we expect. We often cannot see God's leading in the present. But if we stay engaged with God, seek to know God more closely and look for God's hand, then we can see his handiwork clearly as we gaze at the past. Recall the anecdote with which I began the chapter. Life can be like hacking our way through the bush without much perspective. But at times, if we will but pause and look around, we see a larger perspective and see also that even our "wanderings" indeed have purpose. In those moments, we see God's hand. God's surprising work lets us know that it is not we who are in control at all. God is in control.

Second, we are privileged if we have a close mentoring relationship. But in my life I found that I learned from everyone—my wife, clients, clinical supervisees, professors, students, pastors, colleagues, friends, books and the experiences God brought across my path. Sometimes that learning was painful, yet looking back, I could always see God's leading.

Third, I believe it is okay to argue with God. He is strong enough to win. To my shame, I have often argued over God's direction to my life. When I have been obedient, however, the results have been astounding.

God gave me a mission in life at age forty-eight that the poor little boy with the depressed mother and alcoholic father could have never foreseen: To do my best to bring forgiveness into every *willing* heart, home and homeland. Until he calls me home, I must heed that call. What a privilege. What a warm and welcome surprise has been—and I'm sure will be—the journey.

## REFERENCES

McCullough, M. E., Sandage, S. J., & Worthington, E. L., Jr. (1997). *To forgive is human: How to put your past in the past.* Downers Grove, IL: Inter-Varsity Press.

Worthington, E. L., Jr. (1982). *When someone asks for help.* Downers Grove, IL: InterVarsity Press.

Worthington, E. L., Jr. (1985). *How to help the hurting.* Downers Grove, IL: InterVarsity Press.

Worthington, E. L., Jr. (1989). *Marriage counseling: A Christian approach to counseling couples.* Downers Grove, IL: InterVarsity Press.

Worthington, E. L., Jr., & DiBlasio, F. A. (1990). Promoting mutual forgiveness within the fractured relationship. *Psychotherapy, 27,* 219-23.

Worthington, E. L., Jr., Larson, D. B., Brubaker, M. W., Colecchi, C. A., Berry, J. T., & Morrow, D. (1989). The benefits of legislation requiring parental involvement prior to adolescent abortion. *American Psychologist, 44,* 1542-45.

# 3

# A Search for Belonging

*L. Rebecca Propst, Private Practice Psychoanalyst*

Influences on my journey toward the study of the integration of Christian faith and psychology came from many unlikely and disparate sources, and included no Christian psychologists, because I never met any until my career was well established.

## EARLY DEVELOPMENT

When I was twelve years old, Marie Hogue, the wife of the pastor at the little Baptist church I attended in West Virginia, gave me a copy of the book *Dr. Ida*. It told the story of Ida Scudder, the first woman missionary doctor to India, who founded the Women's Medical College of India. I had just become a Christian and this story captivated me. I determined to become a medical missionary. This book started me on a journey of taking academics and school work seriously. Prior to reading that book, my grades were average or below average.

Neither of my parents graduated from high school because of family circumstances during the Great Depression. My father was a West Virginia coal miner, which makes me a coal miner's daughter. My mother, who had only an eighth-grade education, worked in the defense industry during World War II and spent the rest of her life lamenting those days, in which she felt she could outwork the men she worked with. I received unconscious permission from her to achieve, even if for her it meant merely graduating from high school. When I was assigned to the average rather than the superior section of the seventh grade (probably because of our living circumstances), my mother wrote a letter of protest, and she persisted until I was reassigned to the superior section. My parents also devoted a great deal of time to helping both my brother David and me with our homework. I had a great deal of support for academics while a child. My ultimate motivation for studying, however, came from my desire to *go into full-time Christian service,* a standard held out to me by the church I attended as a child. I was the first one in my extended family to attend college and the first one in my immediate family to become a Christian.

My father grew up in Canyon, a company-owned mining town in northern West Virginia. His father was also a West Virginia coal miner and was involved in the organization of the United Mine Workers Union and the West Virginia mine riots of the 1920s, which were portrayed in the movie *Matewan.* Once a week, our entire family visited my grandparents. Every house in town looked exactly alike, as they all were owned and had been built by the coal company. I also remember being afraid of the huge slag pile—a large pile the size of a hill—of half-burning coal taken from the mines. *Red dog* or *gob pile* were also words used to describe this scourge. It glowed at night, an eerie, frightening red. The fire never went out. I must have been five or six years old when I first paid attention to it. To a child, it held a fascinating and frightening attraction, and was an appropriate symbol of the emotional and physical dangers of Appalachian coal mining that my immediate and extended family experienced. Seeing Butcher Holler in the movie *Coal Miner's Daughter* felt familiar.

My grandmother was a Pentecostal preacher, and she was finally ordained to some small Pentecostal sect in 1968, after having been a preacher for some years. I say this not because she had influenced me directly but because my mother detested my grandmother's strong religious beliefs. So, for me to become strongly religious meant that my mother and I would be at odds with each other over my faith. Indeed this is what happened in my life. I learned to be quiet about my faith around my parents, in order to avoid criticism.

I never really knew my maternal grandparents, as my grandmother (born in Alsace Lorraine in western Europe) died long before I was born, and my grandfather died when I was about three. Apparently, my grandfather, who had been an orphan, was raised at least partly in a church-sponsored orphanage, and he felt that he had been treated very badly there. I think my mother must have developed some of her antagonism toward religious faith from her father.

My parents grew up in adverse circumstances. Their resolve and persistence allowed both my brother and me to achieve, and they managed to remain married until death. The latter was not easy, given that during my early years, my father had a drinking problem, which had apparently started during World War II. A few years ago, after both of my parents' deaths, I learned from my aunt that my dad's army unit had been involved in cleaning out concentration camps in Germany. She stated that he said he "had to be drunk to be able to stand to do it." He had never talked about this. When I was about nine, my mother said to my father, "No more drinking!" and he stopped, never to drink again. Such was the resolve of both my parents. I believe this modeled resolve served me well when I determined to focus my research on something that had not been done before.

Even though I had my heart set on being a medical missionary, my mother stated that I would not be attending a church school. If I wanted to go to college, I needed to go to the state university that was in my home town. Looking back, I can see God's hand in that direction.

## MENTORING RELATIONSHIPS

Attending West Virginia University in the 1960s changed my life. My affiliation with InterVarsity Christian Fellowship was that change agent. I adopted Denis and Evelyn MacDowell, faculty advisors to the InterVarsity Christian Fellowship student group, as surrogate parents. Indeed we kept that kind of relationship for many years. I remember our Sunday afternoon Bible studies during my undergraduate days, complete with the peanut butter sandwiches Evelyn always had available, because there was no dinner on Sunday evenings for those who lived in the dorm.

When I came back to Morgantown during holiday breaks while a graduate student at Vanderbilt University, I remember sitting in the study with Denis and Evelyn, drinking hot tea, eating homemade cookies, and talking with them for hours about all of my graduate school woes. They were great listeners. That relational connection brought great healing and great joy to my life, more than any programs or books could ever have done. (Denis was from Northern Ireland, and Evelyn was from Canada, so tea, cookies and small sandwiches were all staples.) Denis, a chemistry professor at the university who had a Ph.D. from MIT, had one of the largest personal libraries I had ever seen up to that point—an entire room filled with just chemistry books and Christian/theology books! It was from here that I first heard about the American Scientific Affiliation, an organization of evangelicals in the sciences. Denis lent me copies of their journal. In this magazine were articles by many in the physical and biological sciences, talking about their Christian faith and their disciplines. Denis also had numerous books from InterVarsity Press, to be lent out or given to students.

When I first encountered InterVarsity Christian Fellowship, I knew I had found home. Here were students who were serious about their faith. We had Bible studies, early morning prayer meetings and social activities. In the late winter of 1970, I even helped organize a large evangelistic project, complete with one of the first Christian rock bands, just before the Kent State episode in which campuses all over the United States exploded in the spring of 1970.

One day in physical chemistry lab during the fall of my sophomore year, I decided that the Victor Meyer experiment was the last straw. I could not get the glass ball to break, releasing my unknown gas into the tube; I was all thumbs. During the 1967 Urbana Student Missions Convention, sponsored by InterVarsity Christian Fellowship that Christmas, someone talked about reaching the university campus for Christ. Something stirred in me.

I immediately changed my major to psychology, and actually "majored" in InterVarsity during the rest of my college days. One of my most comforting memories is sitting in the large living room at Hudson House in Upper Nyack, New York, singing out of the InterVarsity hymnal. I still often recall those images whenever I want to be comforted. In those days, InterVarsity was smaller. The intimate connections, the meals around the small round tables in the dining room at Hudson

House, the long conversations around the book table with staff, and the conversations with InterVarsity staff member Neil Rendall in the University Student Union were all nourishing for me, not just spiritually and intellectually, but emotionally as well. As with the MacDowells, it was in this organization that I found nourishing relationships that brought emotional healing and spiritual growth into my life. *It was not the programs; it was the relationships.* I attended the first Christian Life Institute at Hudson House in Nyack, New York, in 1967, and there I had my eyes opened to the possibility of dialoguing with culture as a Christian. I remember conversations with Neil Rendall and Alice Watts (Fryling), Will Metzger leading the singing, and Harold Burkhart in the kitchen helping with the dishes. I was richly blessed with all these deep Christian relationships and examples in college.

Graduate school, on the other hand, was spiritually difficult. The most difficult part was that I began to experience a loneliness—a disconnect—a lack of belonging that I still experience. If InterVarsity gave me one of the first places where I felt I really belonged, then graduate school propelled me into an emotional space of never really belonging again. I did not have the wonderful comradeship of other students in InterVarsity, when we had had Bible studies or campus outreach projects. I also struggled with fitting into the local church.

Because there were no InterVarsity groups, the anxiety of the academic pressure, coupled with the lack of a small Christian reference group where I could find sufficient emotional connections, made this one of the most difficult periods of my life emotionally. I did attend a small Reformed Presbyterian Church which met initially in a classroom of the Divinity school. Mark Noll, a graduate student in the Divinity school at the time, also attended my church, along with two other graduate students (Bert Hodges and Dorothy Herner) from our psychology department. These connections made graduate school easier. However, two things were missing: (1) This group had a less personal approach to faith than I had found in InterVarsity, and (2) I was no longer a leader. The first problem was more easily solved; I became involved in a Charismatic prayer group that had been started by medical students and residents. The second problem was a different story.

In InterVarsity, I had been one of the student leaders, helping to plan and organize our spring evangelistic project. The leadership role I had had in InterVarsity did much to bolster my self-esteem and give me a sense of self-efficacy. I could plan and execute projects. I began to think it was possible for me to accomplish something for the kingdom of God. InterVarsity Christian Fellowship was unique in the church in the 1960s in encouraging women in leadership roles. The skills and spirit of leadership I gained in InterVarsity freed me to take steps later to do the research I did. Unfortunately, the psychology department at Vanderbilt University also had ambivalence about female graduate students. As of 1975, I was one of only a few female graduates to have received a Ph.D. in psychology from Vanderbilt University.

From time to time in graduate school, I did have some contact with former InterVarsity staff workers. For example, Neil and Jeannie Rendall stopped in Nashville after Urbana one Christmas to visit me. I will never forget that. They also wrote to me regularly, and during one of the darkest periods of my graduate school days, when I felt God was no longer there, I drove up to Hudson House to spend a week with them in New York. They warmly took me in and ministered to me, even when they had a new baby. (It wasn't until years later, when I had new babies of my own, that I realized how difficult that must have been.) They had the ability to just listen.

Over the years, Neil and Jeannie have come in and out of my life, and they have been and continue to be one of the gifts from God to me. For example, one summer in graduate school, I wanted to see them, so I found my way up to Cedar Campus on the Upper Peninsula of Michigan, for the first-ever graduate student conference. That conference, in a small conference center on the north shore of one of the Great Lakes, was another one of those experiences that brought healing into my life at an important time. It was the emotional presence of these people, the opportunity for personal conversations, the opportunity to experience a living faith community, and the opportunity to think about my faith that were all important.

That conference was also a very powerful affirmation of my faith—and of my developing life as an academic. At the conference, I remember meeting James Sire, then the senior editor of InterVarsity Press. From time to time after that we have had correspondence with each other, and he sent me manuscripts from time to time to review. This was also a great affirmation of my sense of selfhood, and indeed of the idea that I had something to contribute to the body of Christ. Given the emotional, intellectual and spiritual connection I have had to Inter-Varsity over the years, it is surprising that I have never written anything else for them, other than an article for *HIS Magazine* in the early 1980s; this chapter is the first. Up to this point, I have seen my ministry to be to the secular academic world, so most of my publishing has been in that context.

If graduate school was sparse on regularly available Christian mentors, it was not sparse on mentors of other types. Donald Thistlethwaite was my dissertation adviser. He was a social psychologist and a rigorous empiricist. He had obtained his Ph.D. at Berkeley in the 1950s, with some of the pioneers of American empirical psychology. I was awed by his ability to organize ideas and to linearly delineate the literature in an area, to prove or disprove a point. Each study of his would be presented to prove a point, until a closely argued tapestry of ideas was present. I followed his pattern of reasoning closely, and lo and behold, I learned about scientific writing. I also learned to find flaws in already published research. It was from this man that I developed an appreciation for the scientific method. Donald Thistlethwaite knew of my first outcome study, on using Christian beliefs in cognitive therapy, which was published in the *Journal of Cognitive Therapy and Research* in 1980. He was very proud of the carefully done empirical nature my work. That was a delight for me.

While a faculty member at Ohio University, I met peers who were at the forefront of research in cognitive therapy. We went to professional meetings and hung out with some of Aaron Beck's early students. Among these individuals, I found support for my work. I also found support among some of the founders of the Society for Psychotherapy Research, such as Allen Bergin. They felt that examining the efficacy of Christian religious beliefs using the paradigm of psychotherapy outcome research was creative and new. I combined the best of rigorous psychotherapy research methodology with the use of the individuals' Christian faith in psychotherapy. No one else was doing that. I often found more acceptance among psychotherapy researchers of that era than I found among Christian writers. Even Aaron Beck was interested in the outcomes of my second study and asked me about it.

Also, at this time I met Pauline Franks, an older lady from the British Isles. Pauline had become a Christian during the London Blitz of World War II. She had absolute faith in her Lord and seemed unflustered by even the most difficult of circumstances. I rented a room from her, so I got to see amazing faith in action day after day, even in a cold house with little heat.

I had not wanted to go to Ohio University after the West Coast because I was afraid of isolation and forever being single. The Lord was calling me to academia, however, and at that point, this was the only open door to a tenured faculty position. I struggled. While taking some courses at Fuller Seminary during this time, I often stayed with a retired missionary couple in Pasadena. Years earlier, this couple, whose names I cannot recall, had served with the China Inland Mission. I had just been offered a tenure track position at Ohio University, but it was the "corn fields," the *back of beyond*, as far as I was concerned. That evening, this elderly woman told me she had not wanted to go to China back in the early 1900s, because she was afraid she would always be single and she felt like it was the back of beyond. She said, however, she met her husband, an Australian, there. I choked up and literally did not sleep that night, until I told the Lord that I would go to Athens, Ohio. And, of course, I did meet my husband, Douglas Campbell, there. He was a graduate student in art history, going to school on the G.I. bill after Vietnam.

At times the Lord's guidance can seem dramatically clear; at other times, it is more subtle.

When I undertook to do my second study, a full-fledged treatment outcome study on the use of Christian faith in the psychotherapy treatment of clinical depression, I am glad I did not know how costly it would be, in terms of time and energy. In part, this costliness was due to the limited amount of research support I had for my work at the time

I was doing my second study, and in part it was due to my attempt to use the identical methodology that was being used in a concurrent National Institute of Mental Health (NIMH) study on the psychotherapy of depression. I did get a few small grants from other sources, but the NIMH was not yet ready to look at religion as a subject for research. These circumstances meant spending ten years on one project, rather than writing numerous books and articles for Christian audiences. It meant that I did not get to be well known in my own Christian peer group. However, now when Christian psychologists write about the clinical efficacy of using Christian spirituality in the actual therapeutic process, they usually quote my study.

Unfortunately, as far as I know, there is still little research on using Christian values in psychotherapy that is published in mainstream psychotherapy research journals, even fifteen years after I published my second major study. This is lamentable. I undertook my study because I felt there was a need for carefully done psychotherapy research using Christian spirituality as an active ingredient, and I felt God calling me to this task. The actual study took about ten years, from conceptualization to publication. I relied heavily on graduate students for the therapy and the evaluations. Creative possibilities are always out there in psychology to do research with limited funds. I was able to work out agreements with two different graduate programs, such that the student researchers received academic credit for their participation in the research. On the final paper I put those students' names who had helped significantly with assessment and logistics (Propst, Ostrum, Watkins, & Mashburn, 1992).

I see my study as a prototype. I hope that other Christian psychologists will commit the time and energy into doing studies of this type, perhaps on many of the topics I suggest at the end of this chapter. I feel a sense of satisfaction in having undertaken something difficult— something for which there was no previous paradigm—something which needed to be done, even if there are no material rewards for the project and very few academic rewards even. When we look back upon our life, the only thing that really counts is obedience and responsiveness to God's leading, even if no others have gone with us and we were going where no one had gone before. The apostle Paul has given us a model: "It has always been my ambition to preach the gospel where Christ was not known, so that I would not be building on someone else's foundation" (Romans 15:20). Sometimes we have to venture out with new research models and with new fields of witness for Christ.

## STRUGGLES

I have already alluded to my struggles. I have usually felt on the borders between the evangelical subculture and the psychological and psychoanalytic communities of which I have been a part. All of my education, including undergraduate school, graduate school and psychoanalytic training, was in secular institutions. All my faculty appointments have been in secular institutions, including Ohio University and Lewis and Clark College. Within the secular academic world, reactions to my work have ranged from curiosity to disdain. I have often heard questions like: "What kind of research are you doing anyway?" or "What is this all about?" Now I rejoice that the larger psychological world now sees the value of religious faith in mental health, and is more interested in investing research funds into that area. This was much less the case thirty years ago. When I began my work, there had been very little published empirical work on the emotional value of religious faith. Colleagues in the Society for Psychotherapy Research understood my research methodology and were usually appreciative of my creative use of that research methodology, often asking me to be on panels at professional meetings. In my own institutions, however, where there was little or no understanding of psychotherapy outcome research methodology, there was a greater knowledge, acceptance and interest gap. Because Ohio University was more of a research institution than Lewis and Clark College, I generally found more acceptance for my work at Ohio University than at Lewis and Clark College.

On the other hand, at that point, the Christian psychological community was writing about the integration of psychology and Christianity from a theological point of view, and it had less interest in the empirical side of things. Of course, exceptions came from places like the Fuller Graduate School of Psychology, whose faculty asked me to give the Finch Lectures there in 1991.

I tended not to write for Christian presses because I felt that my calling was to speak to the wider psychological community, so I was using the language of the wider psychological community. Indeed there was much interest in my work, from a variety of sources. I received a large number of inquiries from abroad. (I still receive regular inquiries about my work from abroad, even though my major paper has been published for seventeen years.) Even the dean of the local medical school came by my office to discuss my work with me.

Another of my major struggles has always been my relationship with the local church. Sometimes churches are just dull, and often the sermons are too trite and simple. In addition, most evangelical churches have not known what to do with academic/intellectual women, so I have usually found myself in "borderline" churches. By borderline churches, I mean churches that don't quite fit into the mainstream evangelical subculture but nevertheless have some measure of orthodox Christian belief. In these churches, I have often had more opportunity to teach Sunday school, and I have even had the opportunity to preach occasionally. I even spent eighteen years as the conference psychologist for a mainline Protestant denomination, and I got a master's degree in theology at a local Roman Catholic seminary. But when my husband and I were seeking out a good evangelical youth church for our sons Joshua and Ian, these places did not work for us as a family. So my husband and I followed our sons to whichever church they have felt comfortable in, postponing our own search for a community of like-minded individuals.

My husband, Douglas Campbell, was a student of William D. Miller, the biographer of Dorothy Day, the founder of the Catholic Worker movement. The title of Miller's biography was *The Long Loneliness*. I have felt *that* loneliness, often feeling caught between two worlds, as Dorothy Day was. I hold to a traditional orthodox, evangelical view of Christian doctrine and the Scriptures and a traditional Christian view of ethics and behavior. I am concerned about the poor, and I have a commitment to nonviolence and pacifism. I strongly believe that Christians should not take a human life, under any circumstances, and I also have traditional Christian personal ethics in the areas of abortion and sexuality.

In the fall of 1994, while on a retreat at a nearby Trappist abbey, the Lord gave me a Bible verse, "By faith Abraham, when called to go to a place he would later receive as his inheritance, obeyed and went, even though he did not know where he was going" (Hebrews 11:8). I wasn't sure what the verse meant at that time, but I felt that being involved in a college campus that was continuously involved in political in-fighting between schools and departments was not good. By the next spring, and after spending every noon in prayer during the weekdays of Lent, I decided to turn in my resignation the Monday after Easter Sunday. That extended period of prayer made it possible for me walk away from a tenured faculty position.

My mother also became terminally ill at that time, so a lot of transition was happening at one time. I will always remember the walk across campus after I had already packed up my books. My husband Doug was waiting on the other side of campus after the last load of books had been loaded into the car. I went back to the graduate school dean's office, to slip the key under his office door. As I walked across campus, I had nothing in my hand. It was a very poignant ten minutes. I had nothing in my hand, and I had given up my academic career. I felt anxious and somewhat stricken. (I had been crying while packing the books.) But I also felt free. I knew I was giving up some status, and that status had been very important to me. God was calling me away from Lewis and Clark College, however. But I knew not where I was going. Even though parts of it were difficult, it absolutely seemed like the right decision. After all, even when the Israelites left Egypt, they still missed the cucumbers.

It is not that I had any special courage; it was more that I felt that the graduate school at Lewis and Clark College was no longer the place for me. I was moving on, but I didn't know where. Object relations theory, a branch of contemporary psychoanalysis, says that our attachment to old objects means that we still live as children of our parents; we act as if we are the young child again, responding to those around us as we responded to our parents. We may do this, even when doing so is not healthy.

If we have lived with critical parents, we often do not see the criticism of those around us. Instead we are inclined to somehow believe that we should have done something differently. In a paper I wrote in 1993, I stated:

> When the Apostle Paul spoke of the powers and principalities, he often did not make a clear distinction between the demonic and the structures of institutions—both meanings were often bound up together. . . . The powers are at the same time intangible spiritual entities and concrete historical, social, or psychic structures. . . . Certainly relationships, including relationships in family and work settings, fit this definition. (Propst, 1993, p. 232)

To decide not to fit into a particular structure means we make a choice to not be part of the powers of that structure. However, it also means that we are opening ourselves up to anxiety and the possibility of something new.

When the Lord moves us into something new, it is often that the Lord moves us into anxiety. When I left Lewis and Clark, I did not know what I would be doing. I knew I would be practicing as a psychologist, but beyond that I did not know.

Not being an academic also meant I had more time with my preschool-age sons, Joshua and Ian. Interestingly, we had wanted children for years, but the Lord had not yet opened the door for that to happen, until I had substantially finished my major research study. I now see this as God's timing. If I had had children earlier, it would have been impossible for me to have committed as much time to my research study.

After one year at the Los Angeles Gestalt Therapy Training Institute, I enrolled in the Northwest Center of Psychoanalysis, a new institute of contemporary relational psychoanalysis in Seattle, Washington. I didn't make this decision myself. In an off moment, I called and asked for an application. In an afternoon, when I had some free time, I decided to fill out the application, to fill the time. To be accepted into the program, I needed to have three in-person interviews, each with a different psychoanalyst. So one day during a hike, I said to my husband,

"Let's do a family trip to Seattle." The Institute set up the three interviews, and I was accepted. I thought I would probably just do a year or two of the institute—I figured that I probably wouldn't finish, since it was a long process, taking at least four to eight years. I spent seven years and finished and became a certified psychoanalyst, much to my surprise. On reflection, all this seems to have been totally directed or orchestrated by God *without my knowing where I was going.*

Leaving Lewis and Clark College and enrolling in a psychoanalytic institute was not something I had ever planned to do. In fact, at the time, I knew nothing about psychoanalysis—certainly not contemporary psychoanalysis. I thought that psychoanalysts were all Freudians. I am still surprised by it all, but I am convinced that it was God's direction for me.

How did I make this decision? It was a moment-by-moment decision, made in the present moment. During my quiet times, each step of the way seemed to be impressed upon me. *Now, in the present, I am waiting to see how God will use this training!* Madeleine L'Engle once said about Christmas, "This is the irrational season, when love blooms bright and wild. Had Mary been filled with reason there'd have been no room for the child."

Recently, I heard a Christian couple from Lebanon speak. They pastor a church among a Muslim minority and share Christ openly. During their brief presentation, this couple laughed with a light-heartedness and a freedom that I had not seen in a long time, and they said there is a term for Christians in their country. They spoke a Lebanese word and said it means "crazy people." One would have to be crazy to put his or her life at risk each and every day, in order to profess Christ in settings where a person could easily be killed for such actions.

## THERAPEUTIC EXPERIENCES

Many therapeutic activities in which I have used Christian faith as an active ingredient in therapy have been unplanned. I often did not set out to say, "I am going to do such-and-such with faith today." Often, in the midst of therapy with a patient, the sense of what might be useful comes up. For example, in my book, *Psychotherapy in a Religious Frame-*

*work* (Propst, 1987), I mentioned the story of a young woman who had been brutally abused (physically and sexually) as a child. One evening, she reported her experiences as a young girl of seven or eight. She had started crying, and her mother proceeded to tie her shoe strings together, turn on the gas kitchen stove, and set her on the burners. I was horrified. It was unspeakable. There were no words. I felt myself drawing back and cringing, with a knot in my stomach. (I later learned that this was my appropriate countertransference to her, because indeed these were her unspeakable feelings.) I didn't know what to say. She was haunted by the memory.

This individual was a devout Christian, so I asked her if she could imagine that Jesus was there with her in the image. I used some language that I had picked up from some training in Ericksonian hypnosis. I asked what Jesus would do. She said, almost immediately, "He would take me off the stove." She started crying, and then I started crying. I don't always cry with patients, but this particular evening, there was a great release.

What happened? I didn't plan it. I didn't say, "I will use religious imagery with this patient today." To be sure, I had had a background of preparation. I had read much about cognitive therapy and therapeutic imagery. I had also read much about inner healing prayer, from sources in both the Protestant and the Roman Catholic charismatic movements.

At that moment, bringing Jesus explicitly into the horrifying image that was almost unspeakable and certainly unfeelable (for both of us) allowed her and then subsequently me to feel. It freed up emotion. It made the experience "safer." That night, as I drove home, I recalled thinking to myself, *There is no hell where God is not,* and I started weeping.

When I wrote the original account of this interaction in my book, I was thinking about it in the context of cognitive-behavioral therapy. Now I would also think about this interaction in the context of relational psychoanalysis. In the original trauma, this young woman had no capacity to feel the terror of the situation (as would be true of most of us). The feeling, and thus the language, of the situation was unformulated (Stern, 1997). Unformulated trauma causes psychosomatic problems, as well as intense feelings that get expressed in other ways. For example, with this young woman, there was suicidal ideation and self-cutting. The only way she could deal with her unformulated trauma was to attack herself, just as her early parental object had done. She had been overwhelmed by her abuser and could not experience her own independent subjectivity. In the suggestion I made about what Jesus would have done in that situation, my patient had someone who was with her—someone who was powerful enough to stand up to her mother and intervene. She had a loving, caring presence. As she acquired some of her own subjectivity, she could cry.

Because of my own subsequent training in contemporary psychoanalysis, I now understand that the most important component of training for a psychoanalyst is the personal analysis of the psychoanalytic candidate. Supervision is second in importance, while coursework is a distant third. This hierarchy is so because our own personal therapeutic experiences—in which we deal with our own pains and our own past traumas—enlarges our own subjectivity about those experiences and thus enhances our emotional ability to feel and experience the pains of others. We can actually process and feel what the patient is feeling. If this does not happen, understanding is lacking, and more of the patient's pain remains unspoken, unformulated and unfelt, resulting in less personal change and less overall resilience. Indeed, it may be eventually determined that unspoken psychic pain may be the cause of much physical illness.

Contemporary relational psychoanalysis is very interested in the role that unspoken and unrealized emotional pain has on real and imagined physical illness (McDougall, 1989). Emotional pain, spoken in the presence of another, is transformed. Psychotherapy for these issues may also be accelerated by work outside of traditional therapy, such as the Feldenkrais method of physical therapy and body work.

Scripture would agree. For example, in the letter to the Hebrews, we read:

For we do not have a high priest who is unable to sympathize with our weaknesses, but we have one who has been tempted in every way, just as we are—yet was without sin. Let us then approach the throne of grace with confidence, so that we may receive mercy and find grace to help us in our time of need. (Hebrews 4:15-16)

In this passage, the word for "sympathize" is the Greek word from which we get our word "empathy," the most important skill of any therapist. I increasingly believe that it is our pains which actually help others.

A second example from Scripture is Jesus healing the paralytic. In Mark 2:1-12, we read of Jesus telling this man that his sins were forgiven. When Jesus understood in his spirit that he was being questioned, he said:

Which is easier: to say to the paralytic, "Your sins are forgiven," or to say, "Get up, take your mat and walk"? But that you may know that the Son of Man has authority on earth to forgive sins. . . ." He said to the paralytic, "I tell you, get up, take your mat and go home." (Mark 2:8-11)

In this passage, it is difficult to find a really clear distinction between physical healing and the forgiveness of sins. This difficulty may be because, in reality, there is no distinction. This, of course, does not mean that everyone who is paralyzed is so because of his or her sin. It does mean, however, that in many cases, there is a close connection between physical illness and psychic pain. At present, we just don't know how to untangle this connection. Contemporary psychoanalysis is exploring the intricacies of this relationship in a way that is quite consistent with Christianity, especially if you consider the point I made earlier about the principalities and the powers, including the social and psychic structures in which we find ourselves functioning. After awhile, these principalities and powers run us down. We don't yet know how to live a radical life of discipleship—one which refuses to bow down to those powers, even when they offer us enticements of power, security, personal acceptance, wealth and prestige. Being under the sway of those powers comes at a deep psychic cost, however. Children in dysfunctional homes are under these powers. Unfortunately, they are so used to these powers that they may never really step away from them for the rest of their lives, because their brain has become used to them.

I also think that we will increasingly find points of contact between different schools of therapeutic thought. For example, cognitive-behavioral therapy is shifting more toward using a unified protocol to treat all emotional disorders, in which one of the most crucial ingredients of treatment is prevention of the patient's emotional avoidance of emotional pain so that individuals can learn to develop more of a tolerance for the pain and change their reaction to the pain (Allen, McHugh & Barlow, 2008). Relational psychoanalysis, on the other hand, exposes the individual to his or her relationship fears in the context of the therapeutic relationship, so that he or she can learn to experience and think about those fears differently. In both theories, the individual has to confront difficult emotions. Confronting our own pains and our own self-delusions is also a mark of Christian maturity.

Finally, if you are planning to be a therapist or to work in the field of psychotherapy integration, then you must immerse yourself into your own personal therapy. The process of growth in personal therapy leads to more anxiety and pain, as well as to more growth and resilience. It also leads to more insight into our patients.

Our own personal experience is important because much of what happens in therapy is not totally accessible by our conscious thought. There is much that is processed through our limbic (emotional) brain. We are a product of all our present and past relationships. Therapy enhances our knowledge of ourselves and of how we affect others. I have also come reluctantly to the conclusion that *many* believers in Christ will *usually* make much more progress in therapy if they can find a therapist who is also a believer in Christ. There is such an immense emotional, intellectual and spiritual gap between these worlds that not having that bridge means that too much psychic energy will be spent trying to bridge that gap. The skill and experience level of the therapist are also very important, however. Sometimes it is difficult, though, to find both the desired experience level and faith background in the same person. How much experience, training and personal therapy has this person had? Therapists who have attended a postdoctoral training institute and who have continued supervision and therapy beyond their residency can teach you more about the process.

During my psychoanalytic training, in addition to my West Coast mentors, I had the opportunity to work extensively with Darlene Ehrenburg and Larry Epstein, two analytic supervisors at the William Alanson White Institute in New York City, the institute of Rollo May, Clare Thompson and Eric Fromm. Darlene and Larry taught me a lot about learning to understand the present moment in therapy and how the present moment relates to other events in the individual's life.

## SPIRITUAL DISCIPLINES

I hope that throughout this chapter it has been obvious that my personal walk with Jesus Christ is the core and centerpiece of any of my integration attempts.

My personal prayer times started as a child, when I read a passage of Scripture every night and wrote a few lines in a diary. In my bedroom, I had a wonderful spot to pray, especially during the summer months. A screen door from my bedroom opened to a second-story porch. On hot summer nights, I could sit in front of the screen door, look up at the sky, and pray. God was a very comforting presence; the entire universe was alive with his love and presence. Later I found this same theme echoed in the Psalms.

During my college years, InterVarsity Christian Fellowship deepened this experience of a daily quiet time. At every InterVarsity conference and training week, we would always talk about the importance of having a daily quiet time, and InterVarsity Press would routinely publish a wide variety of materials on this subject.

When my children were young, I started reading some of the Christian mystics, such as Julian of Norwich (1342/1966), St. John of the Cross (1935/1959) and de Caussade (1733-1739/1975). After a few years, however, I went back to Scripture Union's daily Bible reading guide. Scripture, the Word of God, is authoritative in my life. I have not always succeeded in living my life under the sway of Scripture, but this is my goal.

Christ through Scripture challenges me to live a life of radical discipleship, which I cannot even begin to do, but that is okay. Recently, I read Luke 9:62 in my daily quiet time, "No one who puts his hand to the plow and looks back is fit for service in the kingdom of God." This is in the same chapter that includes Jesus' call to radical discipleship, "If anyone would come after me, he must deny himself and take up his cross daily and follow me. For whoever wants to save his life will lose it, but whoever loses his life for me will save it" (Luke 9:23-24). This means that I move forward; I don't try to hold on to the past—onto any accomplishments, any prestige or any securities. (Interestingly, as we lose our old securities, we may also lose our old anxieties.) In one of my earlier papers (Propst, 1992), I quoted the spiritual writer Thomas Kelly (1941) on this:

> It is an overwhelming experience to fall into the hands of the living God, to be invaded to the depths of one's being by his presence, to be, without warning, wholly uprooted from all earth-born securities, and assurances, and to be blown by a tempest of unbelievable power which leaves one's old proud self utterly, utterly defenseless. (See also Propst, 1993.)

The road to good mental health is not too different from the road to good spiritual health. We must initially leave behind the security of the old way of feeling and doing things. Anxiety is horrible; we try everything to avoid it. Perhaps this is also the problem with the church. Maybe the church's fear of anxiety is why it is sometimes so boring. The contemporary American church wants security, power and safety. It gets it, along with boredom.

Contemporary psychoanalysis and contemporary cognitive therapy, however, both emphasize the importance of anxiety. We cannot change unless we experience our anxieties. In contemporary psychoanalysis, for example, individuals confront their pain in the context of psychoanalysis, because they confront the "other" in the person of the analyst. The "other" represents, in the transference, everyone and everything we have been afraid of in our past. We squirm and move and try to move away from this anxiety—the imagined criticism, and the harshness, the rejection. We struggle with the "harsh other"—the one who may hurt us; the one that may detest us—the gap between what is really there and what we fear is there. The surprising thing, however, is that this gap is the gap we have carried with us our entire life. We writhe. In this process, however, we become more resilient. We become more courageous.

Good psychotherapy is not easy for either the therapist or the patient. Unfortunately, we have bought the mess of pottage that says we will always triumph and be first. If we look at the story of the Transfiguration recorded in Luke 9:28 and following, we see that Jesus' face was altered and his clothing became dazzling white. We see that Moses and Elijah were with him. But what do they speak about? Do they speak of his glory, even in the midst of his glory? No, "they spoke about his departure, which he was about to bring to fulfillment at Jerusalem" (Luke 9:31). Here we see that death and glory are impenetrably linked. This is only understood slowly. The church often fails to understand it and always reaches for glory and security. Recently, we had a Christian Chinese student to dinner, and she remarked that in China, *fortunately,* it was very difficult to be a Christian.

Despite some initial notes on this chapter, its final shape—like the final shape of my professional life—is unknown to me until it is actually written. Likewise, we abandon ourselves to the present moment of Christ—waiting to be healed and taught, as we are living our lives. Otherwise, anything we say is useless.

I believe that as a Christian psychoanalyst, integration happens on an ongoing basis, as I live my life. Integration is a product of my own personal daily walk with Christ and of my own personal daily struggles, with patients and with myself.

As I have reflected on my story, I have noticed that it has many disparate themes, many almost at times contradictory feelings, many varied experiences often seemingly totally unconnected with each other, indeed many different self-states. As I reflect on all these characteristics of my integration journey, I stand outside of them; I stand in the spaces between these experiences, in the presence of God. The Holy Spirit is the teacher who allows me to stand securely in the spaces between these experiences. This standing in the spaces between experiences is also a strong theme in contemporary relational psychoanalysis (e.g., see Bromberg, 1998).

## LETTER OF ADVICE TO THOSE INTERESTED IN INTEGRATION

If I were a young graduate student or scholar who was interested in the integration of psychology and Christianity and I had the perspectives I do now, I would recommend the following to myself.

Follow hard after God. Cultivate a daily habit of prayer and Bible study. As much as possible, understand and try to grasp a truly supernatural view of the universe. As Henry Blamires (1963) said many years ago in *The Christian Mind*, we live in a supernatural universe. Allow your mind, psyche and emotions to be bathed in this fact. God is always present. God is working in all moments and is present in every moment. We must cultivate our hearts and minds to "see" this fact. There is no place where God is not.

Realize that Christ's purposes are not worked out in the worldly ways of power but through weakness, both our own and that of others. Scriptural principles should guide not only what we do, but how we do it. Hudson Taylor, the first modern missionary to China, said that "God's work must always be done in God's way."

If you are still in graduate school, I would encourage you to attach yourself to your professor's research program and learn from her or him. It is too early for most of you to have your own program. Endeavor to work with the best professor possible. If you are attending a Christian graduate school, I would encourage you to do a postdoctoral residency in a secular setting so that you can broaden your range of understanding and also understand what the secular world, to which you are called to witness, is like. If you are in a secular setting, try to hook up with an organization like InterVarsity.

Understand that despite your interest in theology, the secular psychological community is not interested in theology. They are primarily interested in "what happens." Most of American psychology is very empirically oriented, even psychoanalysis. While the latter isn't interested in carefully structured research designs, it is interested in the carefully presented case study that shows how a particular technique or process was helpful to a patient. If you want to impact the larger field of psychology, understand that a strong empirical research program will help facilitate that goal more than anything. I have seen academic psychologists laugh at theoretical articles by Christians in major journals but stop when they saw actual empirical research on Christian topics. Psychology is not yet really interested in one unified theory but instead only in how people are actually affected and changed (Propst, 1997). If theological-psychological models are helpful for you in your personal walk with God or in your work with patients, then by all means use them. But don't try to force everything into one model, as if you had it all worked out. Instead live your professional and spiritual life in a day-by-day walk with God. Live close to Jesus and become thoroughly grounded in Scripture on the one hand, and on the other hand, learn as much as you can about contemporary psychological theory and practice.

If you plan to work in the area of clinical or counseling psychology, social work or psychiatry, then by all means understand that your work will be facilitated by your own personal therapy.

Don't stay in the Christian ghetto. A lot of Christian professionals talk to each other, but they don't talk enough to the broader world. Learn to communicate with that broader world.

Take a radical risk for God. Look around. Where does the church need help with the issues it is struggling with today? Don't just pick the easy issues. There are a few issues that stand out in my mind—areas that are waiting for young Christian psychologists to develop programs combining Christian spirituality with the best of psychological theory, research and practice. First, there is a need for Christians to combine the copious research on the social psychology of attitude change with Christian spirituality, in order to deal with global poverty, climate change and global warming. How do you motivate Christians and others to care for the environment?

Second, Christian spirituality could be combined with the psychological research on conflict resolution and mediation to study how to deal with the ongoing threat of terrorism. For example, a recent issue of

*Christianity Today* contained an article talking about a Christian who works in Afghanistan and talks to the terrorists, emphasizing the role of Jesus as a nonviolent prophet in Islamic thought. Can Christianity and psychology help us to deal more effectively with violence around the world? Jesus did say, "Blessed are the peacemakers" (Matthew 5:9).

Third, the church is going to be increasingly confronted with the issue of homosexuality. For the Christian community, the twin temptations on this issue are either to go along with the world and disregard Scripture as irrelevant or outdated, or to completely withdraw or avoid the issue and react with either harsh judgments or nonengagement. Would we be in a better place with this issue now if the Christian church had engaged with the issue of homosexuality thirty or forty years ago, or even before Stonewall? There is an extensively developing literature in psychoanalysis that deals with gender fluidity, identity and sexuality. This literature could be profitably combined with Christian spirituality and notions of Christian identity to perhaps develop a program and a countercultural voice that could aid individuals who would want help in choosing to change their lifestyle. Both inside and outside of cognitive therapy, there is also an increasing literature on somatic experiencing, which may be helpful. Some work is already being done in this area. Could the Christian community develop a model of nurturing respectful healing that could stand as a model for the world? It is worth thinking about.

Fourth, despite the known successes of programs like Alcoholics Anonymous (AA), which are based loosely on spirituality, there have been minimal attempts to put rigorous research principles together with Christian spirituality in order to rigorously develop and empirically test Christian alternative programs for drug and alcohol treatment. There is a need for vast research and development in this area.

Have you thought about these issues as you think about choosing a direction for your life? Can our findings from contemporary psychology and our Christian faith help us with these problems? If they do, the world will notice. Of course, working on any of these issues entails risk. In some cases, it entails unpopularity and perhaps nonacceptance and hostility from colleagues outside the church—and negative reaction from people within the church in other circumstances. It requires a radical stepping out. Perhaps the integration of radical Christian spirituality with the tools we are developing in contemporary psychology may yet have something radical to give the world. I challenge you, my readers, to accept the challenge of these struggles.

Christians belong to the kingdom of God. This is a kingdom where Jesus is Lord and where greater harmony, healing, justice and unity will exist among humanity. This kingdom is in the process of "breaking in" to our world. It is already here, but it is not yet here. We cannot expect perfection in this world, but we can anticipate shifts in which people become more in tune with God's designs for the world. William Wilberforce understood that attitude in his campaign against slavery in Great Britain in the nineteenth century. In the midst of today's emotional confusion, intense emotional stress, pain and broken relationships, perhaps we can apply the science of psychology and psychotherapy together with our Christian spirituality and provide greater avenues for the relief of pain in the world.

## REFERENCES

Allen, L. B., McHugh, R. K., & Barlow, D. H. (2008). Emotional disorders: A unified protocol. In D. H. Barlow (Ed.), *Clinical handbook of psychological disorders: A step-by-step treatment manual* (pp. 216-49). New York: Guilford Press.

Blamires, H. (1963). *The Christian mind: How should a Christian think?* London: SPCK.

Bromberg, P. (1998). *Standing in the spaces: Essays on clinical process, trauma, and dissociation.* Hillsdale, NJ: Analytic Press.

De Caussade, J. P. (1975). *Abandonment to divine providence* (J. Beevers, Trans.). New York: Doubleday. (Original work published 1733-1739)

John of the Cross, Saint. (1959). *Dark night of the soul* (E. A. Peers, Trans.). New York: Doubleday. (Original translation published 1935)

Julian of Norwich (1966). *Revelation of love* (J. Skinner, Trans.). New York: Doubleday. (Original work published c. 1342)

Kelly, T. (1941). *A testament of devotion.* New York: Harper & Brothers.

McDougall, J. (1989). *Theaters of the body.* New York: Norton.

Propst, L. R. (1980). The comparative efficacy of religious and non-religious imagery for the treatment of mild depression in religious individuals. *Cognitive Therapy and Research, 4*, 167-78.

Propst, L. R. (1987). *Psychotherapy in a religious framework: Spirituality in the emotional healing process.* New York: Human Sciences Press.

Propst, L. R. (1992). Spirituality and the avoidant personality. *Theology Today, 49*, 165-72.

Propst, L. R. (1993). Defusing the powers with Jesus as a model of empowerment: Treating the avoidant personality. *The Journal of Pastoral Care, 47*, 230-38.

Propst, L. R. (1997). Therapeutic conflict resolution and the Holy Trinity. In E. R. Roberts & M. Talbot (Eds.), *Limning the psyche: Explorations in clinical psychology.* Grand Rapids, MI: Eerdmans.

Propst, L. R., Ostrum, R., Watkins, P., & Mashburn, T. (1992). Comparative efficacy of religious and non-religious cognitive-behavioral therapy for the treatment of clinical depression in religious individuals. *Journal of Consulting and Clinical Psychology, 60*, 94-103.

Stern, D. (1997). *Unformulated experience: From dissociation to imagination in psychoanalysis.* Hillsdale, NJ: The Analytic Press.

# 4

# My Integration Journey

## Reflections of a Christian Psychologist and Pastor

*Siang-Yang Tan, Fuller Theological Seminary*

In this spiritual autobiography of my integration journey as a Christian psychologist and a pastor, I will share my reflections and story in the following order of topics: development, mentoring, struggles, spiritual disciplines and meaningful experiences, therapy, and end with a personal letter to you the reader that I trust and pray will be a help and blessing in your own integration journey of faith in Jesus Christ. I have previously written autobiographical chapters and an article covering some of these areas (Tan, 1993, 2005, 2006a), and I will refer to them in this chapter.

## DEVELOPMENT

Singapore, or more formally the Republic of Singapore, in Southeast Asia, is my country of origin. I was born in 1954, and I grew up there until 1973, when I left the country for Montreal, Quebec, Canada, in order to study psychology at McGill University. My father, Siew Thiam Tan, came to Singapore from China, and he met and married my mother, Madam Chiow Yang Quek, who was born in Singapore. In a somewhat typical Chinese-Singaporean family, I grew up with six siblings: three older brothers, an older sister and a younger sister. I was the sixth child in our family of seven kids.

My mother was a conscientious and loving homemaker who brought us up with the help of a housemaid from Canton, China. My father was a businessman who provided for us as the traditional breadwinner in our middle-class family. He had high standards, and he especially valued education and academic achievements. Even so, in his later years, my father mellowed and showed a more tender side of himself.

I have generally good memories of my childhood and adolescent years growing up in Singapore with my family members and my friends in our neighborhood, school and later church and parachurch contexts. I attended Roman Catholic schools (Saint Patrick's School and Saint Stephen's School) right up to junior college level (or "A" levels). In these schools, I received not only a sound education but also an exposure to the Roman Catholic faith. As a young teenager, while I believed in God, and in Jesus to some degree, I still experienced a deep emptiness within me. I searched for answers to my deep fear of death, as well as for the meaning of life. I had external success in terms of academics and other areas of achievement—I had excellent grades, was good in sports (e.g., soccer), and had great relationships with many friends and with my family. However, internally, I felt the void and restlessness acutely.

Thankfully, during that time, two of my good friends in my neighborhood (Kim Lark Lim and Ee Keen Wong) reached out to me and shared the gospel of Jesus Christ. They shared with me that I could be saved from my fear of death and experience deep meaning in life by accepting Jesus Christ into my heart as my personal Lord and Savior and thereby receiving eternal life from God. I did not respond to their caring evangelism immediately, but shortly thereafter I experienced a couple of accidents in which, within a couple of months, my left arm was broken in the same place twice. The first accident happened in June 1968 when I fell off a bicycle that I was riding. The second accident took place on August 12 that same year, when I fell off a slippery, mossy pavement at the beach near my house. That night, August 12, 1968, I finally gave my life to Jesus and by faith asked him to come into my heart and be my Lord and Savior. Although my arm still hurt the next day, I experienced internally a deep peace and joy that I could not explain. It was as if I was "broken but made whole" by the Lord. This was a dramatic and significant conversion experience for me as a young teenager, and it has surely changed my life even to this day. My fear of death was gone, and since then I have entered into a deeply meaningful friendship and relationship with God through Jesus Christ.

My two neighborhood friends were delighted to hear about my conversion experience and brought me to their church, called Bethesda Katong, an open Brethren church. They discipled me in my walk with the Lord, meeting with me regularly for Bible study and prayer. I also met and was blessed by many loving and godly people in the church—people who helped me to grow in my faith and relationship with Jesus Christ. I was baptized in December 1970. Dr. Benjamin Chew was the chair of the elders board then, and I was deeply touched and blessed by his teaching and preaching ministry. He was one of Singapore's most beloved and well-known Christian leaders. He passed away in 1994. I had an opportunity to visit and pray with him several months before his passing. He held my hand for a long while and said to me: "Siang-Yang, write about the psychology of the kingdom (of God) and not the kingdom of psychology!"

I was very involved in my church, especially in Sunday school and youth ministry. I also actively participated in the ministries of Singapore Youth for Christ (or YFC), an exciting youth parachurch organization that was instrumental in bringing many young people to Christ at that time (i.e., the late 1960s). I received excellent mentoring and youth-ministry and leadership training from YFC and its leaders, especially Donald Chia and Harry Quek, men who remain special friends of mine to this day. Through YFC, I also had some training in basic helping and counseling skills. As a result of my YFC and church ministry experiences, I felt the Lord leading me to pursue further advanced training in clinical psychology so that I could be better equipped to more effectively help people with their problems of living.

I had a burnout experience in 1970 that was emotionally and spiritually very painful for me. It included my first "dark night of the soul" episode—a time in which I could not sense God's presence with me and during which I felt spiritually dry. I also experienced feelings of fatigue and depression in this "Job-like" season of my life that was trig-gered by my hectic schedule of activities at school, church and YFC. I had to learn to set appropriate limits in my life and in my schedule; I had to learn to live a more balanced, less driven life, with more regular exercise, sufficient sleep and rest, and proper nutrition. With the sup-port, counsel and prayers of good friends and mentors, as well as with the love of my family, I experienced the healing grace of God, who re-stored me and led me into a deeper and more mature relationship with him. My interest in helping people in their struggles and problems also grew as a result of this burnout experience. I sensed even more strongly that the Lord was leading me to serve him and to serve people in the field of clinical psychology.

I then had long discussions with my father about my future career options, which included law, economics and clinical psychology. He was very gracious in trusting my decision to pursue further university education in psychology instead of law or economics, as well as to pro-vide the financial support I needed to do so. However, he was con-cerned about whether I could find a good job in Singapore after my return from completing my education in psychology. I had to go abroad for this education and training, because in the early 1970s, there was no department of psychology at the local university in Singapore.

One of my older brothers (Siang Yong Tan) went to McGill Univer-sity in Montreal, Quebec, in 1964, to attend medical school on a Co-lombo Plan Scholarship from the Singapore government. He strongly encouraged me to apply to McGill, because it had a well-known de-partment of psychology as well. With my father's and my family's sup-port, with affirmation from close Christian friends and mentors, and with much prayer and reflection, I finally decided to apply to McGill. I was admitted into a B.A. program in personality and abnormal psy-chology, and I left Singapore for McGill in September 1973, when I was eighteen years old.

To complete the chronological and developmental sequence of my life so far, let me briefly mention that I was in Montreal, Quebec, at McGill University from 1973 to 1980, where I graduated with my B.A. First Class Honors in psychology in 1976 and my APA-accredited

Ph.D. in clinical psychology in 1980. Then I was in London, Ontario, Canada, from 1980 to 1983, where I worked as a psychologist in the Department of Psychological Services at the University Hospital that was affiliated with the University of Western Ontario, where I also taught part-time in the Departments of Psychology, Psychiatry and Oral Medicine. Next I was in Toronto, Ontario, from 1983 to 1985, where I taught at Ontario Bible College and served as its director of counseling, and where I also pastored the Malaysian-Singaporean Bible Church part-time. Finally, I have been in Los Angeles, California, from 1985 to the present, where I have been serving as a professor of psychology at Fuller Theological Seminary's Graduate School of Psychology in Pasadena, California, and living in Arcadia, California. Since 1996, I have also served as the senior pastor of First Evangelical Church Glendale, in Glendale, California (see Tan, 1993, for more details on my life history up until 1993).

I met my wife, Angela, in Montreal in 1975 while we were both students at McGill, and we were married on May 21, 1977. In 1977, she graduated from McGill with her Bachelor of Commerce (Honors) degree, majoring in economics and accounting. After her graduation, Angela became a chartered accountant in Canada, and she later went on to become a certified public accountant (CPA) in the United States. I deeply love her and appreciate her constant support and love for me all these years. We have two grown children, Carolyn and Andrew, both of whom were born in Canada.

My father passed away in Singapore in 1976 after suffering his second stroke within a year. When this very sad event took place, I had just graduated with my B.A. First Class Honors in psychology and was about to start my Ph.D. program in clinical psychology at McGill University. I was glad to have spent the previous summer in 1975 back in Singapore, as I had had some good, long conversations with my father during that time. In one of those conversations, for the first time in my life, my father told me that he had attended a Chinese-speaking church when he was much younger, after immigrating to Singapore from China. He also said that he believed in Christ in his own way and that he had a deep respect for my faith in Christ. I am so incredibly thankful that we had those conversations before he passed away the next year.

My mother has been a widow since 1976, and she continues to live in Singapore in the house where I grew up, with a full-time helper. After many years of witnessing to her and sharing Christ with her, she finally received Jesus into her heart as her Lord and Savior several years ago. At her request, I baptized her at her home in November 2006, when Angela and I were back in Singapore to celebrate my mother's eightieth birthday; both of these were truly joyous events.

## MENTORING

I have been blessed by several significant mentors in my life. I have already mentioned the YFC leaders and mentors who deeply impacted me as a teenager and who encouraged me in my interest to pursue further training in clinical psychology.

In addition, when I was at McGill University, I was blessed with two special and excellent mentors, both of whom were professors of psychology: Ernest G. Poser and Ronald Melzack (see Tan, 1993). Poser was my academic advisor as an undergraduate student, as well as my major Ph.D. dissertation advisor. He obtained his Ph.D. in clinical psychology under the mentoring of Hans J. Eysenck at the University of London, in England. Eysenck was one of the founders of behavior therapy. Poser helped to develop behavior therapy in Canada. He directed the Behavior Therapy Unit at the Douglas Hospital Centre in Montreal for many years. It was one of the first clinical treatment and training centers in behavior therapy in North America (see Poser, 1977). He was also the director of clinical training and a professor of psychology at McGill. Poser was an outstanding example of a scientist-practitioner, and he provided excellent mentoring to me during all my seven years at McGill, while I was both an undergraduate and a doctoral student.

Poser helped me obtain a broad education in psychology, including exposure to neuropsychology and clinical health psychology, along with a healthy respect for good scientific research. He has also been supportive of my attempts to integrate Christian faith and clinical practice, particularly within the domain of cognitive behavior therapy. Further, in the mid-1960s Poser did some groundbreaking research on the effectiveness of nonprofessionals (i.e., untrained college students) who, in working with schizophrenic patients in group therapy, achieved comparable therapeutic outcomes to professional therapists (Poser, 1966). His openness to using nonprofessionals or paraprofessionals in helping people has influenced me, and it has led me to develop a major area of experience and expertise in lay Christian counseling (Tan, 1991, 1997, 2002). Poser is now retired in Vancouver, British Columbia, Canada. We still keep in touch, and I have recently visited him in Vancouver a few times.

As I stated above, my other mentor at McGill was Ronald Melzack, one of the best-known psychologists in the area of pain and pain control (e.g., see Melzack, 1993; Melzack & Wall, 1965, 1988). He is now retired from McGill. He served as my interim dissertation advisor for a year (1979-1980), while Poser was away on sabbatical leave. Like Poser, Melzack has also impacted my life and development as a psychologist, helping me to appreciate and understand the neuropsychological and neurophysiological aspects of human functioning and dysfunctioning, including pain. Both Poser and Melzack provided invaluable mentoring for my Ph.D. dissertation research on the effects of cognitive-behavioral skills training on acute pain (i.e., knee arthogram pain) in a clinical setting (see Tan, 1982; Tan & Poser, 1982). In short, Poser and Melzack were significant "intellectual parents" to me. Since then, I have integrated Christian spiritual resources with cognitive-behavioral skills training for clinical pain control in a book I wrote some years ago on managing chronic pain (Tan, 1996a). I have similarly integrated Christian faith resources with mainly cognitive-behavioral strategies in a book on coping with depression, coauthored with John Ortberg (Tan & Ortberg, 2004).

My clinical training and experience in cognitive therapy and cognitive-behavior therapy were further enhanced during the years I worked as a psychologist at University Hospital in London, Ontario (1980-1983). In particular, while there I learned a great deal from Brian Shaw, a student of Aaron Beck (the founder of cognitive therapy) and a key leader in cognitive therapy in Canada. Shaw served as my primary clinical supervisor while I obtained my postdoctoral supervised hours for licensure/registration as a psychologist in the province of Ontario. (I became licensed in 1981.) I learned the finer points of cognitive therapy from Shaw, who was a great clinical supervisor and mentor for me. He was also open and supportive of my attempts to integrate Christian faith and cognitive-behavior therapy.

Gary Collins and Larry Crabb, two key leaders in the integration of Christian faith and psychology, including counseling and psychotherapy, influenced me initially through their books and writings, as well as presentations at conferences. Over the years, we have become good friends, and as informal mentors in my integration journey, they have always been an encouragement and a blessing to me. There have been many Christian psychologists and others in the field who have also touched my life and influenced my work in integration, and the list would be too long if I tried to mention all of them. However, these individuals include the following people whom I have come to know and deeply appreciate: Joe Ozawa, Stan Jones, Gary Moon, David Benner, Ev Worthington, Eric Johnson, Rod Wilson, Tim Clinton, George Ohlschlager, Peter Hill, Richard Butman, Randy Sanders, the late Randy Sorenson and several others.

The Fuller faculty in the School of Psychology have also provided stimulating, challenging and helpful conversations about integration. I am particularly grateful for the earlier support and encouragement of Arch Hart (who was the dean of the School of Psychology at Fuller when I was hired as a faculty member in 1985), Newt Malony, Thom Needham, Paul Clement, Chuck Ridley, Richard Hunt, John Court and Hendrika Vande Kemp, and the encouragement of Winston Gooden (the current dean of the School of Psychology at Fuller), James Guy (formerly the dean, before Gooden), Linda Wagener (formerly the associate dean), Al Dueck, Richard Gorsuch, Warren Brown, Jack and Judy Balswick, James Furrow, Cameron Lee, Alexis Abernethy, and John Martin, as well as many other faculty members. I especially want to mention Jeff Bjorck, who is also a professor of psychology at Fuller, as well as a faithful friend, colleague and prayer partner for two decades now.

Ed Shafranske, who is the director of the Psy.D. program at Pepperdine University and a professor of psychology there, has also been a good professional colleague and collaborator. In particular, I have enjoyed the experience of co-presenting a full-day workshop with him at the annual conventions of the American Psychological Association (APA). (The workshop we co-present is entitled "Integrating Religious and Spiritual Interventions in Psychological Treatment.") Shafranske has edited or coedited a couple of key books on religion and spirituality in clinical practice or psychotherapy published by the APA (see Shafranske, 1996; Sperry & Shafranske, 2005), for which I have contributed chapters (see Tan, 1996c; Tan & Johnson, 2005). At different times, we have also each served as president of the APA's Division 36 (Psychology and Religion).

I also want to mention several pastors who have blessed me deeply and who have encouraged my work in integration. For example, Pastor Don Hamilton at Peoples Church of Montreal fully supported my earlier work in Christian lay counseling, including setting up a lay counseling service at the church from 1976 to 1980 when I left Montreal (see Tan, 1991). Pastor Bill McRae at North Park Community Chapel in London, Ontario, did likewise, as I helped set up another lay counseling service at the church from 1980 to 1983 when I left for Toronto. Pastor McRae became the president of Ontario Bible College and Seminary (now called Tyndale University College and Seminary) in 1983, and at that time, he challenged me to leave my position as a psychologist at University Hospital in London, Ontario, to work at Ontario Bible College, which I did after much prayer and painful reflection together with my wife, Angela. With the full support and encouragement of McRae, I became director of counseling there and also established the Institute of Christian Counseling, to provide training for pastors and lay counselors. McRae had strongly challenged me to further develop Christian counseling in Canada. I should add that Brian Stiller, President of Tyndale University College and Seminary, has also been a real friend and informal mentor to me.

Finally, I want to express my deepest appreciation to Pastor Eddie Lo, former senior pastor at First Evangelical Church Glendale in Glendale, California. Pastor Lo not only strongly affirmed my work in integration and Christian counseling, but he also challenged me to become the next senior pastor of the church, which I sensed the Lord leading me to do in 1995-1996. I was ordained in September 1996 and have been serving as the senior pastor of the church since then. I continue to serve as a professor of psychology at Fuller, on a half-time basis. Pastor Lo passed away into the presence of the Lord on March 15, 2008, and he is deeply missed by all who knew him, including me and my family. He was like a father to us, as well as a mentor, and he showed God's love and grace to us in many ways, for which I will always be grateful.

I am also thankful for the theological mentoring that I have received from the Fuller faculty in the School of Theology, especially from Colin Brown and Donald Hagner. More recently, I have received informal theological mentoring through my meetings with Daniel Fuller, Ralph Martin and presently with Frederick Dale Bruner. Currently, I meet with Bruner every few weeks over lunch, where we engage in stimulating and helpful discussions of theology, ministry and integration, as well as of more personal matters.

Finally, with regard to mentoring, I want to mention my involvement as a ministry team and board member of Renovaré for over a decade now. Renovaré is a spiritual renewal organization that was founded by Richard Foster and is now being led by Chris Webb as president. Serving together with me through Renovaré, Richard Foster and Dallas Willard have been a real blessing to me as informal mentors and friends. The other Renovaré board members have also been channels of God's love and grace to me, and I am deeply thankful for them.

## STRUGGLES

As a phenomenon of interest in the psychological literature, spiritual struggles (e.g., divine struggles with God, intrapsychic struggles with oneself and interpersonal struggles with others in faith contexts) have received more attention in recent years than in the past (e.g., see Pargament, 2007; Pargament, Murray-Swank, Magyar & Ano, 2005). From a biblical perspective, spiritual struggles, including doubts, trials, tribulations, sufferings, persecutions and "dark nights of the soul," can all be used by God to help us to grow in Christ and become more loving and empathic (e.g., see 2 Corinthians 1:3-4). As servants of Jesus Christ, we need to embrace suffering with courage and humility, in the form of a holy and healthy brokenness that is characterized by a deep dependency on God (see Tan, 2006b). Beck (2007) has similarly referred to the interface of complaint (e.g., disappointment, frustration, lament, doubt) on the one hand and communion (i.e., active engagement) with God on the other, highlighting this tension as a phenomenon that needs further understanding from psychological, theological and empirical perspectives. He calls it "the Winter experience of faith" or "the Winter faith experience" (Beck, 2007, p. 68). In a broader context, much attention has also recently been given to the growth that can follow highly stressful life events and trauma, and such perceived growth has been referred to with terms like "posttraumatic growth," "stress-related growth" and "benefit finding" (see Helgeson, Reynolds & Tomich, 2006; Park & Helgeson, 2006; see also Calhoun & Tedeschi, 2006; Tedeschi & Calhoun, 1995).

In this section, I will share my own pilgrimage of faith as a Christian, including how spiritual struggles and painful experiences have been used by God to help me mature more deeply in Christ (see Tan, 2006a). Of course, rather than transform us to become better people in Christ, such experiences can unfortunately sometimes make us more bitter as people. Our responses to these experiences are what will determine if we end up becoming better people or bitter people, and for good or for ill, our responses are based on our beliefs and our thinking, whether biblical or not (e.g., see Hutchison, 2005). Biblical thinking that views trials and suffering as opportunities rather than as obstacles will help us to survive and grow into deeper Christlikeness in tough times.

I have already mentioned my conversion to faith in Christ and my painful experience with burnout as a young teenager in 1970 in Singapore. I have also mentioned how my experience of burnout eventually helped me to live a more balanced life, with deeper respect for proper limits and necessary boundaries. I had a second, similar (but less intense) burnout experience in 1979, while I was doing my Ph.D. studies in clinical psychology at McGill. In addition to my academic responsibilities, my research work and my advanced clinical internship, I was also heavily involved in ministry, including being responsible for directing the Montreal YFC campus life high school clubs division and running a lay counseling service at Peoples Church of Montreal.

For a period, I had to struggle with not feeling God's presence, wondering why a loving God allows suffering in those who love him and whether he would heal and restore me from this second burnout experience. I spent a lot of time in prayer, crying out to the Lord for his healing grace and mercy, even as I was learning to know him and trust him more deeply. During this time, which lasted a few months, I was learning to trust that God really was going to work all things together for good in my life (Romans 8:28), including this painful season of my life. The Lord answered my prayers by providing the loving support and prayers of my close friends, my mentors and especially my wife, Angela. He also helped me to take a much needed break from my hectic schedule of activities and to instead engage in regular exercise (e.g. swimming and working out) and get adequate rest and sleep. I eventually recovered from this second burnout experience, and I was deeply grateful for the Lord's healing and restoration. During that season, I learned more about the deeper and paradoxical aspects of the spiritual life in Christ. For instance, I learned that journeying with Christ includes periodic dark nights of the soul and painful experiences. Moreover, I again learned the need to keep limits and not overextend myself.

As I stated before, I married Angela on May 21, 1977, in Montreal, and I am deeply grateful to have her as my life partner. For over three decades now, she has been a constant source of love, support and prayers in our married life together. While we have experienced many joys and blessings in our marriage, we have also gone through some trials and challenges, as in all marriages. We have learned to appreciate the deeper realities and blessings of what Gary Thomas (2000) has called "sacred marriage"—that is, the idea that God's design for marriage is to make spouses holier more than it is to make them happier. Indeed God has used the crucible of marriage to help Angela and me to grow in deeper Christlikeness and agape love for each other, for our children and for others, even as we have faced periodic conflicts, personality differences and the trials of family life. We have two grown children, Carolyn and Andrew, each of whom has been a joy and blessing to us as parents, as well as a challenge. We have seen them grow up so fast over the quickly passing years. We have also learned about "sacred parenting" (Thomas, 2004) and how raising children shapes our souls and helps us to grow spiritually as parents. As parents, we have loved our children, prayed for them, wept for them in their own spiritual and personal struggles, and rejoiced with them in their achievements and growth. The bottom line is that for my wife and me, we have experienced struggles in our marriage and in our family life, but such struggles truly have deepened our faith in Christ, and they have helped us to know and trust God more.

Finally, I want to share about some other experiences of brokenness, suffering and humbling that I have gone through. These experiences included (1) a job promotion that I had anticipated but did not get, and (2) seeing the personal and spiritual struggles of my children at close range. Through these experiences, I have learned to trust God and his sovereignty even more, as well as to deepen my friendship with him in prayer. I have also learned to come to the end of myself more fully and to depend more completely on God and his grace, which is truly sufficient for me on a daily basis and in which his power is made perfect in my weakness (2 Corinthians 12:9-10).

It has been a painful season of pruning and "shattered dreams" (Crabb, 2001) that has led me to experience greater joy in the Lord, who is completely able to keep us faithful and fruitful through the trials and struggles of life. Such fire-testing seasons of our lives, sent from a loving God, have been called "severe gifts" by Thomas (2002); they are what I have often termed God's "severe mercies." They are an essential part of God's paradoxical, loving and gracious way of working in our lives. My own "severe mercies" have taught me that faithfulness in and loving obedience toward God are more crucial than so-called success. I have learned to no longer try to do great things for God but instead to simply do things for a great God. In short, my focus is now more on the great God than it is on the great things (Tan, 2006a, 2006b). These are precious lessons that have deepened me as a person. They have helped me to become a more authentic, empathic and effective therapist for my clients and pastor and friend for the people who I have opportunities to minister to. They have also helped me to do integration in a way that is more Christ-centered, Bible-based and Spirit-filled (see Tan, 2001b), as well as more culturally sensitive (e.g., see Tan, 1999a; Tan & Dong, 2000).

## SPIRITUAL DISCIPLINES AND MEANINGFUL EXPERIENCES

Staying connected with God on a daily basis is a crucial part of the Christian life (see Tan, 2006a). The spiritual disciplines help me to daily abide in Christ (John 15:5) and be filled with the presence and power of the Holy Spirit (Ephesians 5:18), so that the fruit of the Spirit—chiefly agape or Christlike love (Galatians 5:22-23)—will be produced in my life and in my lifestyle. The spiritual disciplines (see Tan & Gregg, 1997; see also Foster, 1988; Tan, 2003d; Willard, 1988) include disciplines of solitude in drawing near to God (e.g., solitude and silence, listening and guidance, prayer and intercession, study and meditation); disciplines of surrender in yielding to God (e.g., repentance and confession, yielding and submission, fasting, and worship); and disciplines of service in reaching out to others (e.g., fellowship, simplicity, service and witness).

On a daily basis, I take time in the morning to be with the Lord, in what has been called "a quiet time." This time includes the practice of prayer, silence and solitude, meditation on Scripture, and worship. I also usually read the Bible again at night, with a short time of prayer before going to bed. I preach about three times a month at church, and when I am scheduled to preach a certain week, I spend several hours that week studying the Bible and prayerfully preparing my sermon. I also practice the presence of God daily by using "flash prayers" (i.e., brief prayers) many times during the day, to keep focused on God and his presence with me throughout each day. In addition, the study of Scripture, meditation on Scripture and memorization of Scripture have all been crucial means of grace that have helped me know God more deeply. Such biblical foundations and wisdom are also essential for the integration of Christian faith and psychology, including integration in the counseling and therapy room. I also practice the other spiritual disciplines mentioned. I have had varied meaningful experiences of God's presence, from quiet moments of resting in him to more dramatic times of deep communion and rejoicing in him.

Spiritual disciplines, however, can become quite dangerous. If they are practiced in a legalistic and self-absorbed way, they can actually be harmful to our spiritual life, rather than helpful, encouraging self-sufficiency, spiritual pride and self-righteousness. Thomas (2002) has therefore emphasized that the authentic spiritual disciplines (or the "circumstantial spiritual disciplines"), which are not within our voluntary control (see Tang, 2008), are a vital addition to the traditional spiritual disciplines. The so-called authentic disciplines include selflessness, waiting, suffering, persecution, social mercy, forgiveness, mourning, contentment, sacrifice, hope and fear. Thomas explains,

> [These disciplines] turn us away from human effort—from men and women seeking the face of God—and turn us back toward God seeking the face of men and women. . . . This is a God-ordained spirituality, dependent on his sovereignty. . . . This is a spirituality I can't control, I can't initiate, I can't bring about. It is a radical dependence on God's husbandry. All I can do is try to appreciate it and learn from it. (Thomas, 2002, pp. 14-15)

Thomas further points out that the ultimate end of experiencing these authentic disciplines is "learning to love with God's love and learning to serve with God's power" (p. 12).

I have already shared several of my struggles or painful experiences in the previous section of this chapter. They can be seen as examples of authentic disciplines or circumstantial spiritual disciplines God has used in my life to love with his love and serve with his power.

I want to share a specific experience of God's presence and the anointing of the Holy Spirit—an experience that I had at our church's young adults retreat in 1989. Joe Ozawa, my close friend and also a licensed psychologist, was the speaker I had invited for this retreat. God used him in a mighty way, through the messages he gave and the prayer ministry times he led. The majority of the roughly one hundred people who were present were filled more deeply with the Holy Spirit and received spiritual gifts for further service. I was personally blessed with a fresh anointing and powerful infilling of the Holy Spirit (Ephesians 5:18) at this retreat. Since then, I have learned to yield to the Lord and be filled with the Spirit on a daily basis, as well as to minister to people out of a deeper dependence on the Spirit's presence and power, not on myself or my gifts and abilities. I have also learned to make prayer central in my life and in my ministry, taking my need for a prayer covering seriously. In light of the reality of spiritual warfare (Ephesians 6:10-18), I have a prayer shield that is provided for me by a number of faithful prayer intercessors from my church and elsewhere (see Tan, 2006a).

This prayer support and covering has been a crucial part of my integration work and thus of my integration journey. It has also been an important part of my ministry as a pastor who integrates Christian faith and psychology in areas such as preaching, teaching, pastoral care, leadership, community outreach, premarital counseling and organizational research (Tan, 2005). Elsewhere I have emphasized the essential and crucial role of the Holy Spirit in effective Christian counseling and therapy (e.g., Tan, 1999b, 2001b) and in personal or intrapersonal integration, particularly including the spirituality of the integrator. I have highlighted how without the Holy Spirit, integration in the principled (theoretical-conceptual and research) and professional (clinical or practice) areas cannot be substantially achieved (Tan, 1987b, 2001b). I have also written on the appropriate and ethical use of spiritual disciplines (e.g., prayer and Scripture) in Christian therapy (e.g. Tan, 1996b, 1996c, 1998, 2007a; see also Eck, 2002; Hall & Hall, 1997) and in clinical supervision (Tan, 2007b: see also Tan, 2009).

## THERAPY

Most of my work and writing in integration has been in the area of professional integration in clinical practice or therapy (e.g., Tan, 1996b, 1996c, 1998, 2003b, 2003c), and more specifically in the area of cognitive-behavioral therapy (e.g., Tan, 1987a, 2007a; Tan & Johnson, 2005). The professional or practical integration of Christian faith and therapy can be done in an implicit (i.e., covert, quiet) or explicit (i.e., overt, direct) way, along a continuum, depending on the client and his or her problems and needs, as well as on the theoretical orientation and inclination of the therapist (Tan, 1996c). Such integration, however, needs to be intentional and prayerful, with deep dependence on the Holy Spirit's presence and assistance (Tan, 1999b). This has been my approach to doing clinical practice for over thirty years now. I have also just completed writing a major textbook on counseling and psychotherapy from a Christian perspective (Tan, in press).

While my clinical experience and expertise has been mainly in the area of cognitive-behavioral therapy (Tan, 2007a), which emphasizes using specific cognitive-behavioral techniques to treat specific clinical problems, I have found that the therapeutic relationship with the client is a crucial factor in effective therapy. In writing about effective therapy (including cognitive-behavioral therapy) from a biblical perspective, I have therefore emphasized the importance of agape love (1 Corinthians 13), shown in a warm, empathic and genuine therapeutic relationship with the client (Tan, 1987a). Many of my clients have expressed their deepest appreciation for the genuine caring and empathy shown to them in their therapy experience with me. In fact, they often appreciate this genuine care and concern more than they appreciate the specific therapeutic techniques that I have used, although they do often also mention the techniques as being helpful. In sum, I have come to believe firmly that when it comes to effective therapy with clients, empirically supported therapy relationships, including empathy and a good therapeutic alliance (see Tan, 2003a), are just as crucial as empirically supported treatments or techniques (see Tan, 2001a).

My clinical work as a licensed psychologist or therapist with a wide range of clients and clinical problems has also helped me to see the complexity of human functioning and dysfunctioning—and additionally, how hard it is for people to really change. In order to more empathically and effectively help my clients, I have learned to be humble and respectful of my clients, as well as more dependent on God and on the Holy Spirit's guidance during therapy sessions.

My own painful experiences and struggles have also been used by

God to deepen my capacities for empathy and agape love for my clients and their struggles (2 Corinthians 1:3-4). Although I have not received formal therapy, I have been blessed and helped by various mentors and friends who have provided empathic caring and wise counsel for me at various times in my life—times when I needed help myself. My wife, Angela, has also been a special source of such support and help, as my best friend and life partner on earth. My ultimate best friend and wisest counselor is the Lord himself, who has continued to faithfully show me his love and healing grace over the many years that I have walked with him. He has helped me to grow in compassionate caring and agape love for people, including my clients.

## PERSONAL LETTER

My Dear Friend,

I would like to share with you some lessons that I have learned and any wisdom that I may have gained in my integration journey so far as a Christian psychologist and pastor. I trust and pray that my reflections may be of some help and blessing to you in your own integration journey and in your pilgrimage of faith in Christ.

First, I would recommend that you set as your first priority your relationship and walk with the Lord, that he will always be your first love (Revelation 2:4), and that you will love him with all your heart, soul, mind and strength, and love your neighbor as yourself (Mark 12:29-31). The grace-filled practice of the spiritual disciplines on a regular basis will be essential, including a daily quiet time alone with the Lord in solitude and silence, prayer and meditation on Scripture, and worship, and periodic longer personal retreats with him for a day or two or longer. Practicing the presence of God throughout the day, for example by using flash prayers often, will also help much. It is out of such a deep and intimate relationship with the Lord that you will come to know and understand truth more fully, including the psychotheological truth that is foundational for all good integration—that is, for all integration that is Christ-centered, Bible-based and Spirit-filled.

Second, I want to thank God for the many mentors, formal or informal, whom he has so graciously sent into my life. They have made a significant impact on me and on my integration work, as well as on my ministry as a pastor. I have learned so much from them. I wish some of my earlier mentors had taught me more firmly the need to set limits and to not take on too much, as well as to live a more balanced life with adequate rest and sleep, good nutrition and regular exercise. May you learn these precious lessons early on in your journey. I pray and wish for you to have a few good mentors, especially humble, loving and Christlike Christian mentors, who will provide the loving support, intellectual stimulation, rigorous challenge, spiritual direction, and faithful prayers for you on your integration journey.

Third, there is much helpful literature that is now available on the integration of Christian faith and psychology, including therapy (e.g., see Stevenson, Eck & Hill, 2007) that is essential reading for you if you are to do integration work well, whether in the principled (theoretical-conceptual and research), professional (clinical or practice), and/or personal (intrapersonal, including spirituality) areas. Recent work on developing a distinctively Christian psychology that is more substantially grounded in biblical and historical theology, as well as in Scripture itself (e.g., see Johnson, 2007), is also required reading for you and me. In this regard, it is of ultimate importance and value to be saturated with Scripture as the inspired, eternal Word of God (2 Timothy 3:16).

Fourth, learn to be filled daily with the power and presence of the Holy Spirit (Ephesians 5:18), by confession of sins and by yielding to him and to the Lordship of Christ. Each day in prayer, ask him to anoint you afresh with his wisdom, truth, power and love, as well as with the spiritual gifts that will equip you to be a more faithful and fruitful servant of Jesus Christ, capable of doing good integration work. Be prayerfully dependent on the Holy Spirit, who is the Counselor or Comforter par excellence (John 14:16-17), especially in clinical practice or therapy with clients, where his agape love can be manifested in a warm, empathic and genuine therapeutic relationship with clients.

Fifth, be thankful for how we are wounded healers ourselves. In other words, always remember that God can use your own sufferings and struggles to expand and deepen your capacities for empathy and compassionate caring, as manifested in the form of genuine agape love that you can share with your clients and with others who are suffering (2 Corinthians 1:3-4). Gratitude for all that God allows or even sends into our lives will help you to know and trust him more. It will also help you experience growth even through trials and struggles, seeing them as opportunities to become more Christlike and spiritually mature, rather than seeing them as hindrances.

Finally, I would like to suggest that you do not make psychology, therapy or even the integration task to be everything in your life. Integration is not the end-all, be-all of our lives. Instead, seek the Lord and his kingdom first (Matthew 6:33), and always see the bigger picture of God's will and God's kingdom with loving obedience to him, even as we are graced and blessed by him. This means living the eternal kind of life, a life in the kingdom, where he rules and reigns over every area of your life and mine. It includes living a balanced life that allows enough time for yourself and your family, as well as time for the church as a loving community of faith and as the larger family of God. And lastly, it includes leaving enough time for you to reach out to others, especially the lost, the oppressed and the broken—reaching out with the good news of Jesus Christ, who alone can ultimately save us all.

I would like to wish you the Lord's best and deepest blessings, as you walk on with him in your integration journey. God Bless!

With his love and prayers.

Warmly,
Siang-Yang Tan

## REFERENCES

Beck, R. (2007). The winter experience of faith: Empirical, theological, and theoretical perspectives. *Journal of Psychology and Christianity, 26,* 68-78.

Calhoun, L. G., & Tedeschi, R. G. (Eds.). (2006). *Handbook of posttraumatic growth: Research and practice.* Mahwah, NJ: Erlbaum.

Crabb, L. (2001). *Shattered dreams: God's unexpected pathway to joy.* Colorado Springs, CO: WaterBrook Press.

Eck, B. E. (2002). An exploration of the therapeutic use of spiritual disciplines in clinical practice. *Journal of Psychology and Christianity, 21,* 266-80.

Foster, R. J. (1988). *Celebration of discipline* (Rev. ed.). San Francisco: Harper & Row.

Hall, M. E. L., & Hall, T. W. (1997). Integration in the therapy room: An overview of the literature. *Journal of Psychology and Theology, 25,* 86-101.

Helgeson, V. S., Reynolds, K. A., & Tomich, P. L. (2006). A meta-analytic review of benefit finding and growth. *Journal of Consulting and Clinical Psychology, 74,* 797-816.

Hutchison, J. C. (2005). *Thinking right when things go wrong: Biblical wisdom for surviving tough times.* Grand Rapids, MI: Kregel.

Johnson, E. L. (2007). *Foundations for soul care: A Christian psychology proposal.* Downers Grove, IL: InterVarsity Press.

Melzack, R. (1993). Pain: Past, present, and future. *Canadian Journal of Experimental Psychology, 47,* 615-29.

Melzack, R., & Wall, P. D. (1965). Pain mechanisms: A new theory. *Science, 150,* 971-79.

Melzack, R., & Wall, P. D. (1988). *The challenge of pain* (Rev. ed.). Harmondsworth, Middlesex, UK: Penguin.

Pargament, K. I. (2007). *Spiritually integrated psychotherapy: Understanding and addressing the sacred.* New York: Guilford Press.

Pargament, K. I., Murray-Swank, N. A., Magyar, G. M., & Ano, G. G. (2005). Spiritual struggle: A phenomenon of interest to psychology and religion. In W. R. Miller & H. D. Delaney (Eds.), *Judeo-Christian perspectives on psychology: Human nature, motivation, and change* (pp. 245-68). Washington, DC: American Psychological Association.

Park, C. L., & Helgeson, V. S. (2006). Introduction to the special section: Growth following highly stressful life events—Current status and future directions. *Journal of Consulting and Clinical Psychology, 74,* 791-96.

Poser, E. G. (1966). The effect of therapists' training on group therapeutic outcome. *Journal of Consulting Psychology, 30,* 283-89.

Poser, E. G. (1977). *Behavior therapy in clinical practice: Decision making, procedure, and outcome.* Springfield, IL: Charles C. Thomas.

Shafranske, E. P. (Ed.). (1996). *Religion and the clinical practice of psychology.* Washington, DC: American Psychological Association.

Sperry, L., & Shafranske, E. P. (Eds.). (2005). *Spiritually oriented psychotherapy.* Washington, DC: American Psychological Association.

Stevenson, D. H., Eck, B. E., & Hill, P. C. (Eds.). (2007). *Psychology and Christianity integration: Seminal works that shaped the movement.* Batavia,

IL: Christian Association for Psychological Studies.

Tan, S. Y. (1982). Cognitive and cognitive-behavioural methods for pain control: A selective review. *Pain, 12,* 201-28.

Tan, S. Y. (1987a). Cognitive-behavior therapy: A biblical approach and critique. *Journal of Psychology and Theology, 15,* 103-12.

Tan, S. Y. (1987b). Intrapersonal integration: The servant's spirituality. *Journal of Psychology and Christianity, 6,* 34-39.

Tan, S. Y. (1991). *Lay counseling: Equipping Christians for a helping ministry.* Grand Rapids, MI: Zondervan.

Tan, S. Y. (1993). My pilgrimage as a Christian psychologist. In D. J. Lee (Ed.), *Storying ourselves: A narrative perspective on Christians in psychology* (pp. 131-53). Grand Rapids, MI: Baker.

Tan, S. Y. (1996a). *Managing chronic pain.* Downers Grove, IL: InterVarsity Press.

Tan, S. Y. (1996b). Practicing the presence of God: The work of Richard J. Foster and its applications to psychotherapeutic practice. *Journal of Psychology and Christianity, 15,* 17-28.

Tan, S. Y. (1996c). Religion in clinical practice: Implicit and explicit integration. In E. Shafranske (Ed.), *Religion and the clinical practice of psychology* (pp. 365-87). Washington, DC: American Psychological Association.

Tan, S. Y. (1997). The role of the psychologist in paraprofessional helping. *Professional Psychology: Research and Practice, 28,* 368-72.

Tan, S. Y. (1998). The spiritual disciplines and counseling. *Christian Counseling Today, 6*(2), 8, 20-21.

Tan, S. Y. (1999a). Cultural issues in Spirit-filled psychotherapy. *Journal of Psychology and Christianity, 18,* 164-76.

Tan, S. Y. (1999b). Holy Spirit: Role in counseling. In D. G. Benner & P. Hill (Eds.), *Baker encyclopedia of psychology and counseling* (2nd ed., pp. 568-69). Grand Rapids, MI: Baker.

Tan, S. Y. (2001a). Empirically supported treatments. *Journal of Psychology and Christianity, 20,* 282-86.

Tan, S. Y. (2001b). Integration and beyond: Principled, professional, and personal. *Journal of Psychology and Christianity, 20,* 18-28.

Tan, S. Y. (2002). Lay helping. In T. Clinton & G. Ohlschlager (Eds.), *Competent Christian counseling* (Vol. 1, pp. 424-36, 759-62). Colorado Springs, CO: WaterBrook Press.

Tan, S. Y. (2003a). Empirically supported therapy relationships: Psychotherapy relationships that work. *Journal of Psychology and Christianity, 22,* 64-67.

Tan, S. Y. (2003b). Inner healing prayer. *Christian Counseling Today, 11*(4), 20-22.

Tan, S. Y. (2003c). Integrating spiritual direction into psychotherapy: Ethical issues and guidelines. *Journal of Psychology and Theology, 31,* 14-23.

Tan, S. Y. (2003d). *Rest: Experiencing God's peace in a restless world.* Vancouver, BC: Regent College Publishing.

Tan, S. Y. (2005). Psychology collaborating with the church: A pastor-psychologist's perspective and personal experience. In M. R. McMinn & A. W. Dominguez (Eds.), *Psychology and the church* (pp. 49-55). Hauppauge, NY: Nova Science Publishers.

Tan, S. Y. (2006a). Experiencing the grace of God and the God of grace. *Conversations: A Forum of Authentic Transformation, 4*(1), 77-81.

Tan, S. Y. (2006b). *Full service: Moving from self-serve Christianity to total servanthood.* Grand Rapids, MI: Baker.

Tan, S. Y. (2007a). Use of prayer and Scripture in cognitive-behavioral therapy. *Journal of Psychology and Christianity, 26,* 101-11.

Tan, S. Y. (2007b). Using spiritual disciplines in clinical supervision. *Journal of Psychology and Christianity, 26,* 328-35.

Tan, S. Y. (2009). Developing integration skills: The role of clinical supervision. *Journal of Psychology and Theology, 37,* 54-61.

Tan, S. Y. (in press). *Counseling and psychotherapy: A Christian perspective.* Grand Rapids, MI: Baker Academic.

Tan, S. Y., & Dong, N. J. (2000). Psychotherapy with members of Asian American churches and spiritual traditions. In P. S. Richards & A. E. Bergin (Eds.), *Handbook of psychotherapy and religious diversity* (pp. 421-44). Washington, DC: American Psychological Association.

Tan, S. Y., & Gregg, D. H. (1997). *Disciplines of the Holy Spirit.* Grand Rapids, MI: Zondervan.

Tan, S. Y., & Johnson, W. B. (2005). Spiritually oriented cognitive-behavioral therapy. In L. Sperry & E. Shafranske (Eds.), *Spiritually oriented psychotherapy* (pp. 77-103). Washington, DC: American Psychological Association.

Tan, S. Y., & Ortberg, J. (2004). *Coping with depression* (Rev. ed.). Grand Rapids, MI: Baker.

Tan, S. Y., & Poser, E. G. (1982). Acute pain in a clinical setting: Effects of cognitive-behavioural skills training. *Behaviour Research and Therapy, 20,* 535-45.

Tang, A. (2008). Not just for monks: Spiritual disciplines are for anyone who wants to love God and others more. *Asian Beacon, 40*(1), 8-9.

Tedeschi, R. G., & Calhoun, C. G. (1995). *Trauma and transformation: Growing in the aftermath of suffering.* Thousand Oaks, CA: Sage.

Thomas, G. (2000). *Sacred marriage: What if God designed marriage to make us holy more than to make us happy?* Grand Rapids, MI: Zondervan.

Thomas, G. (2002). *Authentic faith: The power of a fire-tested life.* Grand Rapids, MI: Zondervan.

Thomas, G. (2004). *Sacred parenting: How raising children shapes our soul.* Grand Rapids, MI: Zondervan.

Willard, D. (1988). *The spirit of the disciplines.* San Francisco: Harper & Row.

**5**

# Journeying
# Toward Home

*Mark R. McMinn, George Fox University*

Every Monday, Wednesday and Friday at noon—except for those interrupted by pesky academic meetings—I spend an hour on the basketball court. At my chronological age of fifty years, I count it a great blessing to still have joints that allow me to pound the hardwood. I hit some jump shots occasionally, at least if one can call my three-inch vertical leap a jump, and every now and then I stand in and take a charge, which sends me sprawling to the ground with limbs flying in various directions. For the following several days, I limp around, muttering to myself that I need to recognize the disparity between the age I think I am and the age I actually am. It surprises me that I am as old as I am and how fast I got to be this age. Being asked to write this chapter is yet another reminder that I have been around quite a long time now.

## DEVELOPMENT

I have become quite fond of telling people that I am a psychologist who was raised on a nut farm. My parents purchased forty-five acres in rural Oregon in 1959, when I was one year old, and they proceeded to plant hazelnut and walnut trees on the property. Some of my earliest childhood memories are working on the farm with my parents and my older sister. They are good memories mostly, of learning to work and of gaining confidence that all creation yearns to grow.

The farm was large enough to require a good deal of work but not large enough to sustain a family's income, so my parents worked "real jobs" in addition to nurturing their children and their orchard. During my early years, my mother was a homemaker and my father was a teacher. At some point my mother went back to school for her teaching certificate. Then, as my mother started her teaching career, my father went back to school for a doctoral degree. Later my mother went back to school again, this time for her masters in special education.

This kind of educational leapfrog has become common among dual-career couples today, but I remember admiring my parents for their exceptional accomplishments and work ethic. My sister Anne and I picked up that same work ethic; we excelled in school and both went on for doctoral degrees after college—hers in medicine and mine in psychology. I never felt pressured by my parents to achieve. It was more that I felt inspired by their energy and example.

Our family work ethic, along with the growing orchard, compelled us to work on the farm many Saturdays. We worked not only because it was what we knew to do, but also perhaps to mask some of the pain that could not be spoken, and wasn't for many years to come.

I now realize that my mother absorbed a good deal of pain and struggle for the sake of Anne and me, and it stirs me to think how bravely she handled it. My father bore his share of struggle also, and he unveiled a great deal of shame when secrets became known two decades later. I suppose it is not entirely easy growing up in a family with secrets, though my parents protected me well enough that I did not know much of the pain and struggle they faced. I would have told you then that my home was idyllic, and in many ways I would still say so today.

My parents still live, though they live apart. Their marriage survived almost forty years, which speaks to their tenacity. My mother is my hero. Whatever virtue I carry can be traced to her courage, kindness, humility, generosity, diligence and faith. In my father I see a man who survived a difficult start in life with humor, intelligence, faith and friendship. He was adopted from an orphanage at age four, into a home that possessed some of the best and worst things that the Christian religion has to offer. I have all sorts of feelings about my father, with admiration and sadness both on the list.

My high school football coach reinforced the work ethic I learned at home. He used to say—no, he used to yell—"WE WILL BE THE BEST CONDITIONED TEAM IN THE STATE OF OREGON!" Each August, as we endured two weeks of daily triples (daily doubles were for weaker souls), all of us on the team suspected he was right. I loved playing football. It gave me confidence, strength and courage, and it helped me realize that those qualities were worth nothing apart from my teammates.

The bleachers were always full for home games. There was not much else going on in our rural town of Forest Grove, so people came and watched football. Ward Graham had played football at Forest Grove High School a generation before me, so he and his family always came to the games. Ward, his wife, Bobbe, and their four children also attended the First Baptist Church of Forest Grove, where my family worshiped. We had the typical assortment of comical characters in our church, including a godly old man with the name of Harry Rear (actually, he spelled his name Reeher, but it was pronounced the same as Rear). I always wondered why he did not go by Harold.

Ward and Bobbe's third child, Lisa, caught my attention when she walked into the ninth-grade Sunday school class for the first time in 1971. This girl—with soft brown hair, kind eyes, a gentle smile and an adventurous spirit—has walked beside me for thirty-six years now, thirty of them as my spouse. We married early and grew up together. When I look at the classic virtues that Christian philosophers list—temperance, prudence, fortitude, justice, faith, hope and love—I think of Lisa, and I remember how wonderfully God has blessed me with my life partner.

Lisa went to nursing school as I went to college. We were married in the midst of it all—both of us at age twenty, which sounds remarkably young by today's standard. By age twenty-two we were parents of Rae, and at age twenty-four we added Sarah to the mix. I was in my Ph.D. program at the time, and my advisor called me into his office to do an informal mental status exam: What was I thinking, having two children while doing a Ph.D. at Vanderbilt University? Our third child, Megan Anna, came during my internship at Oregon Health Sciences University. One of the other interns asked if we were Catholic.

Our three daughters grew strong. Lisa was mostly an at-home mom when they were young, but sometime later, after she went back to school to get a Ph.D. in sociology, she wrote a book titled *Growing Strong Daughters*. We did. When our daughters were in high school, I joked that Lisa should write a sequel called *Coping with Strong Daughters*. Indeed our daughters have all grown into wise, healthy, good women. No matter how many books Lisa and I may write in our lifetime, the greatest legacy we will leave behind is our three daughters.

I began my academic career at George Fox College in 1984, immediately upon finishing graduate school. After teaching undergraduates for nine years, I was ready for the adventure of teaching doctoral students, and Lisa was just ready for adventure, I guess. So in 1993 we moved our children halfway across the country to Illinois, where I had accepted a position in the new doctoral program at Wheaton College. Lisa spent her first year in Illinois finishing her doctoral dissertation, and then she became an academic also—first at Trinity International University and later at Wheaton College. In all, we spent thirteen years of our lives in Illinois. Wheaton College is a remarkable place. We both feel privileged to have spent part of our careers there.

Near the end of our time at Wheaton, I wrote a little book titled *Finding Our Way Home* (McMinn, 2005). I set out to write this book as a spiritual reflection on our longing for heaven, but in the writing of it, I found myself thinking more and more of my home in Oregon. And Lisa felt it too. We walked almost every evening during the spring and summer months in Illinois, and more and more we found ourselves talking about going home. Our children were all either off to college or beginning their lives after college, and none of them seemed particularly inclined to settle in the Midwest. We were free to dream, and our dreams kept pointing us homeward.

In 2006, Lisa and I drove our U-Haul back across the states we had traversed thirteen years before, and we ended up back where I started my career—at George Fox University. We were about twenty miles from the First Baptist Church where we met as ninth graders. Now we both teach at George Fox—undergraduate sociology for her and graduate psychology for me. We live on five acres, where we built a house (doing much of the work ourselves), planted six hundred fir trees, and terraced a lovely vegetable garden. In our spare time, we maintain a growing forest, raise all sorts of amazing fruits and vegetables, and are part-time beekeepers. We are sort of like Wendell Berry—but with computers and smaller royalty checks.

Our daughters and their husbands have also migrated back to Oregon. We see them often and imagine a future that includes watching our grandchildren grow up nearby. In short, Lisa and I feel as much at home as any two souls can feel outside of Eden.

## MENTORING

In telling my integration journey, I have six mentors to thank, though only one knew much about integrating psychology and Christianity. The remaining five were mentors in one topic or the other but not in both.

Journeys unfold over time, so I will describe each of these mentors in chronological order. And I will mention some other great people along the way too. Sadly, I will inevitably end up overlooking many folks due to my declining dendritic connections and the limited number of pages allocated for this chapter.

*Vanderbilt University.* My primary research advisor through my Ph.D. work at Vanderbilt University was Martin Katahn (mentor #1). Martin was the name that became a household word in the late 1980s when he published his bestselling diet books (Katahn, 1986, 1989), but no one called him Martin. His friends and colleagues all called him Dick. Most doctoral students in my program called their research advisors by first name, but I could never do that. I called him Dr. Katahn partly because I was a socially awkward guy from a farm in rural Oregon, and partly because his name was Dick. I think I could have called him Martin.

Dr. Katahn helped me become a scientist. Each week several graduate students and faculty members would gather for our Vanderbilt

Weight Management Program research meetings. Graduate students arrived with arms full of Statistical Package for Social Science (SPSS) printouts, awaiting the scrutiny of faculty. We discussed ongoing and new research studies, always concerned about scientific integrity and publication potential. While doing my Ph.D. in psychology, I also completed a minor in biochemistry at the Vanderbilt Medical School. In my medical school classes, I memorized the Krebs Cycle and all sorts of other impressive stuff, and then I would go back to my graduate school research meetings in order to explore the psychological significance of what I was learning. I suppose this was integration, but it was not integrating faith and psychology as much as it was integrating medicine and psychology.

Through my biochemistry studies, I learned that losing weight is no easy task. In fact, our bodies sabotage our best efforts to lose weight by cutting back metabolic expenditures as soon as the food revenues slow. It is discouraging news for dieters, but it is also validating to those who have tried, over and over, to lose weight. My dissertation explored how accurate biochemical information about weight loss influences learned helplessness among dieters. In truth I cannot remember what I found, but I do remember being grateful that they let me have the Ph.D. even though my dissertation findings were far from monumental. Dr. Katahn provided helpful guidance as I navigated my way through a rigorous Ph.D. program, and another faculty member—Dr. Kenneth Wallston—did also. I am grateful for their investment in my life.

While being mentored in science at Vanderbilt, I was mentored in the Christian faith at the Gospel Chapel that sat just off Interstate 40, several miles from campus. John Phelan (mentor #2) and George Martin (mentor #3) seemed to see potential in me, and they invested godly wisdom and prayer into my life. John was the full-time worker at Gospel Chapel—a Plymouth Brethren assembly—who invited me to preach every month or two. In addition to motivating me to study Scripture and basic theology, the discipline of preaching helped me discover the teaching gifts that have marked my greatest contribution to the body of Christ ever since. George, a retired postal worker and an avid tennis player, and his wife, Amanda, befriended Lisa and me. George often invited me onto the tennis court, where I was mentored in humility (it is not easy being beaten so badly by a man forty years my senior). He and Amanda also had us over to their home for dinner many times, where we shared conversations about Christian living.

I received my doctoral degree in 1983, at the age of twenty-five. Later in my career I would occasionally hear people say things such as, "Mark McMinn got his doctoral degree in three years," as if this were some marker of brilliance. Actually, my youthful Ph.D. was the result of two strange twists of fate. First, I had my eye on a particular internship that would take me back to my home state of Oregon. There were only a couple American Psychological Association (APA) accredited internships in Oregon at the time, and the one in medical psychology at Oregon Health Sciences University (OHSU) seemed a perfect fit for a guy with a minor from the Vanderbilt Medical School. I knew it would be a tough spot to land, though, because it was the second highest paying internship in the country. During the fall of my third year, I had the impulse to apply for the internship a year early. All my coursework would be finished by the end of the year (at Vanderbilt the fourth year was reserved for dissertation research), so I figured that applying early would give me two chances to secure the internship I really wanted. To my surprise, I was offered the internship with my first application. So I scrambled to get my dissertation done during the spring of my third year and left Vanderbilt a year earlier than initially intended. A second twist of good fate was Vanderbilt's policy to grant the doctoral degree prior to internship. So I left Nashville at the age of twenty-five, doctoral degree in hand, heading home to Oregon and to an internship in medical psychology.

***Oregon Health Sciences University.*** I arrived back in Oregon with more enthusiasm than expertise. About two weeks into the internship, my clinical director, Dr. Arthur Wiens (mentor #4), looked me in the eye and said, "You don't have a lot of clinical experience, do you?" He was right. I had received remarkable research training at Vanderbilt but only minimal clinical training. And so began the most significant clinical mentoring relationship I have experienced. Art was a patient teacher and an inspiring example. After the internship was over, he invited me to continue in a postdoctoral position, as part of his neuropsychology and assessment practice. Over the next couple of years, I administered more Wechsler intelligence tests and Halstead-Reitan batteries than I care to count. We tested applicants for the Portland Police Department and many former auto painters who were experiencing cognitive deficits, presumably related to their heavy exposure to organic solvents. I learned to love assessment and to see it as one of the most important things psychologists have to offer the mental health community.

Perhaps the most important thing I learned about mentoring from Art is the power of his confidence in me. Despite his initial observation that I lacked clinical training, I soon learned that Art believed in me. He saw in me things I could barely see in myself at the time. His confidence was contagious. Soon I began to believe that I could tackle big scholarly and clinical adventures, because I knew Art believed I could. When I look at my most effective mentoring of others over the years, it is this gift of confidence that Art gave to me that I have also given to others. Some graduate students naturally have more confidence than competence. This makes for tough mentoring because it involves helping the student gain humility while learning professional skills, and becoming humble is not easy for any of us. But sometimes I have students whose confidence seems to lag behind, even as they are growing in competence. It is always a delight to help these students grow into an awareness of how capable and talented they are becoming.

Dr. Wiens is retired now. We had lunch last year, after losing touch with one another for many years. We chatted at the restaurant and then returned to his condominium, where he showed me the work he has been doing in compiling his family's history. Art has invested the same energy into his retirement as he did into his career. I admire him more than he knows.

*George Fox College.* Immediately after completing my internship, and simultaneous to doing my postdoctoral work with Art, I began my academic career at George Fox College. It was a small academic community of approximately five hundred students and forty faculty members. The entire psychology faculty consisted of Dr. James Foster and me. Jim, a proud Ohio State Ph.D. and a developmental psychologist, was (and is) an outstanding teacher. We wrote a book together a long time ago (McMinn & Foster, 1990), before he became a science fiction novelist writing under the pen name of James F. David.

Jim and I also wrote an article for *Christianity Today,* in which we defended psychology from some of the outspoken anti-psychologists of the day. After the article came out, Jim and I were invited to join Dr. Gary Collins on *The John Ankerberg Show*—a syndicated Christian television talk show. Gary, Jim and I were the pro-psychology panel, and we were to debate Jay Adams, Martin Bobgan and David Hunt, all published authors who were outspokenly opposed to psychology. Gary was the only well-known person on our side of the debate, having published over forty books by that time. As the date of the taping approached, he felt a deepening conviction to back out. While Jim and I worried that "this was a turkey shoot and we are the turkeys" (Jim's words), Gary pondered whether it would really serve the cause of Christ to get on national television and exchange heated words about the value of psychology. When he decided to cancel his appearance on the show, Jim and I knew we needed to do the same, because Gary was our only hope of credibility. It was a disappointing turn of events at the time, because it seemed like a career-launching moment, but I later came to see Gary's wisdom. And he later became an important mentor in my life.

Jim and I were part of the Social Science Division, and our chairperson was Dr. Ralph Beebe (mentor #5). Ralph was a gifted historian and teacher. He was a humble man filled with uncommon goodness. As is always the case with effective leaders, Ralph's style filtered into the lives of others in the division. It was in the unpretentious context of that Social Science Division that Ralph modeled for me how to be a teacher and a scholar. I watched and learned. With time, I grew to be a professor.

Sometime in my first year of teaching, Ralph gave me a copy of a small book he and a colleague had written, *Waging Peace* (Lamoreau & Beebe, 1980). Though I liked the book for various reasons, I was most influenced by the continuity between the author and the topic. Ralph's words emerged from his character; there was an abundance of integrity connecting his calling, his interpersonal style and his scholarship.

Through self-disclosure, honest confrontation and effective listening, Ralph was all about pursuing peace. Peace is no easy thing, and achieving it can never be done by inertly accepting whatever comes our way. Whether considering inner peace or world peace, it requires action. Peace takes effort. It is something to be waged, not something to be discovered.

Ralph and I still worship together at Newberg Friends Church. He is retired now, an active member of the Friendsview Retirement Community in Newberg and still involved in various ways at what is now George Fox University.

During those early years at George Fox College I was a Christian who was a psychologist. I cared about both psychology and Christianity, so I figured I was doing integration. But it was not until my time at Wheaton College, starting in 1993, that I started to wrestle with the nuances of integrating faith and psychology.

**Wheaton College.** Walking into the Billy Graham Center (BGC) at Wheaton College was a profound experience for me. Words cannot express the deep sense of calling I experienced being part of this community where so much good has been done for Christ and his kingdom. I should add that walking in the BGC was also confusing. For the first month I worked there, I got lost in that building almost every day. And eventually I learned that the big white pillars in front of the building are hollow. That bothers me some, but still I think Wheaton is a remarkable place.

Many of my colleagues at Wheaton helped me understand the essence of integration. My office was just down the hall from the people who have influenced contemporary integration so deeply—people like Stanton Jones, Rich Butman, Sally Canning, Michael Mangis and Derek McNeil. And after the first month, when I finally learned how to weave my way from the mezzanine level to the second floor of the BGC, I discovered some remarkable theologians and Christian ministry scholars who also helped me think about integration. Jim Wilhoit, Dennis Okholm, Tim Phillips, Bob Webber, Walter Elwell and Gary Burge had a profound influence on me as I learned about spirituality, theology and integration. I sat in on as many theology classes as I could fit into my schedule. You could say that I fell in love with theology at Wheaton, and theology helped me fall in love further with God.

During my early years at Wheaton, I had a chance to get to know Gary Collins (mentor # 6) whom I had first met when we were scheduled for *The John Ankerberg Show* several years earlier. Like Arthur Weins a decade before, Gary saw potential in me, and he helped me get a couple of book contracts early in my career (McMinn, 1991, 1996). After I moved to Wheaton, we had breakfast or lunch together fairly often—sometimes as often as once per month. I was drawn to his energy and vision, along with his ability to bring people together for a common cause. Gary still travels all over the world to speak about Christian counseling, and he writes so many books that I cannot keep track of them all. But for me, the most influential interactions came when I saw Gary's heart for Christian service. I recall the time when he flew from his home in Illinois to Colorado in order to help a man who was being released from prison. Gary had been corresponding with this man throughout his incarceration, and he felt called to meet him as he was being released, to spend a weekend helping him find a job and a church community. It touched me deeply to think that a world-famous man still had such compassion for an individual who needed help.

In 1996, at the beginning of my fourth year at Wheaton, I was honored to be named the Dr. Arthur P. Rech and Mrs. Jean May Rech Professor of Psychology. It was an endowed chair position, meaning that the money was in the bank and my salary was paid by the interest on the endowment. As the endowment grew during the financial boom years of the late 1990s, the interest income grew well beyond my salary, which allowed for some creative uses of funds to establish the Center for Church-Psychology Collaboration (CCPC). In that context I had the opportunity to mentor several doctoral students—to give back some of what had been given to me by my mentors over the years.

Mentoring is the greatest honor I have in my professional life. I have been deeply privileged to walk alongside some amazing young people on their integration journeys. Barrett McRay, Katheryn Meek, John Scanish, Connie Valentini, Tim Chaddock, Brent Ellens, Amy Dominguez, Todd Burnett, Heidi Quist, Vitaliy Voytenko, Jeremy

Haskell, Steve Runner and many others have influenced my life even as I have influenced theirs. Some of these relationships have morphed from mentoring relationships into friendship over the years, and I am grateful for that transition.

## STRUGGLES

I have written quite openly about my struggles—perhaps too openly (McMinn, 2004, 2005). Thankfully, not many people buy the trade books I write so I have retained some privacy. Henri Nouwen is one of my spiritual heroes; I have been so inspired by the authenticity of his books that it makes me want to write and live openly too. But with time and age, I am realizing that openness can easily become disorienting and exhibitionistic if taken too far. So one of my struggles is knowing how to best disclose my struggles.

Here I will describe two struggles, though more could be mentioned. First, early in my career Lisa and I faced significant financial struggles. We were both committed to having a parent at home with our young children, which meant that we lived on very little during my graduate school years. Several years later I took a pay cut, moving from one of the best paying internships in the country to a job at a small liberal arts college. My George Fox salary in 1984 just barely covered our house payment. Any other monthly expenses had to be covered with additional employment. Fortunately, I had a clinical postdoctoral position and later a small private practice. If it were not for that clinical income and for Lisa's part-time income as a registered nurse, we never could have afforded for me to be an academic. Through those rough financial years, we worked hard to stay out of consumer debt, to give regularly to our church and to other Christian causes, and to spend responsibly. Those were good patterns for us to establish—both for our own sakes and for the sake of our children, who never had as much as many of their friends at school. Now that Lisa and I both have regular salaries, along with some royalty and speaking income, financial struggles are in the rearview mirror. But we still try to honor the same priorities. Our only debt is our mortgage; we strive to give away more than what comes easily or naturally; and we work to spend responsibly.

God has blessed us financially more than we could have ever imagined. Lisa and I live in a beautiful home on five acres, nestled in the center of Oregon farm country. This idyllic living situation is only possible because we built much of the home ourselves, in order to stay within our budget, and because some of our previous homes have increased in value more than we had anticipated. Living in a house that is bigger than we need, we have sometimes worried about the size of our footprint, so we have consistently made an extra effort to be responsible stewards—for example, by using geothermal energy to heat the home, by building with sustainable products (bamboo floors, wool carpeting, reclaimed wood for cabinets, recycled synthetic decking material and so on), and by making our home available as a gathering place and as a living space for those who need a place to stay.

Second, I struggle with defining myself according to my accomplishments. In God's economy, my value is intrinsic and immense. Still, I have difficulty resting in God's love—and perhaps in the love of those closest to me. As my vita and professional accolades have grown over the years, so has my temptation to base my value on my accomplishments. I fight against it, but I find this insecurity (or is it simply pride?) to be a relentless and furtive foe. Though I have found no solution to the problem, I am greatly helped when I practice times of quiet in my spiritual life. The false self, defined by accomplishments and possessions, tends to have less of a grip on my identity when I faithfully enter into the spiritual discipline of solitude. Nouwen put it well:

> Solitude is the furnace of transformation. Without solitude we remain victims of our society and continue to be entangled in the illusions of the false self. . . . Solitude is the place of the great struggle and the great encounter—the struggle against the compulsions of the false self, and the encounter with the loving God who offers himself as the substance of the new self. (Nouwen, 1994, pp. 81-82)

## SPIRITUAL DISCIPLINES

Growing up in a Baptist church I was taught to read my Bible and pray every day. And being a compliant soul, I did that through most of my high school and college years. As Baptists, we called it a "quiet time," but now that I am a Quaker I realize that it really was not very quiet.

Shortly after starting at George Fox in 1984, my family and I started attending Newberg Friends Church (NFC). Lisa and I returned to NFC after our return to Oregon in 2006. Our congregation is among a minority group of Friends known as *evangelical* Quakers, meaning that we still hold Christ at the center of our faith. The format of our weekly meetings involves instruments, singing and a sermon, in addition to a time of Quaker silence. The silence has given me a new understanding of quiet time. Each week we sit in silence for five to fifteen minutes, not with a prayer list or an agenda, but simply with a goal to sit with God and to listen more than we talk. I find listening is an important discipline to help calm the scurrying, task-oriented self that defines most hours of most days.

The pastor of Newberg Friends Church was once Richard Foster; he left shortly after writing the first edition of his now-classic book, *Celebration of Discipline* (Foster, 1988). Strangely enough, I never read *Celebration of Discipline* until moving to Wheaton.

The transition to Wheaton in 1993 brought some big challenges. My parents' marriage was falling apart at that time, and there were other complexities surrounding those events, which I have never put into written words out of respect for my father. But that did not stop the newspaper journalists from writing their stories, bringing more pain than I could possibly have imagined. Around that same time, I sat in on a spiritual formation class that our doctoral students were required to take, taught by Dr. Jim Wilhoit. I have since referred to this particular course as "the class that changed my life." We used Foster's (1988) book as one of the texts.

For four years after that transition to Wheaton, my greatest joy in life was prayer. I would go to bed at night anticipating awakening the next morning to spend an hour in private worship and prayer. The joy of God's presence was stronger than I had ever known before and, sadly, than I have ever known since. After my time of quiet and prayer, I would often sit in front of my computer and work on a book I was writing at the time. The book was later published as *Psychology, Theology, and Spirituality in Christian Counseling* (McMinn, 1996).

Those four years were my oasis experience, allowing me to drink deeply of God's wisdom every day. The eleven years since have been more of a desert experience. I do not mean that in a pained way—these eleven years have been a great blessing—but I do not experience God as directly or as immediately as I did during my time at the oasis. Still, I am grateful for those four years of intimacy with God. Remembering those years helps me catch a glimpse of the joy of heaven.

And while nothing can take the place of prayer in one's spiritual life, I have found deep spiritual meaning in being close to the land. Planting trees, fruit and vegetables and then watching them grow is indeed a remarkable testimony to God's majesty. I look closely for these moments of grace in the midst of my daily life, and for me, they always seem easy to find.

I have come to think of eating as a spiritual discipline, though writing such a thing feels strange to my inner gnostic. Fasting, of course, has long been recognized as a spiritual discipline, but I also want to consider how I eat during the vast majority of days when I am not fasting. By eating a plant-based diet rather than an animal-based diet, I am able to sustain myself without using as much of the earth's resources as I once did. If I were sitting around a table with six people, I would be careful not to eat more than my share of the mashed potatoes. The earth's table has six billion people around it, but I still want to be careful not to eat more than my share. I have also been persuaded that a plant-based diet is the best way to care for the body that God has given me. But lest this sound like an act of altruism or of deprivation, I should quickly add how much joy I find in eating. I experience great celebration—*spiritual* celebration even—in eating spinach salad, curry lentil soup, oatmeal cookies, whole wheat pasta with pesto, and a whole host of other foods that I could describe in more detail than anyone would care to read.

Materiality and spirituality are tied together in Christianity. The eternal Word became flesh and lived among us (John 1:14). And so as we pause before a meal to say grace, we ought to be awed by the immense blessing of God's material creation and to bow in reverence to its Creator and Sustainer.

## PERSONAL THERAPY

Getting my doctorate at age twenty-five had some advantages, I suppose, but I had to do a lot of growing up after my degree. As a young professional without much knowledge of myself, I struggled with managing my relational boundaries well. In those days I believed (naively) that a man and a woman could be friends in the same way that two women or two men could be friends. This troubled Lisa, of course, because she felt displaced when I became close friends with a female colleague at work. I was sure that the problem was her insecurity; she felt sure that the problem was my poor self-awareness. We were both partly right and partly wrong, but it took us four years and many tense conversations to figure that out. The way out of that maze was personal therapy. Our therapist opted to see us individually rather than conjointly.

Dr. Price was an unusual sort of psychodynamic therapist. She kept her door to the waiting room open throughout the entire session, and she sat behind a big oak desk as we talked. She was aged. I remember wondering if she would die before we finished our work together—and then feeling ashamed to think of her in such a way, as if she existed solely for my healing. She died a few years after Lisa and I were done with our therapy; I recall a resounding sadness when I heard.

There was one session that I remember more than all the others. I had just poured out my emotions, expressing how deeply I longed to be accepted for who I am, without any sense of demand that I should become who another person expects me to be. I was expecting her usual empathic response, but instead she looked me in the eye and said, "Mark, that sounds like a narcissistic fantasy to me." I was taken aback—shocked and hurt—but I later realized the wisdom of her pointed comment.

Looking back these many years later, I realize how deeply helpful personal therapy was in my personal and professional development, but I also recognize that the deepest fault lines in a person's character are not easily mended, even with therapy. As a tenderhearted and compassionate man, I still find it easier to draw close in friendship to women than to men, and it causes both Lisa and me confusion and pain at times. Over the years we have learned to listen and learn from one another better than we once did as I work to find the proper balance of freedom and caution in my friendships with women while deliberately pursuing closer friendships with men.

I separate my life as a therapist into two halves—before personal therapy and after. Before, I was a cognitive therapist who assumed clients wanted to get done with therapy and out of my office as quickly as possible. Now, I focus more on the relational dimensions of therapy, even though that sometimes entails saying difficult things such as what Dr. Price said to me. Over the years I have come to see myself as an integrative psychotherapist (McMinn & Campbell, 2007), drawing on both cognitive and relational aspects of effective interventions.

## CONCLUSION

I have titled this chapter "Journeying Toward Home" because I see this as the grand theme of my life. The good lessons I learned way back on that forty-five-acre nut farm have served me well: work hard, take good care of God's creation, prune back wayward growth, get your hands dirty when the need arises, be attentive and kind to the person working beside you, and be grateful—always grateful—for the One who provides the fruit of your labor.

## LETTER

Dear Reader,

Yesterday, Lisa and I were browsing a gift shop in Depoe Bay, Oregon, where we had escaped to watch whales for our thirtieth anniversary (being in the gift shop tells you what little success we were having seeing any whales). We came across a souvenir plaque with words that caught our attention: "Thank you, God, for this good life. Forgive us if we fail to love it enough."

Sometimes in the midst of our stressful work, and in the midst of the graduate schools that credential us for that work, it is easy to lose sight of life's goodness. But remnants of Eden are here, all around us, evident in the beauty of freshly fallen snow, the swelling of an ocean wave, the grace of a deer, the purr of a cat, the laughter of a good friend, the touch of a lover, the smell and taste of freshly baked bread. Creation is tainted by our sin, of course, but still this creation is magnificent and ought to be celebrated. And our victorious God, the triune maker and sustainer of all life, is worthy of all praise and honor and glory.

If asked to offer one word of sage advice, I suppose this would be my word: Remember that life is beautiful. Wherever you go, see the beauty and goodness in life, and help others see it too when they have lost their way. We are never as far from home as it may seem.

May God's grace and peace be with you,
Mark R. McMinn

## REFERENCES

Foster, R. J. (1988). *Celebration of discipline: The path to spiritual growth* (Rev. ed.). San Francisco: Harper & Row.

Katahn, M. (1986). *The rotation diet.* New York: Norton.

Katahn, M. (1989). *The T-Factor diet.* New York: Norton.

Lamoreau, J., & Beebe, R. (1980). *Waging peace: A study of biblical pacifism.* Newberg, OR: Barclay Press.

McMinn, M. R. (1991). *Cognitive therapy techniques in Christian counseling.* Waco, TX: Word Books.

McMinn, M. R. (1996). *Psychology, theology, and spirituality in Christian counseling.* Wheaton, IL: Tyndale House.

McMinn, M. R. (2004). *Why sin matters: The surprising relationship between our sin and God's grace.* Wheaton, IL: Tyndale House.

McMinn, M. R. (2005). *Finding our way home: Turning back to what matters most.* San Francisco: Jossey-Bass.

McMinn, M. R., & Campbell, C. D. (2007). *Integrative psychotherapy: Toward a comprehensive Christian approach.* Downers Grove, IL: InterVarsity Press.

McMinn, M. R., & Foster, J. D. (1990). *Christians in the crossfire.* Newberg, OR: Barclay Press.

Nouwen, H. J. M. (1994). *Show me the way: Readings for each day of Lent.* New York: Crossroad.

# 6

# Confessions of a Tortoise

## Slow Steps on the Integration Journey

*M. Elizabeth Lewis Hall*
**Rosemead School of Psychology at Biola University**

*The tortoise was a strange fellow, and sat all day under his own big shell, which was shaped rather like a basin upside down. Now and then he would poke out from under the shelter of the shell, a small flat head, and four small flat feet, and take a slow walk into the water and out again.*—The Hare and the Tortoise *(Winder, 1965, p. 54)*

**M**any of the contributors to this book have wonderful stories to tell, and many of them are "hares," with action-packed life voyages that are real page-turners. The story I am about to tell is not like that; it is the story of a tortoise. My story is not a story with exciting turns and twists. Instead, it is a story of small, subtle steps in my life and in my soul—steps that have shaped me and compelled me on my integration journey. The steps in my journey may not be fast-paced, but they are very real. They have occurred as I have encountered ordinary events in ordinary life: growing up, getting an education, becoming a wife and a mother. Perhaps some of you will identify with this kind of journey—the journey of a tortoise.

## DEVELOPMENT: INTEGRATION AS
## A CROSSCULTURAL JOURNEY

Fortunately, finding the starting line for my integration journey was not a challenge. Long before I had heard the phrase "the integration of psychology and theology," the concept of trying to see life the way God sees it was familiar to me. In fact, I have never known a different way. Integration is not something I learned during my years in Christian higher education; rather, those years in Christian higher education taught me the labels and vocabulary for something I had learned much earlier. Let me explain.

Integration is a process of tearing down walls, of bringing together pieces of life that have always belonged together, but which have been artificially separated because of opposing worldviews, the development of distinct academic disciplines, with their own vocabularies and intellectual histories and, of course, sin. These pieces of life include knowledge about living the life that God gives us—in his Word, in the world around us and in the lives of others. These pieces of life also include the head and the heart, knowing about the world and actually living out that knowledge in real life. The walls that separate these pieces of life can be incredibly strong, thick and difficult to penetrate. As I look back on my own developmental history, I experience it as a blessing that some of those walls were never erected in my heart and mind.

One important piece of that was growing up in a home where my parents modeled a life without walls. My parents' faith was integrated with their lives. The important life decisions they made, their time commitments, their financial practices, their parenting choices, all reflected their desire to live life well in God's eyes. "God talk" was not reserved for Sunday mornings or devotional times but came up naturally during the course of everyday conversations. My parents behaved in the home the same way that they did in public, respecting each other and their children as much behind closed doors as they did at social gatherings. I did not realize how unusual this consistency was until much later in life. I still remember the shock, as a teenager, of being on the phone with a friend and hearing her father, whom I had always experienced as a friendly, benevolent man, yelling at her in the background.

My father also modeled the practice of integration as a mental health professional. Of course, I was not privy to his therapeutic work with patients in his psychiatric practice, but I did know that his motivation to go into the field of psychiatry was based on the need he saw in his work among university students with the Argentinean branch of Inter-Varsity. I observed how much integrative work my father put into preparing messages and retreat materials that addressed applied topics such as marriage. I also saw him at his desk most mornings, with his Bible open in front of him, surrounded by commentaries and his "maté" (i.e., a gourd that is used to drink yerba maté tea). Further, I had access to my father's library, which included works by some of the earliest integrators, such as Paul Tournier and Gary Collins. As a teenager, I would plow through these books, not understanding very much but surely laying the foundations for an integrative mindset. In short, I was exposed to integration long before I first learned about mainstream psychological theories.

Another piece of my history that, in retrospect, facilitated my experience of not having walls was growing up moving back and forth between Argentina and the United States. My father is American, but his parents were missionaries, and thus he was raised in Argentina since the age of four. Consequently, my father grew up bilingual. My mother is Argentinean, the granddaughter of European immigrants. My parents met, married and had their children in Argentina. When I was two, we moved back to the United States, and then we moved back down to Argentina when I was ten. While living in Argentina, we had little contact with American culture. Apart from our occasional trips to visit relatives in the United States, we spoke Spanish (with a little English thrown in at home), ate Argentinean food, attended public school, fellowshiped in an Argentinean church, and had almost no contact with other Americans. The point here is that I was truly immersed in Argentinean culture; I did not think of myself as American or of the United States as my home.

How is all this related to integration? Cognitive psychologists speak of "metacognition," the ability to think about thinking. There is some evidence that bilingual and bicultural individuals have an advantage in developing metacognitive abilities. Such a finding makes sense when you think about it. For example, at the most basic level, there is a difference between words and the objects to which they refer. You can call that furry, long-tailed object a *cat*, but it is also a *gato*. Reality is not the same thing as the labels that are attached to those pieces of reality. Reality can be seen from different perspectives, and through language, it can be organized in different ways.

Living in two different cultures has made me aware of how language shapes experience and even how it can shape character. Let me give you an example from my own cultural history. For various historical reasons, Argentineans have the reputation of not taking responsibility for their actions. "Yo, argentino"—literally, "I'm Argentine"—is an idiomatic expression for communicating, "I had nothing to do with it!" This attitude is embedded in language in interesting ways. If I am (accidentally) causally responsible for a glass falling and breaking, I say, "se me cayo el vaso," which loosely translated means, "the glass was made to fall from me," once again emphasizing that I had as little to do with the act as possible. So words shape experiences, and are in turn shaped by experiences—but being able to say the same thing in two languages highlights that the words are not themselves the experience.

At a broader level still, living in two cultures has made me aware of the sociocultural water I swim in. Most people do not notice that the water around them is blue, but because I have lived where the water is aquamarine, I can tell that this water is indeed blue. Cultural assumptions that seem to be "just the way things are," are not taken as easily for granted when you have lived fully in two cultures. The way time is structured, the way relationships are prioritized, the moral values that hold more weight than others—all are influenced by culture; they are all part of the water of our cultural worldviews.

What does this have to do with integration? It has everything to do with it. Some scholars have pointed out that the task of integration involves translating concepts from one domain to another. In other words, they have asserted that at a minimum, integration involves realizing that a certain concept in psychology is relevant to a certain concept in theology, even though each perspective's vocabulary and framework may be very different from the other. Integration involves looking at the same experience from the vantage point of two "languages" and two "cultures." One is the language of the Bible, written in a variety of genres, including historical accounts, genealogies, songs and letters. The interpretation of that unique language is then influenced by the "culture" of Christianity, and additionally it is filtered through the unique subculture of the particular Christian branch, denominational heritage, and church community. (For example, if someone tells you she has a "God story" to tell you, you can bet the farm that she is part of a contemporary evangelical church with a seeker-sensitive service.) The other is the language of scientific discourse, embedded in the culture of modernism, positivism and empiricism. It is a language of clearly defined constructs, of causal relationships, and is thick with numbers intended to clearly represent the material world. These languages, and the cultures they represent, do not just provide labels for our experience. They also shape our experience, profoundly influencing our way of seeing the world. It often seems a daunting task to get beyond the different languages and cultures in order to access and describe a common facet of human experience or a broader reality. Becoming a good integrator involves seeing that beyond the language and paradigms of the disciplines is the ontological reality that they represent, which God sees and knows perfectly.

My husband, Todd Hall, and colleague Steve Porter coined the term "referential integration" (T. Hall & Porter, 2004, p. 167), and this concept fits nicely with the notion of integration as a translation process. Hall and Porter argued that integration requires referential activity. Referential activity is a moving back and forth between the subsymbolic (nonverbal, experiential) and symbolic (verbal) domains. We grapple with an integrative question intellectually, reading up on the psychological information and perhaps meditating on relevant biblical passages or reading relevant theological sources. Then this knowledge sifts down into our nonverbal experience and sits there, working itself out, largely outside of our awareness and without a conscious sense of being in control of the process. Linkages are being made; common experiences underlying the disciplinary structures are merging. Then something pops up in the form of an insight or integrative understanding, which we then put into words, returning the integrative concept to the verbal domain. In this way, our underlying experience can be reorganized along qualitatively new dimensions, categories and concepts, resulting in rich, thick integration. Because of the need to access experience, referential integration relies heavily on self-reflection, "a 'tuning in' to one's subsymbolic [nonverbal] experiences and drawing out the underlying emotional meaning" (T. Hall & Porter, 2004, p. 172). This back-and-forth process is at the heart of integration.

So integration is a crosscultural (or at least crossdisciplinary) journey, which requires some skills in "translating." These "translation skills" are facilitated by referential activity, which in turn relies on self-reflection, a topic to which we will later return.

## SPIRITUAL DISCIPLINES: INTEGRATION AS A COUNTERCULTURAL JOURNEY

The Christian subculture in which I was raised is the Argentinean version of the Plymouth Brethren. Our small local church was the hub of our social world. We were at church whenever the church doors were open. Every Sunday we celebrated the Lord's Supper, with the pews lined up in a circle so that we could face each other. Wearing a skirt, so as not to be in men's clothing, and wearing a lace covering on my head, to demonstrate my submission to men, I listened to men in the congregation, led by the Spirit, offer exhortations, pray and share insights from Scripture. In between movements of the Spirit, we waited in silence. We sang hymns a cappella and then passed around bread (never crackers) and wine in a common cup. I can identify with Garrison Keillor, also raised in a Plymouth Brethren church, who wrote in *Lake Wobegon Days:*

> In a town where everyone was either Lutheran or Catholic, we were neither one. We were Sanctified Brethren, a sect so tiny that nobody but us and God knew about it, so when kids asked what I was, I just said Protestant. It was too much to explain, like having six toes. You would rather keep your shoes on. (Keillor, 1985, p. 101)

When I read Scripture, echoing in the background are the values and customs of this denominational group. The Plymouth Brethren give a high degree of authority to God's Word, and they tend to be extremely biblically literate. They have no official clergy, and teaching responsibilities are shared by many of the men in the church, requiring the congregation to know their Bible well. This biblical literacy has multiplied the impact of the Plymouth Brethren. In spite of their small numbers, a disproportionate number of leaders of the contemporary evangelical movement have come from a Plymouth Brethren background: martyred missionary Jim Elliot, of *Through Gates of Splendor* fame, psychologist Larry Crabb, Argentinean evangelist Luis Palau, British theologian F. F. Bruce, emerging church leader Brian McLaren, spiritual formation leader James Houston, and *Sojourners* founder Jim Wallis. Though I now attend a Baptist church, I am grateful for an upbringing in which I learned to love my Bible and to see it as an inerrant source of truth for living life well. Although intellectually I understand that other Christian traditions view the Bible differently, in my gut I still experience a wave of aversion when I encounter Christians who dismiss sections of the Bible as being outdated or irrelevant.

The Plymouth Brethren are also countercultural. They believe that living as God desires may require you to be seen as different or even backward by others (particularly so in Argentina, where non-Catholics were a small minority). In truth, for them, "fitting in" with culture is not a priority. The Plymouth Brethren also cling tightly to tradition, just in case the tradition is really what God wants. They sing a cappella, because neither organs nor guitars are mentioned in the New Testament. In a culture of coffee drinkers, they drink tea with milk during fellowship times—not because they necessarily prefer tea to coffee, but because the good English missionaries who brought the gospel to Argentina a century earlier all drank tea; therefore, so did we!

Both of these influences—the high view of Scripture and the countercultural trend—have shaped my commitment to integration. Though the language and logical flow of biblical writings may not be as easily understandable to me as a recent article from a psychology journal, I know with all my heart that it contains wisdom for my journey. Consequently, it is worth the effort to dig deeply into it. If what I find in Scripture does not fit well with prevailing theories from my discipline, then so be it. The social pressures to conform can be incredibly strong, but I grew a backbone during my time with the Plymouth Brethren. The choir at my public school was invited to events all over the city, including religious ceremonies. I remember singing in Mass with my school choir and standing alone in silence while my Catholic classmates knelt to participate in the liturgy. As they relate to my role as a psychologist, these embodied memories make it easier for me to take public stands on controversial issues.

A couple of controversies have recently taken place in integrative circles, and on both issues, I have found myself compelled to take the "politically incorrect" side, based on my understandings of scriptural teachings. First of all, many passages in the Old and New Testaments suggest that our soul exists even after our body is dead and before the resurrection. Therefore, I am a dualist, even if such a position flies in the face of the materialistic biases that pervade our discipline. So be it. Second, many passages in the Old and New Testaments prohibit homosexual activity; therefore, I see the practice of homosexuality as morally wrong. This stance is possibly the most politically unpopular position that could be taken in our field today, yet I am compelled to take it. So be it.

In both these cases, the integrative tensions have led me to explore the issues from both psychological and biblical sides, more thoroughly than I might have explored without my integrative commitments. If I am right in believing that integration gives the most accurate picture of reality and that all truth is God's truth, then both intellectually and spiritually, I have nothing to fear from exploring these issues. I have found this conviction to be resoundingly true. I have discovered that dualism is an intellectually defensible position, is compatible with research connecting brain activity tightly to behavior, and is more compatible than monism with research showing some independence of the mind from the brain. At the same time, my reading of theology has led me to reject older forms of dualism that are not compatible with research and that denigrate the body. In short, I feel that I am in a better position now to function as an embodied soul and an ensouled body.

Something similar has happened for me with the topic of homosexuality. A former student of mine, who is now doing graduate studies at a major secular university, recently came to visit me. He recounted how one of his professors had made a strong statement about the genetic basis of homosexuality, but when my former student e-mailed her later to request the relevant literature, he was told that this finding was so well established that she could not pinpoint any specific articles to recommend to him. I was able to provide him with the most recent literature on the topic, including the study that has definitively established that there is no direct genetic link to homosexuality (though there may be other biological bases; see Bailey, Dunne & Martin, 2000). Keeping up with the literature has brought me closer to the often-difficult experiences of homosexual individuals, including the discrimination they face, their internal struggles as they live in a culture that puts sexuality at the core of identity, the lack of options they are given, and the alienation they experience from Christian groups.

Embracing an integrative perspective has forced me to expand my soul, to cultivate a place where I can believe that living a homosexual lifestyle is not part of the flourishing life designed by God while simultaneously being interpersonally open and accepting to the gay men and lesbian women that I encounter in my life. This place is not an easy one to live in. It would be much easier for me to either wall myself off from practicing homosexuals, as many fundamentalist groups do, or to change my moral stance on homosexuality, as many liberal and even evangelical Christians do. I have come to believe that this internal place of holding truth in tension is necessary in many parts of the Christian life. Believing that God is love and that he is holy can produce tension. Only in allowing that internal place to expand can we begin to understand that these are not ultimately in tension. God is love, and that is why he hates sin—because it destroys us.

## THERAPY: INTEGRATION AS THE PURSUIT OF THE FLOURISHING LIFE

*"Good Mr. Fox," said the tortoise, "Mr. Hare and I are going to run a race." "Ah, and what is the prize?" asked Mr. Fox. . . . "There is no prize," answered the tortoise with great dignity. "We are going to race for honour and glory." (Winder, 1965, pp. 55-56)*

If I had to give just one definition for the word *integration,* as I have experienced it, I might say that integration is *living life well.* Although I am intellectually fascinated by the ways that psychology and Scripture intersect with each other, these intersections are not what integration has primarily been about for me. The way I see it, I only get one chance to live this life. One chance to be a good wife, a good mother, a good daughter, a good friend. One chance to make a meaningful contribution to God's kingdom. One chance to live out my calling within that context. One chance to make an impact as a professor, a therapist, a Sunday school teacher. In other words, I have one chance to live a flourishing life, and I am going to be as intentional about living that life as I can be. That is where integration comes in. God knows what it takes to live well, and he has chosen to let us know much of what is involved in doing so, whether it be through clear teachings of Scripture or through the patterns of wisdom that can be gleaned through our study of people. The whole of my integrative journey to this point can be seen as my autobiography. In fact, just about every piece of integrative scholarship I have done has emanated from my own attempts to live well. Let me illustrate.

For me, the last few months at Rosemead before heading out on my predoctoral psychology internship were very difficult. Goodbyes to significant people and places were happening, and our psychodynamically oriented school (Rosemead School of Psychology at Biola University) was not about to allow us to "terminate" in some kind of truncated way. We wallowed in the throes of disengaging from each other. Among some of the most painful goodbyes were those with my clients, a couple of whom I had been seeing twice a week for two years. The crux of my difficulty was that I was not convinced that they would be okay after I left. Both of these clients had been very damaged by past relationships, had unstable current relationships and were at odds with God. In prayer, I begged God to change these clients, to heal them, to provide for them and to please do it quickly. But God did not seem to be responding. Heaven was silent, and my clients continued to struggle. One even decompensated in light of our untimely termination.

My own life, in contrast to theirs, had been relatively happy and secure. I had never struggled with major loss, betrayal or abuse; I had been loved and respected by those closest to me. In walking with my clients through their struggles, for the first time, I was faced with the reality of evil and despair in a personal way, and I wrestled with God for my clients. Even after termination, voices lingered: *Why couldn't God have intervened? Didn't he care? Was he too weak to do anything in the face of life's difficulties?* In response, God brought to mind the story of Job, struggling with devastating loss, with no answers. Job had also struggled with God, and ultimately he had found satisfaction, not in answers but in the presence of God.

God also brought to mind a lecture by self-psychologist Robert Stolorow, whom I had heard speak some months previously. In that lecture, Stolorow had talked about trauma, and how the effects of trauma were moderated by the victim's suffering being both acknowledged and understood by the victim's caretakers. The caring presence of a significant other helped the victim carry the burden of the trauma and process it, minimizing its negative effects. A light went on. God had responded to my clients—and to me. While he did not necessarily respond the way I would have liked him to, he gave my clients and me something more important—his caring presence and his ability to tolerate our anguish, along with the certainty that he had faced even more suffering (M. Hall & Johnson, 2001). As a therapist, I had been God's mediator, listening and caring for my clients. And God had other people in his service, capable of showing his presence and power. I felt relief.

An integrative perspective has also been helpful at other points along my journey as a clinician. After my predoctoral internship, my husband Todd and I moved to a small town in southeastern Arizona. The army, which had paid my husband's way through graduate school in psychology, had assigned him to work at the outpatient clinic in Ft. Huachuca. Eager to start accumulating hours for licensure but without many options in Sierra Vista, our new home town, I took a job at a Christian counseling center in Tucson. For two years, I commuted an hour and a half each way, three days a week.

But the commute was not the hardest part of my job. Fresh out of training, with no other doctoral-level psychologists on staff and with a "marathon" supervision only once a month, I bore the weight of my clients' care alone. I acutely felt my lack of experience, and at the end of each day, I drove home carrying the burden of my clients' hopelessness and despair, wondering if I had given them anything of value. I found myself increasingly dreading the long, lonely commutes and the long, lonely days of listening; I cried out to God to ease my burden. The answer came unexpectedly, as I prepared for a talk I was giving at a women's chapel group. In a book whose title and author I have forgotten after all these years, I found a section that emphasized the role of the therapist and the role of God in the counseling process. I read how my role was to listen, to care, to be in relationship and to offer my skills. In comparison, God bore the lion's share of the responsibility; his role was to change, to heal and to provide. For the first time, I understood that in the counseling process the burden was not mine. No matter how strongly clients tried to place the burden on me, no matter how easy it was for me to take on burdens that were not my own, and no matter how much I wanted to help, the truth remained: *The burden was not mine.* This insight has stuck with me over the years. For example, even this morning, as I sat through a particularly difficult session, I prayed silently, handing over my client's burden to God.

## STRUGGLES: INTEGRATION AS EMBODIMENT

Almost twelve years ago, an extremely strange and bizarre thing happened to me—I got pregnant. The pregnancy itself was not a surprise; my husband and I had been married for five years, graduate school was behind me, and we had planned on starting a family. The shocking thing was not that we found ourselves pregnant—it was the *being* pregnant that was so strange. The changes that were occurring to my body were of course largely out of my control. For example, my body projected beyond the limits that I had been used to my entire adult life; I was constantly bumping into things. Hormonal changes were reflected in emotional swings that I had been a stranger to until that time. And, strangest of all, something was inside of my body that was not *me*. Something in my belly moved at its own volition, sometimes reflected in small ripples across my stomach, and at other times in intrusions on my bladder or stomach.

For the first time in my life, I noticed my embodiment. I suppose it is a blessing that I had not noticed the fact that I had a body before then. I had always had a quick metabolism, so I had never struggled with weight; I was pretty enough to not think about it, and not pretty enough to think much about it. I was not an athlete, so I had not come to notice my body through that channel. But now, at age twenty-eight, there was no avoiding my body. And my own newfound body did not become less demanding of attention after that point, as I struggled with weight loss after my pregnancies, and, in more recent years, began to cope with small signs of the aging process.

How was I to deal with this newfound discovery of having a body? A relationship that had been so taken for granted, for so long, now became complicated. I struggled with body image. I fought with aging. I wondered what the balance was between "freshening up my image" and capitulating to our culture's ageism and overemphasis on looks. I also began to notice clients' body concerns more readily (e.g., eating disturbances, aggression against the body in the form of cutting, discussions regarding whether to have cosmetic surgery). I was at a loss. What did a healthy relationship with the body look like, both for myself and for my clients?

I searched the psychological literature and found that others had explored this very topic. For example, French philosopher Merleau-Ponty (Madison, 1981) had written about the phenomenology of having a body, and I discovered that even in my own psychodynamic tradition, Fairbairn and Guntrip had wrestled with having bodies (see Jones, 1999). In learning about the exquisitely designed functions of our body, which are so crucial to maintaining relationships, I gained a renewed appreciation for my body. During this time period, I also participated in a faculty development seminar in which we explored the life of Jesus for a week, under the tutelage of systematic theologian Millard Erickson. In this context, I worked on a paper with a colleague, theologian Erik Thoennes. We explored the implications of what it meant for my embodiment that Jesus had taken on a body himself. In considering the incarnation, I learned that my body is part of God's good creation; in following Jesus, I should care for my body, enjoy the pleasures of the created world through my body and discipline my body (M. Hall & Thoennes, 2006).

Some time later, I ran across objectification theory, a psychological theory about the effects that being culturally treated as objects has on women's embodiment. This theory, which suggests that health involves an emphasis on the body's functionality over its appearance, opened up new avenues of thought for me. Thus far, all the psychological literature I had read had convinced me that God had exquisitely designed our bodies for relating with others. Did the Bible have anything further to say about the function of our bodies—that is, what bodies are for? To my amazement, the answer lay clear as day in a verse I had read many times but had never noticed: your body is for the Lord (1 Corinthians 6:13)! It turns out that my body (and yours) has a clear function: to glorify God and to show his presence and power (Hall, 2010). As do most embodied souls (as opposed to the disembodied ones, I suppose!), I continue to wrestle with my embodiment. However, for me the framework for doing so is now much clearer: how much is my focus on maximizing my body's function of showing others who God is?

The birth of my children also led to another interesting development. Perhaps I should have expected it, but again, it caught me by surprise. Not only did my pregnancies result in my having children, but they resulted in my becoming *a mother*. However similar these might appear, they are actually quite different phenomena. I am a mother to my children in that I have given birth to them and behave toward them in mothering ways. But I have also become someone different—at least in everyone else's eyes. I have moved into the category of "mother." I have passionately loved having children and mothering them, though I have been less thrilled with being in the category of mother. Let me explain.

I discovered, even before my first son was born, that as a mother, people had all kinds of expectations of me. Rather than being an individual, with talents, passions, callings and interests, I had degenerated into a collective identity of Mother. A woman at church assumed that I would be quitting work after the birth of my child, and she was surprised when I said that I would not be. An acquaintance was amazed that mothering my child did not completely fulfill me, making my career irrelevant. A sermon at my church condemned working mothers for their selfishness and greed. At work, my commitment to the counseling center I worked for was questioned. On the one hand, I felt like I had been admitted to an exclusive club, where experiences with pregnancy, childbirth and the latest developments of my child were the subject of hours of conversation with other mothers. On the other hand, no one seemed interested anymore in the other contributions I might be able to make or in the other interests I might have aside from those related to mothering.

What's a girl (who is also trained as a clinical psychologist) to do? I went to the psychological literature, and once again, I found company in the thoughts and experiences of others who had gone before me. I read about how gender stereotypes intersect with discrimination—that is, women can either be (a) competent, cold and disliked or (b) warm, incompetent and liked. Research has found that motherhood often moves you into the latter category, at least in the minds of those around you. Unknowingly, I had moved from having a brain and not having a baby to having a baby and not having a brain. Apparently, the transition I had made in becoming a mother was a bigger one than I had anticipated! In the psychological literature, I also ran across the concept of "motherhood ideology" (e.g., Glenn, 1994), the idealized image of the good mother that is culturally transmitted and internalized. I learned that in our era, the motherhood ideology is more demanding and intensive than it has been at any other point in history.

By this time, I was back at Rosemead, on faculty. Standing in line before commencement, a colleague named Tammy Anderson and I swapped stories about being working moms. By the end of the evening, Tammy and I had decided to organize a research group on the topic of motherhood. Our first project was a qualitative study of mothers working in Christian academia. How did they balance their work and their mothering? How did their Christianity impact the ways they thought about their job, their parenting and their identity? Since that time, I have had the opportunity to further explore the small psychological literature on motherhood (as opposed to mothering) and to think more fully about what God wants from women who are also mothers. He calls us to a vocation of motherhood, and often he also calls us to vocations outside of the home. I have become more aware of pressures to be a "good mother." I have been able to examine those pressures in light of what the psychological literature shows that children actually need, as well as in light of what God seems to expect from me with respect to my children. Once again, integration has brought me sanity and perspective.

## MENTORING: INTEGRATION AS CHARACTER FORMATION

*Mr. Tortoise, under his shell, was more wide-awake than he had ever been in his life. Slowly and surely, slowly and surely, he made his way . . . his funny little feet moving steadily under his shell. (Winder, 1965, p. 57)*

I turned forty a couple of months ago. A woman of forty really has no business writing a life narrative! But since I am asked to tell my story, let me tell you something about integration and being forty. The older I get, the more I am convinced that the distinction between theoretical integration and personal integration is an artificial one. At forty, I am finally settling into who I am, without so pressingly struggling with who others think I am or who they want me to be. At forty, I am finally living more in the moment, without feeling overshadowed by deadlines or internal productivity quotas. At forty, I am finally learning to sit quietly in God's presence. And often, as I sit there, God will bring to mind new understanding of situations or of myself, based on both my psychological training and my spiritual convictions. I have done the hard work of furnishing my mind and soul with the rich knowledge of our discipline and the God-breathed truths of our faith. And as those come together, they prompt me to grow, to change and to live life more fully.

For example, in the last few months, God has been challenging my shell. As a deeply introverted individual, I often wander through life immersed in my own internal world, completely oblivious to the world around me. People greet me and engage me in a conversation, and while I may recognize their faces and engage in conversation with them, I often do not have a clue what their name is and how I know them! Consequently, I sometimes jokingly describe myself as "functioning barely above autism." I shared this self-description with my spiritual director, who shared a laugh with me about it but then challenged me to ask God for "seeing eyes." How can I love others well when I do not really see them? While my "shell" of introversion is unlikely to disappear, I am learning to be more intentional about poking my head out, opening my eyes, and being truly present with whomever I am interacting.

There has been a long debate over whether integration is (a) primarily (or exclusively) conceptual or (b) primarily (or exclusively) experiential (for overviews, see M. Hall, Ripley, Garzon & Mangis; T. Hall & Porter, 2004). With postmodern challenges to epistemology, this debate has indeed intensified in recent years. However, at this point, there is no doubt in my mind that integration involves both types of integration, and furthermore, these two types of integration are interwoven. They require each other. Experiential integration informs conceptual integration, and conceptual integration informs experiential integration. As I have grown and matured, I have provided a richer space for my integrative notions to take root and produce fruit. And as I have interacted with my world through both conceptually and experientially integrative perspectives, I have increasingly fertilized and nourished my internal world.

Our field of psychology, particularly the subdiscipline of clinical psychology, relies heavily on conceptualizations of human nature and functioning. Thus, integration in our field depends on our implicit, experiential knowledge of relationships. This knowledge, in turn, relies on safe, consistent relationships which nurture and shape us. I am grateful for the many people who have shaped my integrative path: my parents, who modeled a life without boundaries; my husband, who sees every part of me and provides acceptance and challenge; my professors and colleagues, who have shaped my intellectual commitments and modeled integrative lives; and my spiritual director, who has kept me intentional about my spiritual development.

My own journey led me into spiritual direction about four years ago. At the time, I found myself in a very dry place, spiritually speaking. My two boys were young, and every minute of my waking hours was being spent either getting work done or attending to the constant demands of my young children. At night, I would collapse into bed, falling asleep instantly. I would sporadically try to squeeze in a "quiet time," but I was inevitably either interrupted by one of the boys or I would doze off. Even when I managed to stay awake, prayer felt like a great effort, as I tried not to fall into a rote grocery list of requests but kept feeling drained by the demands of keeping up a monologue with God.

I asked for advice from an older woman whose spiritual insight I admired. She told me to tell my husband to watch the kids for an hour each day, so that I could have uninterrupted time with God. Internally I sighed, realizing that this single woman had no idea what life as a mother of young children was like. I could not even go to the bathroom for two minutes without having children banging on the door, asking what I was doing and whether I was done yet. When my husband was home, both our hands were full, and we barely had time to finish a sentence to each other! An hour alone? I resigned myself to an extended season of drought.

When I decided to seek out spiritual direction, the first question I asked my spiritual director was whether she was a mother. She was not only a mother, but she was a grandmother too, and she had lived through what I was going through. After hearing of my experiences, the first thing Myrna introduced me to was the concept of being silent before God. From her, I learned to rest in God's presence, without feeling the need to fill the time with words. Later on, I learned from her to pray the prayers recorded by other Christians, and I found out that some of these prayers had been offered to God for centuries. Reciting these prayers relieved me of the effort of having to find words in my tired, sleep-deprived state. These were prayers I could say even when my children woke up and climbed into my lap for an early morning cuddle. In short, my relationship with God was no longer in competition with my relationship with my children.

This was several years ago. Even today, my children still wander into my room and sit with me as I am finishing up my time with God. But many other things have changed. God has used my time in spiritual direction to quiet my heart and to help me attend to the present. I now have space for self-reflection, a space which is so necessary for the integrative task to flourish. My reading of Scripture has become more meditative, drawing on the ancient practices of *lectio divina* and the Ignatian practice of using imagination. These practices further feed my soul, and they also furnish it for the integrative task.

My time in spiritual direction has also opened my eyes to the larger context in which I do integration. For the last two years, my spiritual director has led me through an extended version of the nineteenth annotation of the Spiritual Exercises of Saint Ignatius of Loyola. The Exercises consist of a series of reflections and exercises, with a special focus on the person and ministry of Jesus. In particular, one series of reflections has impacted my view of integration by providing an overall context for my integrative efforts. In a postmodern culture that denies metanarratives, I have found a metanarrative that is so compelling that it is able to encompass all my life—I have found my metanarrative in the lordship of Jesus.

It may sound odd that I have lived for forty years in a Christian context without being grabbed by this. Sure I have heard and even used the phrase "Jesus is Lord." But I always thought about it in a purely individualistic sense: that is, he is Lord over my life. My recently acquired metanarrative is much larger: it presents Jesus as Lord of all. Ephesians 1:10 speaks of the fulfillment of time when "all things in heaven and on earth" will be brought together under Christ.

Hebrews 2:8 and 1 Corinthians 15:26-28 affirm that everything is under him and will be subject to him. Perhaps the most evocative passage that speaks to this metanarrative is Colossians 1, where Paul builds a captivating image of Jesus' centrality, culminating with the statement that God, through Christ chose "to reconcile to himself all things, whether things on earth or things in heaven, by making peace through His blood, shed on the cross" (v. 20). Jesus' call to his followers (including me) is for us to participate in establishing his kingdom—that is, the place where he rules. This kingdom includes "all," "everything" and "everyone," and it certainly includes the field of psychology. I can do my part in bringing Jesus' rule over the study of human behavior, starting with my own little integrative endeavors. What a meaningful context for my efforts!

## LETTER: FROM MY JOURNEY TO YOURS

I do not know what your background is or whether your journey has led you along some of the same paths as mine. Even so, wherever you are in your journey, hopefully the following advice will be helpful.

Do your best to prepare for the task of integration. Preparation involves dedication to a continuous, lifelong learning process that leads to expertise in both your area of psychology and in the area of Christian theology and Scripture. Many of us have opportunities to grow in the knowledge of our discipline that are built into our work lives. The same is not always true for the side of biblical and spiritual knowledge. Do not be satisfied with "Sunday-school knowledge" of the Bible. Meditate on Scripture. Read challenging spiritual authors. Practice the spiritual disciplines. As you learn and grow in these areas, they will seep into the experiential domain and, outside of your control, ripen into integrative insights. Furnish your mind and heart with the good stuff we have access to. If shallow theology or pop psychology is what you consume, then your integrative output will also be deficient.

Develop self-reflection. It is necessary to access deeper levels of yourself, because these are the places where good integration will be both conceived and birthed. Maybe you can learn to be quiet and in the moment a little earlier than I did. Integration does not just come from the head; it emanates from who we are at a deeper level. Allow God to shape you.

Practice integration. In addition to requiring knowledge and personal characteristics, it is a skill. For most of your life, cultural pressures have probably trained you to keep these parts of your life separate. To the degree that this is true of you, you will need to make intentional efforts to pull these together. Surround yourself with people who also do this. We need others to challenge and shape us.

Enter the story of Jesus' lordship. If you have not made him Lord of your life, I encourage you to take this step into a flourishing life. After all, he came so that we could have life abundantly. And if he calls you to the task, become a reconciler of Jesus, bringing your practice of psychology under his lordship.

## REFERENCES

Bailey, J. M., Dunne, M. P., & Martin, N. G. (2000). Genetic and environmental influences on sexual orientation and correlates in an Australian twin sample. *Journal of Personality and Social Psychology, 78,* 524-36.

Glenn, E. N. (1994). Social constructions of mothering: A thematic overview. In E. N. Glenn, G. Chang & L. R. Forcey (Eds.), *Mothering, ideology, experience, and agency* (pp. 1-32). London: Routledge.

Hall, M. E. L. (2004). God as cause or error? Academic psychology as Christian vocation. *Journal of Psychology and Theology, 32,* 200-209.

Hall, M. E. L. (2010). What are bodies for? An integrative examination of embodiment. *Christian Scholar's Review, 39*(2), 159-76.

Hall, M. E. L., & Johnson, E. (2001). Theodicy and therapy: Theological/philosophical contributions to the problem of suffering. *Journal of Psychology and Christianity, 20,* 5-17.

Hall, M. E. L., Ripley, J. S., Garzon, F. L., & Mangis, M. (2009). The other side of the podium: Student perspectives on learning integration. *Journal of Psychology and Theology, 27*(1), *15-27.*

Hall, M. E. L., & Thoennes, E. (2006). At home in our bodies: Implications of the incarnation for embodiment. *Christian Scholar's Review, 36,* 29-46.

Hall, T. W., & Porter, S. L. (2004). Referential integration: An emotional information processing perspective on the process of integration. *Journal of Psychology and Theology, 32,* 167-80.

Jones, J. W. (1999). Embodying relationships: An object relational perspective on the body. *Gender and Psychoanalysis, 4,* 387-98.

Keillor, G. (1985). *Lake Wobegon days.* New York: Viking Penguin.

Madison, G. B. (1981). *The phenomenology of Merleau-Ponty.* Athens: Ohio University Press.

Winder, B. (1965). *Aesop's fables retold by Blanch Winder.* New York: Airmont Publishing.

# 7

## Practicing
## Convicted Civility

*Mark A. Yarhouse, Regent University*

**S**everal years ago I sat in on a session at the American Psychological Association (APA) Convention. In this session, leading gay psychologists were talking about religious persons who were sorting out sexual identity questions. They talked about how they as a community had failed their own people and drove them away from the gay community and into the conservative religious community, a group that in their minds often takes advantage of them and misrepresents research to the detriment of sexual minorities. While I disagreed with the conclusion they came to, I appreciated hearing for the first time that these leading gay psychologists thought of the people I saw in my clinical practice as having more in common with them than with me. It changed my heart toward the debate and gave me hope that while we would certainly disagree about fundamental issues related to sexual identity and behavior, we could share some common ground in our regard for the people under discussion. In fact, that session led to personal relationships with the various speakers and discussants who one year later would eventually comprise the first-ever panel to dialogue on these matters at the APA (Yarhouse, 2000; Yarhouse & Burkett, 2000). That dialogue would lead to several others over the years and define the early stage of my career in psychology. I would be challenged to sort out how to live and relate to others with "convicted civility."

## DEVELOPMENT

There is a family story we tell: when we were kids my cousin pulled my sister aside and asked her, "Which of your parents is the *religious* one?" My sister looked confused for a moment and then replied, "Both." Indeed, both of my parents were Christians and fostered a family environment in which my siblings and I would come to experience our faith as a real and normal part of our daily lives. My father did not grow up in a Christian home but had a conversion experience as an adult. Like many adults who convert to Christianity, my father was more aware of what a life-changing commitment being a Christian can be. This was evidenced in how he and my mother raised us, how they approached their work, their involvement in the local church and in related parachurch ministries (e.g., my mother served as teaching director or assistant teaching director for eleven years in Community Bible Study; both served on our local Young Life steering committee), their relationships with neighbors, and so on. You could say that my mother grew up in one denomination and my father in another, but I think it would be a mistake to identify either of them with a denomination. They selected churches in my childhood and adolescence based on whether a particular church taught that Jesus was the Son of God, died for us and was resurrected; denominational affiliation as such was of little importance in that regard.

Christianity became especially salient to me during high school. I was active in Young Life and in our local youth group, but it was not until a youth group retreat one fall that I had a personal conversion experience. This marked a conscious assent to the claim that Jesus is Lord and Savior for me personally. Over the next several years, my youth group leader subsequently invested a lot of time meeting with me, helping me grow to greater spiritual maturity. This discipleship relationship was one of the most defining relationships of my adolescence. In fact, I originally thought I would be a physical therapist like him, but he really helped me to recognize the other gifts that I had and to realize that I could listen to God directing me toward a career that would utilize those gifts and that I would enjoy. I wondered then whether I might become a pastor or a counselor, though I had little sense at that time as to what either might entail.

When decisions were being made about college, I decided on Calvin College, a small liberal arts school in Grand Rapids, Michigan. My sister had attended Wheaton College, and I was the kind of person who wanted to try his own thing and was probably too insecure to follow in her footsteps. So I packed up and headed to Calvin College, the school of the Christian Reformed Church denomination. My experiences at Calvin were very positive, both socially and academically. It was at Calvin where I grew in my own understanding of the intersections between Christianity and various areas of study.

At Calvin, I double-majored in philosophy and art, and I minored in psychology. I had been interested in art since I was very young. Art had been a part of my mother's life and my grandmother's life, and I wanted to "punctuate" that interest by completing a degree in that area. I specialized in lithography and also enjoyed watercolor painting and pen and ink drawing. I minored in psychology because I believed I would attend graduate school in psychology one day. I think I had a sense of calling to the counseling field even at that time, and I started to contemplate the possibility of serving in a Christian college counseling center. I chose to also complete a major in philosophy because I believed it would better prepare me for how to read and critique position papers, as well as assist me in developing reasoned arguments in any field, including psychology.

When I graduated from Calvin, I worked at a youth home in Grand Rapids, Michigan, in part to confirm my sense of calling to the counseling field. My wife and I had just been married, and she was completing her last semester at Calvin. I then applied and was accepted at Wheaton College for the M.A. in Clinical Psychology program. It was during this time that I met Stan Jones, who was then the department chair at Wheaton. Stan hired me as his research assistant, and when I completed that two-year degree, he and others encouraged me to go on and get a doctorate. For my doctorate, I decided to stay at Wheaton. In fact, I was a part of the first cohort in Wheaton's new doctoral program in clinical psychology. This was an exciting time to be at Wheaton. I continued to work with Stan formally and informally during that time, and by the time that five-year program was completed, I had also been able to earn an M.A. in Theological Studies.

During my graduate studies, a time that encompassed seven years from beginning to end, my wife and I attended an Episcopal church, St. Mark's Episcopal Church in Glen Ellyn, Illinois. I was drawn to the liturgy, to the sense of the church calendar and to tapping into more of my own senses during worship, as well as exposure to more contemplative prayer and silence. During this time I went through a one-year discernment process to determine whether I was being called to seminary. The Episcopal Church provides for this time of discernment in which a group of people with various gifts and insight meet together monthly for a year to discern with you whether in fact you are currently being called to ministry. At the end of that year we concluded that at that time, I was not being called to leave graduate school and enter seminary.

It was also toward the end of my training that my wife and I decided to start a family. We thought it was as simple as just planning when to have children, and we were surprised and disappointed to find that we were unable to conceive a child. The next year or more was spent exploring the various issues surrounding infertility. We decided at the end of that process to pursue adoption. The experience itself is difficult to communicate. It was a painful time, a time of tremendous grief, of loss and isolation, and at times even of questioning God and his sovereignty and purposes in our lives. It was also a time for making new connections with what I experienced as an "underground" group of people in the church. They were underground because they were not particularly visible as people who were going through similar loss and grief in their own lives. But they were tremendously important to us, and they stayed with us during this time and taught me a lot about humbly recognizing that we do not always have easy answers to the pain and difficulties we face in life.

I can now say that God is good, that God provides, but those truths would have been difficult to claim at the time. Every couple facing infertility makes a decision about what procedures they are comfortable with and how far to go with various medical options. When we reached our limit, we decided to pursue adoption, and this decision would prove to be a life-changing experience and a tremendous blessing for us both. Over the next several years, we adopted three children—each from a racial minority background. At the time, while we tried to understand the implications of transracial adoption, we had little idea how trans-formative it would be for us, particularly in terms of how it opened us up to recognizing and addressing racial/cultural issues, both in the church and in the broader culture.

When I graduated from Wheaton, in terms of my career, I antici-pated working at a local community counseling center, serving diverse and underserved populations in the Chicago area. Although I had some interest in an academic career, there were no openings in the Christian integration programs with which I was familiar, and I felt that if I were to be in academia, the best fit for me would be an integration program. After all, much of my training was in that kind of program, and I had a heart for mentoring Christian students who were interested in the study of psychology. As it turned out, there was some delay in working out the specifics of the position at the community counseling center, and during this time, one opening in an integration program became available—at the new Psy.D. program at Regent University in Virginia Beach, Virginia. I interviewed there and accepted a position, and since 1998, I have been part of the core Regent Psy.D. faculty.

When I thought of starting my career, I was faced with what to focus on as primary research area. I had interests in marriage and family therapy, but as a research assistant in graduate school, my primary work had been in the area of homosexuality. When I graduated I did not see many other Christians in psychology who were engaging the topic, and I felt some sense that I should be a good steward of what I knew and understood of the subject. So I began a research program at Regent, and that program eventually evolved into the Institute for the Study of Sexual Identity, a research institute I have directed since 2004. The institute has provided me a place to mentor students and to conduct original research on sexual identity. We have studied such topics as how sexual identity develops and synthesizes over time and what types of challenges are faced by Christians who are sorting out their sexual identity in light of their religious identity.

In addition to the study of sexual identity, I have also enjoyed reflecting on areas of interest to me, thinking about them from the standpoint of a Christian worldview. This has led to collaborative, Christian integrative writing projects on psychopathology (Yarhouse, Butman & McRay, 2005) and on family therapy (Yarhouse & Sells, 2008). Just writing about these projects reminds me of how much I enjoy collaborating with others, as well as how important mentoring relationships have been to me in my career.

## MENTORING

Mentoring has been one of the most important parts of my personal and professional development. I respond and learn best in the context of a relationship. For me, mentoring relationships trace back to my high school youth group leader, who invested so much of himself in my spiritual development at that time. My youth group leader modeled for me a kind of selfless investment in me that others would also provide over the years and that would later serve as a model for the way I want to invest in the lives of others.

Other mentoring relationships have included academic relationships with people who either inspired me or challenged me in various ways. For example, while I was at Calvin College, I had the opportunity to study under Nicholas Wolterstorff and Mary Stewart Van Leeuwen. Although I would not say either person formally mentored me, both had an impact on what I saw as possible ways to relate Christianity to my areas of interest in the field of psychology. In Wolterstorff, I saw how Christianity could form the fundamental foundation for approaching any topic of study. I particularly learned the importance of examining "control beliefs," or ways in which religion (in my case Christianity) functions as "a fundamental determinant of [my] hermeneutic of reality" (Worlterstorff, 1993, p. 270). I recall the impact of his book *Reason Within the Bounds of Religion* (Wolterstorff, 1984), which challenged the view that it was religion that had to be kept "in its place" in scholarship. In Van Leeuwen, I saw a desire to respectfully and intelligently engage both sides of any given argument. Her area of expertise is in gender studies, an area of significant disagreement among conservative Christians. She modeled how to walk with students as they wrestle with theological issues and with Christian integration in an important and controversial area.

In graduate school my primary mentor was Stan Jones. In Stan, I saw a tremendous grasp of theology and science, as well as the ways in which theology and science can help Christians form a meaningful critique and engagement with psychological theory and practice. We worked together for several years, and even to this day we continue to enjoy collaborating with each other from time to time. I learned a great deal about critically engaging the field of psychology from a Christian perspective and about rigorously critiquing my own work. I think that this last point has really stayed with me. In essence, I learned that when it comes to your own scholarship, it is best to be your own toughest critic—to anticipate how others will challenge your work and to address such challenges directly. I also learned about taking risks—about how to stand up for positions that may be unpopular but that are today areas of great importance in the church and in society. There is a real cost to this kind of sacrifice, but the cost is consistent with what Scripture teaches that believers will face.

## STRUGGLES

On a personal level, God has also allowed me to have what I have at times thought of as a "thorn in [the] flesh" (2 Corinthians 12:7). For those unfamiliar with that terminology, the apostle Paul used those terms to describe a condition he had—something that God allowed—perhaps a physical concern such as an eye condition. Whatever "thorn" Paul was describing, I believe it must have helped Paul avoid pride, helping him remain aware that he was not being used by God because of his own natural abilities but instead because God uses whom he chooses to bring about his will. For me, this condition has been vitiligo, a chronic skin condition in which melanocytes fail to produce skin pigmentation in various areas. This condition is known to be associated with autoimmune diseases, but its etiology is not fully understood at this time. I would be among the last to over-spiritualize this condition, but I do understand it as a reflection of the Fall (that is, to borrow from Neil Plantinga, it is a reflection of things that are "not the way they are supposed to be"). Many of us (perhaps most of us) have these conditions or limitations or areas of struggle or insecurity. It is often precisely in these areas of struggle that God meets us, communicates his love for us (despite our struggles), and conveys that he can use us despite our insecurities. For me, this condition can be an area in which God continues to work out his concerns for me and for my spiritual life, as well as his concerns for my relationships with others. I think that suffering from vitiligo has helped me to empathize with others and to be sensitive to the struggles they might face.

This experience has also helped me to reflect on what it means to live in a fallen world—to remember that sin is not just what we do wrong or fail to do. Rather, sin is also a part of our fallen world: a world in which some people have lower levels of neurotransmitters that contribute to depression or anxiety; a world in which some people develop psychosis or whose biological blueprint unfolds in any number of irregular ways. It has not helped me fully answer the more challenging questions regarding the problem of evil, but it has helped me understand how far-reaching is the impact of our fallen world, from neurotransmitters to melanocytes to cognitions and schemas to social learning and reinforcement schedules and beyond.

Another personal struggle is the struggle my wife and I faced with infertility. It challenged my assumptions about control, my life's timeline, expectations for how God would answer prayer and meet needs. I also learned a lot about how well-intentioned believers could cause me pain in their efforts to be supportive. This taught me to be quiet but present in the suffering of others, to resist the urge to offer words that were—if I was honest with myself—intended to be reassuring to me rather than to the person who was suffering. I think this kind of lesson can make a difference when we are counseling others through very difficult struggles.

There have also been professional struggles. Although I have written Christian-integrative textbooks on areas such as psychopathology and family therapy, my primary line of research has been sexual identity, with a concentration on homosexuality. For me personally, it has truly been challenging to be involved with the controversial topic of homosexuality. I do not particularly like to be disliked. I know that some people really seem to thrive in that role, but that does not fit either my temperament or my personality. I genuinely enjoy the friendships I have formed over the years and what it means to connect with others in meaningful ways. So to be viewed as someone who *must be unkind* (or complete the sentence any way you like—intolerant, bigoted, angry, prejudiced, etc.) for writing about homosexuality from a Christian worldview has indeed been quite a challenge at times.

There are also challenges associated with presenting material accurately, even if the presentation goes against the expectations of the audience. For example, one year early in my career, I was asked to present the same scientific findings at two different churches in the same week. I went to a conservative church first and presented the latest research on the prevalence estimates for homosexuality, the etiology of homosexual orientation, the status of homosexuality as a pathology, and the evidence for whether or not sexual orientation can change. The audience responded favorably to the research on low prevalence estimates, which indicate that the prevalence of homosexuality in the general population is much lower than the ten percent prevalence rates that have often been cited in the past. They seemed to respond favorably to the data that suggests that various mental health concerns are often associated with homosexuality, as though they expected that homosexuality would be associated with elevated rates of depression, anxiety, substance abuse and so on. However, they did not care to hear about studies suggesting a biological predisposition toward homosexuality for some persons. They questioned that material at length.

Later that week I spoke at the more liberal church. I gave virtually the exact same talk. The audience there agreed with the material on biological predispositions to homosexuality, but they reacted with suspicion to the prevalence rates being lower than expected and to the data that suggested that some persons are able to experience substantive change in their sexual orientation. That week I learned a valuable lesson: Being responsible and honest about all of the scientific evidence will not necessarily win over an audience. They often have in their minds the conclusions they expect you to reach, and an accurate presentation of the data often leaves people conflicted. Indeed, I tell students studying with me that if they have finished making a presentation on homosexuality or sexual identity and someone is patting them on the back for too long, they have probably not accurately conveyed the complexity of what we know and do not know about homosexuality and sexual identity. This is a complicated area of research, and the findings are often more complex than advocates on either side care to admit.

Since that time, there have been several instances in which my work has been appreciated by both "sides" of the debates on homosexuality. But I have also had a few occasions when some have reacted quite negatively to what I have written and have used different situations to attempt to discredit me. That has been challenging, as the criticisms go far beyond rational debate and discussion of ideas and into taking advantage of circumstances to foment emotions people have about the "Religious Right" or evangelical Christians or Republicans or whatever someone wants to bring into the discussion to get an audience upset. For the most part these strategies have been seen by others for what they are, but occasionally they have strained existing relationships I had formed within the gay community, and people who did not know me have at times made assumptions about my beliefs and values about a number of issues related to homosexuality.

Though these difficulties have sometimes challenged my view of what it means to be in relationship with those with whom I disagree on important issues, it has not kept me from pursuing dialogue and from turning to scientific findings as the language through which psychologists are to communicate. I have been able to continue meaningful dialogues with members of the gay and transgender communities, both in professional settings and in less formal venues. These opportunities have included discussing the meaning of marriage with members of the gay community and with conservative Christians, as well as providing therapeutic services to sexual minority youth and other individuals (see Yarhouse, 2004, 2005; Yarhouse & Beckstead, 2007).

One result of the tensions that sometimes are part of this area of scholarship was to spend more time in prayer about the spiritual dimensions of the work we do in psychology. I have also tried to prayerfully reflect more on various projects and professional opportunities. I have a limited amount of time and energy to do the work I do in the field. In which project should I invest my time and energy? Someone once told me that I would eventually have to choose between good alternatives, which means saying no to important projects because I am working on other important projects. I have found that to be true.

Finally, engaging the field of psychology in the areas of homosexuality and sexual identity is not just about potential conflicts and misunderstandings. It has also been about sorting out what I actually believe about homosexuality. I was faced with what I was taught about homosexuality growing up, as well as what one gathers from historical Christianity in terms of doctrines associated with human sexuality and sexual behavior. But at some point I had to evaluate all this, reflect on the existing scientific research, and then decide for myself what I believe. Of note, this process did not take place in a vacuum; it took place within the context of personal relationships with friends, students, colleagues and acquaintances who identify as gay. So I feel a desire to communicate a perspective that addresses the issues raised by people on all sides of the debate. These are not purely theoretical debates either; real people's lives are affected by the discussions and debates that are taking place in the church and in the broader culture.

The challenges associated with engaging a controversial topic as a Christian have helped me work toward what Richard Mouw refers to as "convicted civility." As I understand the concept, convicted civility refers to the idea that Christians retain their beliefs and values ("convicted") while they still engage others in ways that convey mutual respect and a high regard for those with whom they disagree ("civility"). My experience is that most Christians struggle with how to hold these two dimensions together. For some Christians, conviction is the most salient; they know what they believe about homosexuality and they approach dialogues with that rigid certainty, often to the detriment of constructive and meaningful engagement with others. For other Christians, civility is most salient; they focus so much on being in relationship that they fail to see how their faith informs the discussion, providing them beliefs and values that can be difficult to articulate when they are facing potential disagreements.

On controversial topics, there are often two "sides" that appear to be at odds. Practicing convicted civility has meant recognizing the truths that can be found on both sides, while clearly and respectfully articulating areas of disagreement. What is challenging is that both sides can be fairly demanding and try to pull you toward them by criticizing your perspective or by making reference to exaggerated expressions of the view they fear you represent to them. I have found this to be true among some in the gay community, and I have found this to be true among some in the conservative Christian community. It has been helpful to convey what we know and what we do not know in a spirit of humility and with an openness to hear perspectives that differ from my own.

Practicing convicted civility can be emotionally draining, however. I think it is exhausting because there is a cost associated with caring about and demonstrating respect for others. It would be less draining to advance a political agenda, because this typically means looking past people to further a particular cause. The alternative is to move toward others, to engage them in a meaningful relationship, which necessarily entails emotional connections that can sometimes be conflicting, and this is the part that can be draining. For me, it has been important to receive emotional support from people who care about me personally and understand my attempts to practice convicted civility.

## SPIRITUAL DISCIPLINES

Coming from the Reformed perspective, I tend to be drawn the most to certain spiritual disciplines, such as prayer, fellowship, reading of Scripture and corporate worship. Because there are so many other streams of Christian spirituality, I often find myself drawn to other disciplines (e.g., solitude, meditation or contemplative prayer), in part because they were not emphasized in my upbringing. During graduate school, I had the opportunity to meet with a spiritual director who helped me structure some of my prayers and to find images and ways of praying that I still use today.

I suspect that is why my wife and I were drawn to the Episcopal Church for a season. We were drawn to the church calendar, the liturgy and the use of incense, chants in minor keys, and colors for seasons to draw on other senses in a corporate worship environment.

We currently worship in a multiethnic church that emphasizes trans-ethnicity (the idea that believers recognize and celebrate cultural backgrounds but can also transcend them in our kingdom identity with one another). We chose a multiethnic church mainly because of our family composition (we had adopted three children from a different racial background). We wanted our children to be surrounded by models of leaders who share their racial identity. Admittedly, this church is a departure from the Reformed background we had, and it is also a departure from the quiet, reflective aspects we appreciated in the Episcopal Church. There is more of a praise and worship emphasis in this church than we have ever experienced, and so we are tapping into another area that has perhaps been underdeveloped in my own spiritual life.

For years my wife and I have also engaged in the spiritual discipline of service to others. I finished my two-year master's degree in clinical psychology, and then we prayerfully considered whether I should go on to get a five-year doctoral degree. We talked about not setting aside ministry and service during the time I would be working toward my doctorate; we wanted to not only commit to a specific ministry during that time but to be more active in the local faith community as well. We subsequently joined the youth ministry team at our church, getting our fill of "lock-ins," youth retreats and so on. More recently at our church, my wife and I have co-led a small group and have taught Christian education. Over the years, we have also been involved in other service opportunities.

## THERAPY

Therapy was highly recommended for all students in my doctoral program. I benefited from seeing two therapists during the course of my training. They helped me understand some of the issues that have been challenging for me personally and professionally, providing me insight into various intrapersonal and interpersonal dynamics. They have also influenced how I view the work I do in providing clinical services.

I have learned a tremendous amount from the people I have counseled over the years. When I think of my specialty area and my work with those who are sorting out sexual identity concerns, I have learned about the challenges associated with living in a way that is consistent with one's beliefs and values. When people are sorting out how to live and how to identify themselves and they decide to follow what we might refer to as the orthodox Christian view of sexuality and sexual expression, they really are saying no to something that the broader culture is telling them they have every right to enjoy. In fact, the broader culture tells such persons that they have every right not to just enjoy this aspect of their lives but to achieve actualization by embracing it. When a person who struggles with same-sex attractions chooses to follow an orthodox Christian view, he or she essentially chooses to pursue other ways of actualizing one's potential, typically focusing on what Christians have historically referred to as sanctification (Yarhouse, 2010). He or she learns what it means to steward one's sexuality, a lesson that is really crucial for all believers to learn but that is often not realized. But I have found that their choices are acts of courage that I do not myself have to choose in the same way. I do not struggle with the same issues, and frankly, the concerns I struggle with personally often get a "pass" in the local church. But those who struggle with sexual identity concerns do not get that same "pass," and they learn and have taught me valuable lessons about spiritual maturity.

Of course, not all sexual minorities make the same decisions about their religious and sexual identities. While some move in the direction of sanctification as I have described, others leave the faith tradition of their family and find greater resolution of tension in a gay identity and in support from the gay community. Others join different faith traditions that allow them to maintain aspects of their faith and also identify as gay. There are many others who do not appear to find resolution; rather, they come into counseling for help navigating the terrain. In any case, I have found it deeply meaningful and humbling to be involved in some small way in what is such a personal and often painful journey toward congruence.

There has been some pressure to practice reorientation therapy. I defend people's right to pursue such therapy, even if many people who do so appear to make fewer gains than they had anticipated. My own therapy model focuses instead on sexual identity, which I see as a more holistic approach, one that facilitates personal congruence, so that a person is able to align behavior/identity with beliefs/values.

Several sexual minorities have pulled me aside or written me notes to thank me for my work on sexual and gender identity issues. It is not that I have discovered something especially novel, but they say to me that they appreciate that someone for whom this is not a personal struggle is willing to invest time in something that matters to them, and to do so in a way that avoids polarization and still holds high regard for orthodox Christian teachings on sexuality.

## LETTER

Spring 2009

Dear Reader,

I meet many students who come to graduate school with a genuine and straightforward faith. They have a faith that is simple in the best sense of the word but that becomes complicated in the course of their studies. It has been said that simplicity is found on the other side of complexity, and that is what I hope you can find as a Christian working in the field of psychology.

In the field of psychology, we are inevitably going to face challenges to our faith. But we cannot be surprised when non-Christians in our field fail to appreciate a Christian perspective on any given subject. That is one of many reasons why being in the field of psychology and thinking about the field as Christians is so important. There is a need for Christians to critically engage and critique existing theories and practices within psychology, as well as to provide constructive models of how to conceptualize and intervene in the lives of others. I want to encourage you to stay engaged in the field, to draw upon your faith as a Christian, to take hold of courage in areas of potential and real conflict, and to engage others with what Richard Mouw terms "convicted civility." At the very least this means forming and sustaining genuine relationships with others with whom we disagree, recognizing that such disagreements typically arise from our Christian worldview. Practicing convicted civility can be emotionally draining, so be sure to take care of yourself and be in encouraging, supportive relationships with others.

In closing, remember to live your life, including your professional life, in a way that gives God glory for all that he has done for you. That may mean working with the underserved, or it may mean tackling difficult topics in a spirit of humility, or it may mean developing novel approaches to helping people to find and experience God's redemptive plan for their lives. But whatever God calls you to do in this field, I think God wants you to delight in that area, both as you serve him and as you serve others around you.

In Him,
Mark A. Yarhouse

## REFERENCES

Wolterstorff, N. (1984). *Reason within the bounds of religion.* Grand Rapids, MI: Eerdmans.

Wolterstorff, N. (1993). The grace that shaped my life. In K. J. Clark (Ed.), *Philosophers who believe: The spiritual journeys of 11 leading thinkers* (pp. 259-75). Downers Grove, IL: InterVarsity Press.

Yarhouse, M. A. (Chair). (2000, August). *Gays, ex-gays, ex-ex-gays: Key religious, ethical, and diversity issues.* Symposium conducted at the meeting of the American Psychological Association, Washington, DC.

Yarhouse, M. A. (Chair). (2004, July). *Sexual identity confusion during adolescence: Religious, diversity, and professional issues.* Symposium conducted at the meeting of the American Psychological Association, Honolulu, Hawaii.

Yarhouse, M. A. (Chair). (2005, August 18). *The many meanings of marriage: Gay and conservative religious perspectives.* Symposium conducted at the annual convention of the American Psychological Association.

Yarhouse, M. A. (2010). *Homosexuality and the Christian: A guide for parents, pastors, and friends*. Grand Rapids, MI: Bethany House.

Yarhouse, M. A., & Beckstead, A. L. (Co-chairs). (2007, August 17). *Sexual identity therapy to address religious conflicts*. Symposium conducted at the American Psychological Association's Annual Conference.

Yarhouse, M. A., & Burkett, L. A. (2000, August). Respecting religious diversity: Possibilities and pitfalls. In M. A. Yarhouse (Chair), *Gays, ex-gays, ex-ex-gays: Key religious, ethical, and diversity issues*. Symposium conducted at the meeting of the American Psychological Association, Washington, DC.

Yarhouse, M. A., Butman, R. E., & McRay, B. (2005). *Modern psychopathologies: A comprehensive Christian appraisal*. Downers Grove, IL: InterVarsity Press.

Yarhouse, M. A., & Sells, J. (2008). *Family therapies: A comprehensive Christian appraisal*. Downers Grove, IL: InterVarsity Press.

# 8

# Living the Legacy

## A Letter to My Students

*Jennifer S. Ripley, Regent University*

**A**bout a month before I got married, my mother and I were visiting with our next-door neighbors. These neighbors were a delightful family; they are now missionaries in a Third World country, serving persons who suffer from leprosy and similar diseases. At that time, they were beginning to plan their move overseas, and they offered my husband and me some hand-me-down kitchen and household items, in order to help us set up house after our wedding. This gesture was very kind, and my mom and I loaded up a box. Unfortunately, it was dark and raining outside, *but* we had an umbrella. The neighbor offered to carry the box for us in the rain, but we innocently insisted: "Oh no, we're women of the 90s! We can carry a box. It's just next door." Little did we know. So we each took one end of the box and stuck the umbrella down in the center to help keep us dry. As we walked, that umbrella slowly started to fall forward. Just as we hit the halfway mark, it completely blocked our view. We couldn't fix it, since we needed all four of our hands to hold the box. We (poorly) tried to work together to find where the front door was, but our klutzy nature took over and our path was soon hopelessly off course. Yet we were *still* determined to handle it ourselves. Before we knew it we were in the azalea bushes near the ditch, blinded by the umbrella and desperately searching for a way to the front door. Mom said, "women of the 90s, huh?" and we got to laughing at ourselves while the rain really started to pelt us. Later my mom called her mom to tell her of our "women of the 90s" funny story, and she giggled and said: "Why didn't you just turn around so the umbrella was behind you so you could see where you were going?"

This chapter gives me a chance to stop and think, turn and look behind me to share how I developed into a Christian psychologist today. I have had the privilege of becoming a Christian psychologist primarily through my attachments to important family, church and professional colleagues. My beliefs, values and practices are built on the foundation of those relationships. Attachment theory teaches that people learn their interpersonal stance and how to live their lives through their attachments to important people in their lives. Some of my stories are about people whom I am attached to. Some of my stories are not even about my life but about the life of others who have come before me. I am intentionally including their stories here because I believe that my personal narrative is the culmination of more than my own life; in other words, I view myself as part of a larger, collective story. Ultimately the lead character in our collective story is Christ—everyone else points to him. In my life, those key figures who have pointed me to Christ have taught me many things.

## DEVELOPMENT

I grew up in a fairly "typical" Caucasian evangelical family. My parents had been in the Youth for Christ movement in the 1960s and early on rooted themselves in a missionary-oriented denomination called the Christian and Missionary Alliance. I was almost a missionary kid, but one of the leaders of the church talked my parents out of being missionaries and into being lifelong church lay leaders. My mother has been a children's ministry leader since before I could talk, so our home was enriched with Christian teaching. My father was made a church elder at twenty-two years old (he didn't recommend that anyone that young be made an elder, by the way), so he was always a bulwark of the faith. They were the lay leaders that planted a church in my elementary school years in Alabama. When we moved to Minnesota when I was in junior high, they were leaders who helped counsel people when a larger church in the community had alienated people and the wounded started showing up in our church. They were leaders when we lived in Williamsburg, Virginia, and leaders when they moved on to Boston after I was married. They were personally blessed with four children who loved them deeply, a mature marriage, good standing in my dad's engineering career, love for the stay-at-home-mom role my mother enjoyed and respect in the community. It was a good childhood in their home.

I was honestly afraid of getting in trouble a lot in my adolescence, so I avoided the party scene and was heavily involved in Young Life club. Primarily out of fear, I went to a Christian college. In my first semester there I had one my first experiences of seeing how God was working in my life. I was disenchanted with the spiritual-growth opportunities on campus (a fact that I now believe is a necessary step for all Christian college students to mature) so I began to pray about it. When I returned from Christmas vacation, I talked with my roommate about it. She said she had been praying the same thing. That night we invited a group of friends to come help eat a box of goodies my grandmother had sent to us, and we stayed up talking all night long. We discovered that all eight of us had been praying the same thing. So we began a Sunday night prayer circle. The amazing thing is that this Sunday night prayer circle persisted throughout our entire college years together. It was the first time that I took my faith development and fellowship not as something given to me by my parents or other leaders, but as something that was my responsibility. As friends we knew God put us together for that purpose.

When I graduated from Nyack College, I married my childhood sweetheart, whom I met in Minnesota when I was twelve. He actually has a bit of a prophetic gift. When I moved away from Minnesota, he wrote me a letter that things weren't over for us yet; I didn't believe him. I was fifteen. But when he was in the Navy and was stationed near my parents' home when I was eighteen, his premonitions were fulfilled. We married when I was twenty-one, moved to Richmond, and Jeff started college. After a difficult and isolated first year, I applied to graduate schools, and we then settled into life at Virginia Commonwealth University (VCU) together. I was mentored by Ev Worthington at VCU (another author whose integration journey is chronicled in this book). We attended Christ Presbyterian Church, a charismatic PCUSA church, which provided rich opportunities for growth, maturity and good friendships. Jeff started working in grassroots roles in politics, a passion and calling he continues to enjoy today. Actually around that time, Kirby Worthington (Ev's wife) had an insight from God about our lives: She talked about us being like two people in an envelope, looking out of the clear opening, protected from outside attacks. I don't want to give the impression that my childhood or early marriage was ideal. There were some difficult things about moving often in childhood, and I threw more than a few frustrated pillows at my new husband in our first years. But these seem like small struggles compared to what so many people face early in life.

## STRUGGLES: DIFFICULT THINGS ARE ALWAYS THE MOST VALUABLE

*And provide for those who grieve in Zion—*
*to bestow on them a crown of beauty*
  *instead of ashes,*
*the oil of gladness*
  *instead of mourning,*
*and a garment of praise*
  *instead of a spirit of despair.*
*They will be called oaks of righteousness,*
  *a planting of the LORD*
  *for the display of his splendor.*
  *(Isaiah 61:3)*

My husband and I sat down in our study on a warm Friday evening in June 2007. We had planned to take our daughters to the oceanfront for an evening of playing flashlight tag with the fiddler crabs that cover Sandbridge beach at dusk. Instead, we sat down with my parents, and my father told me that he had just gotten back from the doctor, who had informed him that he had late-stage cancer, with an unknown future. At the time, my dad was fifty-seven. After sharing the news with us, the four of us prayed together, and I will never forget my dad praying the words: "You are my friend, Jesus, and you have blessed me." He died sixteen months later, just four months before I started writing this chapter.

A few weeks before he died, my dad wrote down some reflections that I would like to share with you.

> A day after getting the news of fourth-stage kidney cancer and a very poor prognosis, a Psalm from the Bible rang clear and true—as it has from David of Israel through all the ages, perhaps ignored by those like me that we often referred to as baby boomers, but burning true to a few of us who are faced with life-threatening prospects.

> Show me, O LORD, my life's end
> and the number of my days;
> let me know how fleeting is my life.
> You have made my days a mere handbreadth;
> The span of my years is as nothing before you.
> Each man's life is but a breath.
> Man is a mere phantom as he goes to and fro:
> He bustles about, but only in vain;
> he heaps up wealth, not knowing who will get it.

> But now, Lord, what do I look for?
> My hope is in you. (Psalm 39:4-7)

> The creed common to my fellow baby boomers, "I did it my way," characterizes the materialism of selfish desire. I see us riding the fence between being a success in this world and God's eternity. It takes on an up front and undeniable dilemma when examining life in the rear view mirror. As I soon came to understand, my plans of early retirement, a life's reward for my successful efforts in aerospace and the silicon micro-machining world, was coming to an end. My life's ride into peace and eternal joy perhaps in only a few months [it was actually a few weeks after this writing that he died] was not my planned boomer trajectory. Yet it did help me to focus on finishing well with my heavenly Father and not living life for twenty-plus more years. I soon was reminded that

life should be lived in the joy of today, by being a blessing to others. This new revelation of what God had planned for my wife and I, married thirty-nine years, turned on the brilliance of a spiritual Technicolor that gave us much to experience and share. (R. Sulouff, personal communication, June 20, 2008)

It is in *those* kinds of moments of life—the most difficult, the most unknown—where something can happen that can only happen in those kinds of moments. In those kinds of moments, the fog of day-to-day living is lifted, and we see in "spiritual Technicolor" exactly *why* we are living this earthly life.

In our most difficult times in life, true character is revealed. I watched my mom tenderly care for my dad, faithful to his last day. She is now mourning him wholeheartedly. She can do that because she has a lifetime of building faith and honesty, making her an oak of righteousness. During that year of surgery and treatments, my parents sent encouraging notes to dad's doctors, and they reached out to friends who either had cancer themselves or who had lost someone to cancer. During my dad's treatments and tests, while I tried to encourage *him*, my dad always looked out for opportunities to be an encouragement to those around him. I once said about a sour nurse, "don't worry about her, let's just focus on you right now," and my dad's response was "no, we don't do that, we always encourage others." Even in dad's final days, he did things to bless the nurses who cared for him in the ICU. In fact, three days before my dad's death, I watched him say words of encouragement to that sour and burnt-out nurse who had mishandled him earlier that day. His word turned her into a laughing woman, and she then started to talk with me about some stressful things in her life. I am truly blessed to have had two parents with such demonstrated character, who loved their God and rooted themselves and their family in the faith. But what has shaped me so deeply as a woman, wife, mother, psychologist and community member is not really my parents. They were certainly good people, but it was not them who shaped me. They carried a legacy from well before them, all the way back to Christ, and they faithfully passed it on to me. In other words, what shaped me was not my parents per se—it was *Christ in them*.

Christ was the suffering servant. Suffering is not something to run from. Former White House Press Secretary Tony Snow, who died shortly before my father, called cancer "an unexpected blessing" (Snow, 2007). A student of mine, Amy Smith, sent me Tony Snow's reflections on the blessings of terminal cancer, and in talking about Snow's comments, my father and I had such wonderful conversations about how all things are redeemed to Christ—especially suffering. As C. S. Lewis pointed out, suffering is indeed like a megaphone to all of us who are deaf and are so focused on everything that does not really matter in life that we easily miss the wisdoms and important things that really *do* matter. While I will always wish that I had not only been able to grow old with both my parents but that my children could have fully known their grandfather, I cannot say that my father's cancer was not a blessing. It was not a failure, and it was not a curse. Even though it has been the most difficult thing I have been through in my life yet, it has also deeply blessed me with a rock-steady understanding of this truth: Difficult things are the most valuable. They strip away all pretense, pride and self-centeredness, leaving us with only God.

To my students I want to say: In your work as a psychologist, there will be very difficult things that you will face. There will be unethical or burnt-out coworkers, unspeakable client trauma stories, and frustratingly stuck therapy situations. You will face difficult life experiences in your personal life and then have someone with that same situation come and sit down in your office, asking for your help. You will stare at them blankly, because you know that you are struggling with that very thing in your own life—struggling even just to sleep at night. Do not pull back from all that those difficult situations have to offer you. Of all life's situations, *those* are the ones that truly offer the best opportunities for growth. Do not seek after an easy road, characterized by wealth, fame, security and predictability. Clinical psychology is not an easy road. It is in truth a profession in which you never know what suffering will walk in your door next. Our job is to walk *toward* suffering, sit down with it, listen to it and help our clients (and ourselves) find great meaning in it.

In his aforementioned reflections, Tony Snow (2007, para. 8) wrote:

God relishes surprise. We want lives of simple, predictable ease—smooth, even trails as far as the eye can see—but God likes to go off-road. He provokes us with twists and turns. He places us in predicaments that seem to defy our endurance and comprehension—and yet don't. By his love and grace, we persevere. The challenges that make our hearts leap and stomachs churn invariably strengthen our faith and grant measures of wisdom and joy we would not experience otherwise.

## DEVELOPMENT REVISITED: PRACTICE HUMILITY BY LAUGHING OFTEN

*He will yet fill your mouth with laughter*

  *and your lips with shouts of joy. (Job 8:21)*

I come from a long line of Southern women with great senses of humor. This genealogical fact is kind of ironic, because while I laugh easily, my own funny stories never seem to end up quite as funny as I had hoped. Perhaps these things skip a generation.

One of the funniest women in my recent family history was my great-grandmother Bertie Scarborough. My great-grandma grew up on a farm in northern Florida and married a Baptist preacher. I remember her as a sweet and spunky woman who cooked the best Southern food and had a deep Southern accent. Still today, the stories her three daughters tell about her put the entire family into stitches. One such funny story happened when my grandmother was rather elderly and living in a trailer on her daughter's property. One morning she went to make up her bed, and as she stepped around the end of the bed, her foot caught in the skirting that lay loose on the floor. It was a Chenille type bedspread, so it was kind of thin and clingy. She tried to get out of it by stepping further away, but her other foot slipped, and she was thrown off balance. As she twisted and began to fall, she grasped for her bedspread. The bedspread started wrapping itself around her and wrestling her down to the ground. Around her it went until that bedspread had wrapped itself around my great-grandma like a little hot dog in a bun.

She rolled right down to the floor. She was wrapped in that bedspread and could not get out. She was really elderly at this time, and she could have gotten seriously hurt, but somehow she did not. She just lay there laughing, even though she was a little worried about how she would get out of that bedspread. Thankfully, her daughter Claudette soon walked in. "Mama, where are you?" she asked. My great-grandma quipped: "I'm in here honey! The bedspread got me!"

My great-grandma's ability to trip up gracefully was one of her most steadfast characteristics. She went to a wedding once when she was having the best time with friends and family and wanted to get some punch. Now the punch and cake were up on risers you had to step up on. My great-grandma wore long skirts all her life, the kind that go all the way to the floor. On this particular occasion, when she stepped up on the riser, my great-grandma tripped on her long skirt. She tried to regain her balance, but she ended up doing the two-step all the way across the riser, passing in front of the wedding party and then falling, sliding right under the wedding-cake table. Now everyone might not have noticed the spill except for the fact that from across the room, my great aunt had seen her mother falling and yelled out: "Maaaaamaaaaa!" Everyone in the room turned and watched it all happening, gasping that this elderly lady had fallen. But true to form, my great-grandma just picked herself up and giggled at herself; it was a pretty good two-step for a Baptist preacher's wife!

To my students: You will start out graduate school with self-assurance. You do not get to go to college or graduate school without a good measure of success in life. You might even succeed in grad school and in your career. For many of us, it is important to try to "prove" that we are special, as if it were necessary for us to do so. If you are not careful, you may start to actually *believe* that you are special—and not the kind of "special" that is God-given but the kind you earn and create all by yourself. It is easy to fail to give credit to those people who held you up, created you, formed you, educated you, mentored you and corrected you along your professional journey. Once you start seeing clients, it is tempting to think that you are *causing* the outcomes of treatment, whether those outcomes are positive or negative.

It is clear that we have a role in our clients' treatment outcomes, but sometimes the bedspread is just going to attack and roll both you and your clients up like a hot dog, leaving you each helpless on the floor. First, check for bruises; next, call for help; and then just laugh— together.

## MENTORING: RELATIONSHIP ALWAYS TRUMPS INTELLECT

*Two are better than one,*

*because they have a good return for their work:*

*If one falls down,*

*his friend can help him up.*

*But pity the man who falls*

*and has no one to help him up!*

*Also, if two lie down together, they will keep warm.*

*But how can one keep warm alone?*

*Though one may be overpowered,*

*two can defend themselves.*

*A cord of three strands is not quickly broken.*

*(Ecclesiastes 4:9-12)*

I met Everett L. Worthington Jr. on a snowy January day in 1993. When I met him, I was trying so hard to be impressive—I had even borrowed my mother's brown suit. Ev was casual and easy to talk to. We ended up talking some about his daughter, who was at William and Mary at the time, and some about his work in the areas of marriage and forgiveness. I later joined Ev as one of his graduate students; for over fifteen years I have been mentored by him and collaborated with him.

Ev has this pattern of mentoring. He intentionally lives out the discipleship of Christ in his mentoring, as much as students are willing and able to participate in it. Mentees are not just disposable slaves to a clinical or research project. Likewise, they are not just temporary teaching assistants to use like a workhorse and then disregard. Most fundamentally, Ev expects a great deal from his students, believes in them and invests in them. For example, he spends quite a lot of time meeting with his students each week. Once I became a professor, I realized how many professors only interact with their students in the classroom. This realization helped me appreciate Ev's passion for investing in his students all the more; it helped me realize just how much of a priority mentoring really is for Ev. I realized how time with students is not really all that productive toward the many classes, committees and research work that calls for attention in department life. Meeting with students will not impress a tenure-review committee or free up time to learn a new hobby. I know that if you meet with students, it can mean having to work late or having to work weekends so that you can still meet deadlines. Time is a great window into seeing what is important to us, since we all have the same amount each day, and how we use it largely reflects our relative priorities.

In mentoring relationships, it is not just time together that creates the attachment between mentor and mentee—it is personal investment in its many forms. Take for example the first draft of the first article I ever wrote under Ev's direction. It was so covered with red ink and rewriting that about halfway through the draft, Ev stopped and left a note for me to come talk with him about it. Honestly, as a professor now, I might have been tempted to conclude that this student simply did not have the background and ability to write well. I perhaps just might not have offered additional writing projects and articles. But Ev did not do that. He persevered on behalf of his student, mining out my potentials. When it comes to professional academic life, Ev and I both love academics, writing, ideas and theories. Even so, while all these things are fun and important, over the years Ev has implicitly taught me that they are secondary to what is learned in and through the mentoring relationship. In other words, it is my relationship with Ev that has changed me. Somehow this realization has freed me up to view edits and corrections not as threatening but as an investment in me. What a gift! Essentially, I learned from Ev that mentoring relationships need to be characterized by investment, by careful tailoring of feedback to the individual needs of the student, and by respecting the calling that God has placed on that student's life. And above all, the relationship must be consistently characterized by patience, a quality that is exceptionally difficult to fake.

As graduate students, my classmates and I would travel to conferences with Ev. On our drives to and from various conferences, we would often discuss how Ev's Christian beliefs impacted his work as a psychologist. For example, once three of us were driving back from a conference in Maryland: fellow doctoral student Terry Hight, Ev and I. At the time, we were discussing a new book that Ev had read—*The Sunflower* by Simon Wiesenthal (1998). In this book, various writers responded to a situation in which a Nazi war criminal, an SS officer from a Nazi death camp, was on his death bed, asking a Jewish person to forgive him for all his crimes. We discussed how difficult it must have been for the contributing authors to write about this situation. We wondered about such things as whether there are some crimes that should never be forgiven in this life, whether the role of justice in forgiveness is primary or secondary, whether a person can forgive when the larger offense is still happening, whether the character in the story had the right to grant forgiveness on behalf of others who were not there (particularly those who had been killed or harmed). Above all, we wondered what God would have us do in a similar situation. How would being representatives of Christ and his forgiveness matter in such a scenario? In this and similar discussions, Ev would always share his thoughts with us, but most of the time, for me, these discussions were academic and intellectual.

All that changed when Ev's mother was murdered on New Year's Eve in 1995. I found myself pondering: How would this tragic event affect Ev? He had just published a book on forgiveness, and I knew his theory of forgiveness well. But I wondered: In this real-life experience, will Ev's academic ideas really mean something? As Ev struggled to sort through his ideas on forgiveness and his feelings toward his mother's murderers, I was in my third year as his graduate student. Like Ev, I was seriously wrestling with the issue of how you forgive someone, regardless of the severity of the offense, when you did not see justice. I followed Ev around as he spoke about forgiveness at conferences and on various television programs. In addition, Ev started engaging in re-search on forgiveness. It would have been so easy for him to withdraw from it all. It also would have been easy to fake it. He could have talked about self-care and proper boundaries—but only as a veil for disengag-ing from the very rocky road that God had put him and his family on. I know that Ev was tempted to do so.

Ev forgave the murderers very shortly after the murder, and the amazing part is that he continued to struggle through and hold on to that forgiveness over a long period of time, when no justice came. It has now been over ten years since the murder, and Ev has come to recog-nize that when it comes to the murder, he will probably never see justice done in this life. Before losing his mother, Ev had been following Christ for a long time; since losing his mother, he has just trusted Christ with the injustice. For awhile, he still struggled to emotionally put this deep offense behind him. And yet, eventually even these emotions were re-deemed. In fact, it was out of that redemptive struggle that the aca-demic idea of emotional versus decisional forgiveness was born. You can read about it in his work *Forgiveness and Reconciliation* (2006).

Ev has indeed developed some academically excellent theories on forgiveness, but without my relationship with Ev, these theories never would have changed my life. It was our relationship that made all the difference. Ev invested so much in me, even as he invests so much of himself into whatever and whomever God brings his way. And while my youth and inexperience limited my ability to glean all I could from that mentoring relationship at the time (I was just twenty-two when I entered grad school), what I did glean I still carry with me to this day. For example, as I have faced different situations in which forgive-ness was needed, I have found it so much easier to forgive because of that relationship. Moreover, as I have mentored students who are struggling in various ways (academically, clinically, personally), I can hear Ev's voice as I talk with the students. Lastly, as I have personally endeavored to invest whatever knowledge and gifts God has given me into my work, I remember Ev doing the same, even while he was grieving. Ev is truly an amazing person—as a professor, as a mentor and as an individual. But recognizing that, I also recognize that it is not Ev that I carry—it is Christ living in Ev.

In addition to Ev, there are some wonderful people whom I have had the privilege to know, work with and even get attached to—ranging from fellow faculty who support and challenge me to those fellow congregants who serve with me in children's ministries at our church. Right now in my life, I am working to develop deeper and more authentic kinds of relationships with people in my life; that is not something that comes really naturally for me. (With a wink, Ev once kindly told me that I only exist online and not in the real world, and this comment definitely strikes a true note with me.) In actuality, I often prefer interacting with words and ideas rather than relating deeply and consistently with others.

In one of our long talks during his illness, my father confessed to me that he never really enjoyed being around people, and I have some of that "isolationist" mentality too. Ironically, sharing that day together with my dad was one of the best moments of relating that my dad and I ever had. I think that what made it so meaningful was that we both knew that to carry on the legacy of Christ, we must put aside our love for ideas and fully relate with other people. This realization is part of why I maintain a relationship with my grad school mentor, Ev. It is also part of why I must retain relationships with people who knew me before I was Dr. anybody. It is why I often put aside the never-ending "to do" pile and have lunch with a friend or my mother. It's why this chapter is full of stories of my mentors, parents and people who invested in me. It is why I remain active in the Christian Association for Psychological Studies (CAPS), a small Christian-integrationist, nonprofit organization where for fifteen years now I have had the privilege to develop relationships with Christians in the field of mental health. All the things that I have described in this chapter may not be terribly flashy or impressive, and I certainly do not view my work as necessarily "cutting edge" or brilliant. I guess when it comes down to it, what matters to me most in my integration journey are the relationships that I share with the people in my life. As I learned from Ev, I have carried on the legacy that relationship always trumps intellect.

To my students, I say invest deeply in a few people. Set aside the intellectual ideas of books and theories and look up at the people around you. Enjoy relationships with faculty and fellow students, and make relationships with some nonuniversity people too. It's tempting to want to write the next bestselling Christian psychology book or amazing theory explaining the psychology of religion. Straight A's in classes or fabulous class essays make you feel great about yourself. If you are practicing, there's considerable pressure to try to squeeze ten forty-five-minute sessions into an eight-hour day. You'll feel like being a good parent means working that extra time instead of giving the time to your kids. There's pressure to give the bare minimum to supervisees or staff that you work with. It's tempting to withdraw from church or community leadership because dealing with people can be exhausting, the next urgent situation is always five minutes away, and these things do not increase your productivity. Dedicate yourself to the people you love, help, mentor, train and develop. That is your legacy, the legacy of Christ you carry on through your life.

## SPIRITUAL DISCIPLINES AND GRACES

I was twelve, and the preacher at a youth rally was bemoaning the sins of rock-and-roll music and miniskirts. My heart was pricked with conviction and I went forward, knelt at the altar and prayed for forgiveness for my rock-and-roll music. My parents would never let me wear miniskirts, especially at age twelve. Actually the only rock-and-roll music I listened to was some old Lettermen albums and occasionally Rick Springfield on the radio. But I so wanted to be good. It's funny how this trait in me—we psychologists would call it conscientiousness—bleeds into my spiritual disciplines throughout my life.

The evangelical brand of Christianity that I grew up in was heavily focused on appearances—at least that's how I internalized it. Even as a child and young teen, I wanted to look like a "real" Christian. I am thankful that another youth rally convicted us to read Scripture daily and that a youth program I was involved with had us memorize entire books of the Bible. These experiences moved me a little beyond the somewhat limited experiences I was having in my church. They helped me come to know the real Christ individually, through Scripture. I was definitely genuine in my seeking, but I was immature. Even so, if I was to live the legacy of Christ and carry on his name, it was absolutely essential that I learned who he was. Today I read Scripture regularly, but this bent to just "be good" means that I need to try to walk in grace more often. It also means that I often struggle with the enigma that too much spiritual discipline dries up my faith, while too much grace leaves me with no faith.

As a result, my personal spiritual disciplines are varied. They include good Christian readings and studies (like C. S. Lewis, A. W. Tozer, Beth Moore or Philip Yancey), Scripture readings, writing my prayers and leading devotionals with my children at home or with students in my classes. At times in my life, I have done regular outreach to those less fortunate than me, but until my daughters are old enough to join in that practice, I am currently in a season where I don't directly practice that. I serve a good deal within our church—my mother and I have often led children's ministries; my husband and I have continuously led small groups together for eight years; and I have sometimes temporarily led women's ministries or Bible studies. Attending smaller, sometimes struggling churches has helped me develop certain graces that I probably would not otherwise have developed. For instance, it has helped me remain ever mindful of not taking on too much in Christian service—all in some kind of effort just to "be good." I cut back in ministry when I feel tired, and I have developed the habit of taking summers almost completely off from formal ministry. This understanding of grace has taught me to live with the imperfection of my spiritual life when I haven't sat down for a devotional time for days, when my only Scripture memory comes from my kids' AWANAS class assignments, or when the stresses of work/family/life multiple roles make me too grouchy and tired to open up to the very nurturance that Christ offers and I need to fulfill those multiple roles. God is good to me in this struggle with my "be good" pride.

## LETTER: CHRIST AS LEGACY

When I was still a new professor I tried to invent my own theory. I wanted to develop a creative and compelling theory that would help researchers and clinicians better understand marriage—specifically religious marriages. I thought that great ideas and great theories were really what academic life was all about. But I had no great ideas. To be honest, nothing would come to me, and when it did, it would inevitably turn out that someone else had already thought of it, written about it, and researched it with an army of graduate students and an abundance of grant funding. I got kind of depressed that I just could not come up with any original ideas. I had borrowed the idea of marriage as covenant from a blend of covenant theology and a sociologist named David Bromley, who had written about it in scientific-theoretical terms. This idea of marriage as covenant helped shaped my first research projects. I had also taken the Hope approach to marriage counseling from Ev Worthington and started to empirically investigate that clinical theory as well. In short, in my academic pursuits, I was reading and taking great ideas from a variety of psychologists and researchers, but I had no great ideas of my own. I began to wonder: What do I have to contribute?

Then I had a spiritual revelation. There was a lesson for me. At this time in my life, God had another path for me. He wanted me to carry legacies on, not to create new ones. This was true not only in my research but also in many other parts of my life. For example, in terms of our family life, my husband and I have collectively carried on a legacy of raising our daughters in the traditions of our families (at least I hope the positive ones). In terms of our church life, we have not searched out the most new "happening" place, but instead have carried on the legacy of investing deeply in a small and sometimes struggling church body. In terms of my psychology classes, I have carried on the legacy of various theories and research findings by passing them on to the next generation of students. Lastly, in terms of my research, I have carried on the legacy of the Hope-Focused approach to couples counseling. In short, in my own integration journey, I have come to recognize that my service to Christ is to build his kingdom by carrying legacies on—passing them on to my children, to my congregants and to my students.

As I look back on my life so far, I see that I am not wandering on my own path; I am following—carrying on the legacy of Christ that was passed to me. As we follow and carry on that legacy, we live the fullest, most unpredictable, stomach-churning, off-road, joyful life. Although my heart still cries for smooth roads and clear paths, I believe that sharing life with Christ will inevitably involve facing suffering. For my husband and me, I would like years of peacefully bringing up our daughters, celebrating feasts and holidays, enjoying retirement and mentoring our grandchildren in the faith. I hope for a gigantic fiftieth wedding anniversary party and a peaceful passing into eternal life. And yet, of course, even with all these desires, I do not know what life will bring. Consequently, my highest desire is to welcome whatever calling God brings my way, whether planned or not, whether peaceful or off-road. In short, I have come to realize that when it comes to our "integration journey," our greatest calling is to carry on the legacy of Christ, wherever he may lead us. The experiences I have discussed in this chapter have collectively convinced me of this truth.

So to my students, if your life brings praise in suffering, laughter in humbling circumstances and long-time authentic relationships within collective communities, then you will have carried on the legacy of Christ. Perhaps you will write your own story one day and teach me what part of the legacy of Christ you have lived. I hope so.

## REFERENCES

Snow, T. (2007, July 20). Cancer's unexpected blessings. *Christianity Today, 51*. Retrieved from www.christianitytoday.com/ct/2007/july/25.30.html.

Wiesenthal, S. (1998). *The sunflower: On the possibilities and limits of forgiveness*. New York: Schocken Press.

Worthington, E. L., Jr. (2006). *Forgiveness and reconciliation: Theory and application*. New York: Routledge.

# 9

# Honoring My Tradition

## Particularity, Practice and Patience

### *Alvin C. Dueck, Fuller Theological Seminary*

*The story is told of an Amishman who is queried whether he is saved by a tract-toting evangelical Christian. The Amishman looks at him but says nothing. He ponders. Then he asks the inquirer whether he might have a pencil and paper with him; he does. The Amishman writes what appears to be a list. He stops to think, and then writes more. Finally, the Amishman turns to the evangelist, gives him the list, and says: "Here are the names of my friends who know me well and who know how I live. Please ask them, and they will tell you whether I am saved."*

I tell my children that the Amish are my spiritual first cousins. We share the same four hundred years of history as Anabaptists, those who in the sixteenth century would not baptize their infants, chose not to solve problems with violence, and who believed the church was God's way to change the world (Dyck, 1993). These are my particular people, the Mennonites, and you would not know who I am without knowing who they are—nor would you know how I "integrate" faith and practice (Dueck, 1995, 2002a, 2002b). In this essay I will honor the gift of my tradition by making connections between my scholarship and my experience of being a Mennonite.

As is apparent from the anecdote above, deeds are more important than words. The Mennonites have always worked from a few basic convictions outlined in the Schleitheim Confession (1527) and constructed from communal discernment of the Scripture. For Mennonites, more important than finely nuanced theological propositions is the simple call to follow Jesus in showing compassion, loving mercy and being reconciled with one's enemies. With respect to the latter, we recognize that peace might not come immediately; it requires patience.

## ON BEING DEVELOPED

I grew up an ethnic minority. My parents were German Ukrainian immigrants, and I distinctly remember shortly after World War II being called a "DP," a displaced person. We were different. We had our own Saturday schools for learning German and the Bible; we also had our own private high school and our own periodicals. In short, ethnic particularity has remained an important theme in my scholarship (Dueck & Reimer, 2009). I have always wondered how a "thick" ethnic religious voice will be honored, empowered and integrated—whether in society or in therapy.

My mother raised my brother and me in a house that was not much larger than eight hundred square feet, and we lived on welfare for the first few years after my father's death. Mother cleaned the homes of the wealthy in Winnipeg, and I earned money by delivering newspapers in order to attend our Christian high school. Friends and relatives helped us through those difficult times. And so, as I travel through Kenya, Guatemala or China, empowering mental health professional and missionaries (Dueck, 2006a), I see the indigenous poor and constantly feel the contrast with how wealthy I am. I think about the paucity of mental-health resources that are available to them, about what kind of therapeutic help would actually be helpful, and about whether they have even eaten today. I continue to be troubled by the large percentage of North Americans who have neither health insurance nor mental health insurance. In fact, one of my first published essays was on educating for justice (Dueck, 1977).

It was the modeling of my mother that eventually led to my work as a psychologist, though she never understood what it meant to be a professional psychologist. I told her that it was somewhat like a being pastor. I should have told her it was like what she did for a troubled family in our neighborhood as I was growing up. For example, on one particular occasion, I remember that the mother in this recently arrived immigrant family was having a "nervous breakdown." Her husband was away at work, while she managed her children in an alien Canadian environment. My mother cared for her. I remember the children arriving at the door to tell us: "Mutti weint schon wieder" (Mother is crying again). And so my mother would trudge to their home through the snow, to help them in the midst of a miserably cold Manitoba winter. Mother was not a psychologist, but she knew what it meant to be present to others in distress. She would do what she could to address this family's immediate needs, whether that meant getting a washing machine repaired, enrolling the children in school or getting medical assistance. Years later, having met with the grown children, she related to me with deep satisfaction how well they were doing. As you can imagine, God comes to me as a gentle mother.

But I would not want to understate my mother's intuitive skills. Some years ago I came across a book by psychiatrist Doris Brett (1988) titled *Annie Stories*. I bought the book, without even opening up to the table of contents. I simply wanted a copy of the book, to remind me of how my mother told stories to her grandchildren. As a teenager, my niece came over after school to tell Grandma her current woes: school work, boyfriends and so on. My mother listened quietly and then continued a story she had begun much earlier about an emerging adolescent girl. Woven into the story were the very problems that were confronting her own granddaughter but with some creative additions—ways the main character went about resolving the same problems, addressing the same hurts or forgiving the same offenses. Ironically, when I finally read Dr. Brett's book, it turned out that my mother was in fact practicing what this psychiatrist was recommending, but she was doing so instinctively. Not surprisingly, stories are important to me as well, both in and out of my counseling office (Dueck, 1989, 1993; Parsons & Dueck, 2002; Reimer & Dueck, 2006).

An uncle once told me that, like my mother, my father was a storyteller. At bedtime he would spin tales for his brothers—tales that would continue night after night. I have no memory of my father, but being told of his creativity has certainly influenced me. It has drawn me to study the work of psychologists like John Friesen, Virginia Satir and Carl Jung, each of whom honored the role of the imagination in therapy. Spirituality too needs to be balanced between the concrete and the imaginative (Dueck & Taylor, 2003). Hence, whether in therapy or in a spiritual formation seminar, I invite clients or students to imagine alternatives to their present pain, to allow the contours of the presence of God to emerge, or to engage in a conversation with a departed saint.

My father related to the Mennonite tradition in his own unique way. As an adolescent he grew up in the city of Ekaterinaslav in the Ukraine. When his family fled to Canada in the 1920s, they ended up in a small town in Saskatchewan, Canada. The contrast was too great for my father to bear. In fact, it was so great that he eventually left home (i.e., ran away!). He rode the railcars, took odd jobs and fiddled at barn dances. The latter, clearly a taboo in his conservative Mennonite community at the time, brought considerable consternation to his parents. On occasion my father would come home, violin in hand. Upset that such a worldly instrument was in her home, his mother would hide the violin, hoping her son would decide to reform his ways. In no time he would somehow acquire another. It is not exactly clear to me how this story has influenced me, but those who know me would not say that I tend to sacralize received traditions, whether theologically or psychologically. Lamarckians (people who believe a parent can pass on attributes developed in their lifetime to their children), and perhaps my detractors, might even think that I have inherited my father's nonconformity.

I come from two generations of widows. My maternal grandfather died shortly after arriving in Canada in the 1920s, and after my father drowned, my mother never remarried. I was close to my maternal grandma, as she was my earliest caretaker. She filled my young mind with frightful images and harrowing stories of the dangerous journey from Russia to Canada. They had narrowly escaped death in the Bolshevik Revolution. Years later I read historical novels on the Mennonite holocaust in the Ukraine, during which a third of our people were massacred. Two things I learned: (1) there is blatant evil in the world, and (2) narratives construe identity. As a therapist I am cognizant that not only is pathology shaped by neurons and society, but there is also deliberate malevolence. This biblical conviction is only further reinforced by my reading of Carl Jung (Ulanov & Dueck, 2007). But I know that in therapy, a client's painful stories can be reframed. A new plot can be imagined and a different life lived (Dueck, 1995, chap. 3). Ultimately, I believe that the story of Jesus is salvific. And so, to this day I am an avid reader of novels, listening for traces of redemption wherever I might find them—often in dramas such as those constructed by Susan Howatch, Wendell Berry, Annie Dillard, Wallace Stegner, Marilyn Robinson, Haruki Murukami, Ian McEwan or Chaim Potok. (In college I almost chose a major in literature.)

Growing up, I did not want to become a psychologist; rather, I wanted to become an electrician like my father's youngest brother—whom I idealized. This uncle taught me how to drive his truck, how to write an essay and how to be playful. In high school, and later while attending a small Bible school, I wanted to be a pastor. Then, as I learned more about my Anabaptist faith, I discovered that even more important than a call to be an electrician or a pastor was the call to be a follower of Jesus. That was my vocation; the rest was avocation. The first was to be reflected in the second. Thus, my journey toward practical "integration" began. It was clear: My work was to mirror my confession.

After an early conversion experience and my baptism as a twelve-year-old came not only adolescent spiritual malaise but also recommitment. For me, the latter meant not simply "rededication"; it meant coming to grips with how I was living—that is, with my adolescent peccadilloes. For instance, I had pilfered food from uncle's grocery store, slipped a drill bit into my pocket at the hardware store and jumped the fence to gain free entry at a football game. *These* failings seared my soul, not theological conundrums. I had learned from my mother that the way to right a wrong was to confess it and to make restitution. Consequently, I apologized to my uncle, sent money to the store and mailed a two-dollar bill to the administration of the sports arena. (It was less expensive to make restitution in those days!) My conscience was clear. I could move on—a journey that would eventually include both more confession and more restitution.

In my undergraduate studies, I majored in psychology, philosophy and theology, and I fell in love with ideas, especially those of Carl Rogers, Søren Kierkegaard, Martin Buber and Karl Barth. In my graduate and postgraduate schooling, I focused on cognitive psychology, psychotherapy, and theology. My training in psychology was completed at secular institutions, but it was as I taught at two small liberal arts schools and at a seminary that I acquired the kind of education I needed to engage broadly in integrative scholarship. I began reading original works. My colleagues read Gadamer, Marx, Hauerwas, Lyotard, Levinas and Horsley—and to converse intelligently, I read them as well. But more than ideas, what moved me deeply were (and are) the stories of those who sought to follow Christ—people like Elizabeth Bingen, Dirk Willems, Peter Friesen, Gandhi, Iulia de Beausobre, Andre Trocmé, Dorothy Day and Anne Lamott. More important than being a modern or postmodern psychologist, more than any other prayer I utter, is my yearning that I might love the way these people loved Jesus, humanity and God.

As a child, while not an accomplished artist in any field, I learned to play a little piano as well as a little violin (no surprise there). Neither a Picasso nor a Monet hung on the wall of our little home, but the arts were very much a part of our Winnipeg Mennonite culture. (Decades later, while standing near the actual lily pond that Monet painted so often, I marveled at how he had transformed the Japanese bridge with his own impressions.) In the past fifteen years, I have learned to throw clay pots. I derive much joy in the unpredictable shapes that emerge, and I delight in the appreciation that I see on the faces of those who receive my simple creations as a gift. In my classes, I lecture as I mold a pot, drawing out the analogies to therapy, such as preparing the clay and one's heart, the importance of centering, maintaining multiple perspectives, making a critical intervention, being comfortable with unpredictability and knowing when to stop.

## MENTORS: SOUGHT AND ACCIDENTAL

Walking across the campus of the Mennonite Brethren Bible College that was situated next to my high school, an elderly man once stopped me. "I think I know who you are," he said. I was worried that I had been trespassing. "Your father is the one who drowned in British Columbia. Well, you may be interested to know that I sang in a quartet with him in the years before he died." What followed was a conversation about my father and a friendship with this man that lasted for years. This man, Dr. Frank C. Peters, was among the first in my Mennonite Brethren denomination to have studied both theology and psychology, and he encouraged me to do the same. I did.

I chose to attend a college, now called the University of Winnipeg, which was related to the United Church of Canada. It reflected a British influence in that many of the faculty were trained in England. Dr. Robson, my first psychology professor, would come flowing into class in his black gown, like an English don. I listened to him, spellbound. Ancient philosophy taught by Dr. Taylor continues to influence me as I teach the history and philosophy of psychology. And Dr. Ridd's course on the religious quest in the modern world was so formative in my education that it has resulted in my constant use of novels in my courses to this day.

Upon completing my graduate studies, our young family moved to rural Kansas, where I taught at a small Christian liberal arts college. Here I found wonderful mentors like John Toews, who wondered what it meant for me to be a psychologist and an Anabaptist. I began reading original sources from my religious tradition. I had taken courses in Mennonite history ad nauseam, but it was then that it became a live tradition, relevant to my work and faith. After reading John Yoder's (1972) *The Politics of Jesus,* I pondered the political context of modern psychology. With colleagues, I have written about the role of an empire mentality in America and its influence on psychologists' involvement in the military (Dueck, Langdal, Goodman & Ghali, 2009; Dueck & Reimer, 2009). As a result, the ethical context of psychology became increasingly important to me (Dueck, 1992b, 1995).

Jewish novelists, philosophers, painters and historians have also mentored me. In Potok's (1972) *My Name is Asher Lev,* I found a deep affinity for the tension between communalism and creativity. Together with Viktor Frankl's (1959) *From Death Camp to Existentialism,* both books continue to be reading assignments in my courses. Seeing Chagall's (1938) painting *White Crucifixion,* depicting Jesus on a cross, with a prayer shawl as loincloth, spoke to me of the renascent conflict in Jewish and Christian communities over the meaning of Jesus' death (Green & Baker, 2000). The hostility toward Jews over the centuries, as recounted in James Carroll's (2001) *Constantine's Sword,* reminded me of the suffering of my Mennonite forbears in Russia—though on a smaller scale. I read and reread Martin Buber and then moved on to Emil Fackenheim, Franz Rosenzweig, Abraham Heschel and finally Emmanuel Lévinas. I find myself moved by their ethical and historical view of psychological identity, as well as by their disenchantment with extant ontological and essentialist readings of human nature (Dueck & Parsons, 2007; Dueck & Goodman, 2007).

Then I discovered the ways in which exegetes across the centuries have downplayed the Jewish context of Jesus and of Paul. Geza Vermes (1973) and Amy-Jill Levine (2006) have transformed the way I view the life of Christ. Krister Stendahl's (1986) book on Paul's life and ministry among the Jews and Gentiles was critical for me. Stendahl argued that Paul saw himself as Jewish, that his conversion was more of a call, and that his vocation was the reconciliation of Jew and Gentile. I am convinced that as researchers and clinicians, if Jesus is at the heart of our work, then recovering the Jewish context of Jesus will make a difference in our understanding of God and of ethnicity. I believe that making Jesus central is the critical mandate for the contemporary church and for our integrative work as psychologists. However, my thoughts on how we accomplish the latter are still embryonic.

The influence of international students and scholars on my life cannot go unmentioned. In the early 1980s we provided lodging for Arabic students who came to Fresno, California, to learn English. I discovered how being a Muslim meant that all of life was impacted by a decision to believe in Allah and be a follower of Mohammed's teachings. In other words, I learned that Islam was not a collection of beliefs but was instead a way of living that was, in our experience, a very peaceful one. Our Muslim guests maintained their prayer regimen, ate food blessed at the mosque and kept Ramadan. In the past decade, my colleagues and I have interviewed spiritual exemplars from the Muslim, Jewish and Christian traditions (Reimer, Dueck, Neufeld, Steenwyk & Sidesinger, 2010). In completing these interviews, I have been challenged by the depth of conviction and the commitment to service that members of each tradition have exhibited. In another study, some colleagues and I have interviewed Muslim and Christian peacemakers and encountered persons who are deeply committed to justice and reconciliation in both traditions (Dueck, Reimer, Morgan, & Brown, 2009; Brown, Reimer, Dueck, Gorsuch, Strong & Sidesinger, 2008).

## STRUGGLES, TENSIONS AND CONTRADICTIONS

There are at least four primary issues that I have struggled with: the absence of a father, the psychological effects of intellectual scholarship, Western ethnocentrism and choosing to be an Anabaptist. Here I will examine each in turn. First, growing up in a single-parent family certainly left its impact on me, but I am not always sure what its actual effects were. I have nothing with which to compare it. While in personal therapy, I realized that my father's death is a continuing wound. I explored how it might affect my response to authority, to powerful males, and to demanding institutions. When my therapist suggested that there would always be scar tissue, I was discouraged. Eventually, I realized that while the wound would heal, I need to respect the sensitivity of the scar tissue, to be aware when I feel myself starting to respond with either too much passivity or too much aggression. Thankfully, though I grew up without a father, I was ensconced in a cohesive community of friends, neighbors and relatives. In this community, I had many fathers—at times more than I needed or wanted.

After several decades in academia, I was living too much in my head. I knew that emotionally I was missing important cues in my work as a therapist. My personal therapy was a process of softening, of moving from head to heart. Just before my first session of therapy, I had the following dream:

> I am taking our son Kevin to the hospital. He is around twelve at the time and the event takes place somewhere in Canada. I cannot remember the reason for hospitalization, but I do remember boxes in the aisles which I have to avoid. While I am waiting for the examination to end, I hear over the intercom that Kevin is being rushed into emergency surgery. I next remember standing in the surgery room watching as they wheel Kevin in. He is lying on a gurney with doctors hovering over him. The surgeon pours a thick red liquid on him that resembles blood. It gathers on the side. He then takes a knife and begins to cut once lengthwise and once crosswise. I begin to cry uncontrollably, am discovered, and ushered out into the lobby where many relatives have gathered. (Dueck, 1995, pp. 237-38)

The critical images in this dream are blood, the cross and surgery. I took this dream to be a reminder for me to attend to the issues of the heart, to be willing to suffer and to embrace the process as necessarily painful. It was not my son's heart that needed radical surgery—it was my own.

I struggle with the ethnocentrism of our discipline and profession. Our purview is our own Western culture. Our training of psychologists seldom includes the history of psychological thought in other cultures. When we invite international students to study with us, we assume that they must learn our way of being a psychologist and that they have little to offer from their indigenous cultural perspectives. We export our theories, our research and our manuals with the naive assumption that no harm is being done in the process—and yet, the evidence suggests otherwise. Our theories displace local understandings of human nature. Our research questions dominate their journals, even when there may be more pressing local questions. In such environs, modes of healing that have been practiced for millennia are traded in for classic psychoanalysis, Rogerian nondirective therapy, cognitive behaviorism and EMDR (Gergen, Gulerce, Lock & Misra, 1996).

In the past decade I have increasingly traveled internationally, and to my horror I have witnessed the effects of our ethnocentrism. No doubt

Western psychology has made positive contributions, but my experience has also revealed the other side. One of my most transforming experiences in the past few years was writing a book with Dr. Gladys Mwiti on African indigenous Christian counseling (Mwiti & Dueck, 2006a, 2006b). The book and accompanying DVD are now being used in a variety of seminaries across Africa. After one of our workshops in Nairobi, with eyes brimming with tears, a therapist asked me: "Are you and Gladys really telling us that it is okay for us to use our ancient proverbs in therapy? We were always told that as Christians we needed to leave behind our past." How deeply troubling. As a result, the impact of colonialism and of an empire mentality is the focus of some of my recent publications (Dueck, Ting & Cutiongco, 2007; Dueck & Reimer, 2009). Conversely, I have found myself moved by the indigenous theology and pastoral counseling practices of my Chinese friends (Dueck & Walling, 2006; Wang, 2002).

In relationship to what evangelicals call integration, the conversation between psychology and my Mennonite convictions has proven to reveal some interesting contrasts and similarities (Dueck, 1982, 1988, 2002b; Dueck & Lee, 2005). Often it is assumed that there is one correct way of intellectually integrating a standardized Christianity and a monolithic psychology. I have come across more than one book titled *The Christian Approach to Counseling,* a title which assumes such a universality. The use of the word *integration* may well belie confessional particularities. Some religious groups tend to use this term more than others, and they do so with the assumption that integration is bringing together the thoughts of two very different disciplines: theology and psychology. Not all theological traditions assume that such an approach is the critical way for Christians to engage culture. For example, the late Quaker/Covenant psychologist Randall Sorenson once commented:

> I even had one early leader of integration tell me in a personal conversation that he was baffled why I was publishing integrative articles that were sympathetic to Anabaptist theologies. He said, "Randy, that's not integration!" Later, when our conversation touched on dialogue about a Reformed theologian, he thumped the table with approbation: "Now that's integration!" (Sorenson, 2004, p. 186)

Over the decades, I have persistently pondered what the dialogue between faith and psychology looks like from an Anabaptist perspective. Catholics and Protestants alike persecuted the Anabaptists in the sixteenth century. (The tension persists. One article I wrote for a Protestant journal needed to be vetted first by a non-Mennonite theologian.) Perhaps the discomfort that the religious establishment had with the radical Anabaptists came because of the latter's refusal to make the state ultimate and their insistence that we focus on Jesus as the model for what it means to be human—a model which included loving one's enemies. In my writing I have drawn on our communal history, the experience of suffering that comes with radical discipleship, the critical importance of particularity, the humility to serve others and the refusal to make the received tradition of a profession a "calling." I choose not to create global Christian models of integration but to encourage time-delimited and space-specific models. For example, rather than the broad question of the relationship of sin to pathology, I would prefer asking something like this: How is one uniquely faithful to one's particular Christian tradition when working with a couple where one partner is suffering with Alzheimer's disease?

## SPIRITUAL DISCIPLINES IN CONCRETE PLACES

I grew up in a home and in an evangelical subculture where the measure of one's faith was a regular devotional life. Such a view may be pious, but it is not enough. I have had clients who assented to the creeds of the church but violently abused a spouse. What is missing in these and other instances is faithful practice (Dueck, 2008). It was many years before I began to understand what it means to be a follower of Jesus. And then it even took many more years to learn to actually practice imitating Jesus. More than piety, concrete practice became important to me. Being a member of an intentional neighborhood, being active in congregations that eschewed violence, loving God in the company of gentle friends—these have been my most important spiritual disciplines. I attend a house church these days where we begin with a meal and communion, sing hymns in four-part harmony, share the joys and struggles of everyday life, reflect on Scripture or discuss a book. As a result of my participation in this worshipping community, I have expended considerable scholarly energy discussing healing structures in the church (Dueck,1992a; Dueck & Herrera, 1999) and reflecting on violent versus peaceful modes of coexistence (Dueck, Becker, Goodman & Jones, 2005).

How does God come to me? What nurtures my soul? Poetry, novels, music, meditation on art and throwing pots. But most importantly, God comes to me in the friendship of believers, in the look in the eye of a student who has made a connection or in the tears in the eyes of a client as she recounts her abuse. My spiritual disciplines are concrete as well as introspective. For me, integration is not merely a rational and theoretical process. Providing psychological assistance to the poor is as much "integration" as is comparing Freud and Augustine theoretically. Theory does not trump practice. Indeed our day-by-day journey is itself a form of integration, as Abraham Heschel recounted in the following experience he had walking with Martin Luther King in the 1960s:

> For many of us the march from Selma to Montgomery was both protest and prayer. Legs are not lips, and walking is not kneeling. And yet our legs uttered songs. Even without words, our march was worship. I felt my legs were praying. (Kimelman, 1985, p. 1)

As I walk I pray and wait for the unexpected. I would like to be surprised by God in everyday life, much like Anne Lamott (Lamott, 1999).

## THERAPY: ON BEING TAUGHT

I have been changed by the students and clients that I have cared for. By their questions, students constantly remind me how little I know. Knowledge is an interconnected web, and one bit of information is connected to many strands about which I know very little. Then there are my international students who, when they are not seeking to be Western, value wisdom over intelligence, otherness over self-confidence, and obligation over autonomy.

In my experience, by sharing their innermost thoughts and feelings, clients often point to the mystery of what it means to be human. Granted, on occasion I have been gratified by clients whose changes were consistent with my own intuitions and theories. But more so, I am grateful for those clients who have stumped me, who have left me with nothing to say except "I don't know." Among many things, my clients have taught me patience, and they have taught me that change often comes slowly.

Additionally, I have benefited from reading the accounts of therapy by Irving Yalom (2002) and from watching the tapes of therapy being conducted by Helm Stierlin at Heidelberg. The experience of being a therapist has made me aware of my own areas of weaknesses and areas of needed growth. Therapy is for me a process of self-emptying, or *kenosis*. Kenotic self-emptying is a process that has also been nurtured by living in community, by being married and by participating in personal therapy with a gifted therapist.

The latter was a Catholic and a Jungian; he was both nurturing and forthright. Indeed, my therapy was concurrently spiritual direction. Often when I came in for a session, I could tell that my therapist had been reading the "Book of the Hours" (Catholic Church & Franciscans, 1965). He stunned me by asking at one point why my spirituality seemed so sterile, but he also encouraged me when a client committed suicide. I remember an emotional session that transpired after we had been meeting for some six months. During that session, I complained that he knew so little about who I was, about where I came from and about what it meant to be a Mennonite. He listened quietly, made a brief comment, and therapy moved on.

I came to realize that, in fact, he did know much more about the Mennonite tradition than I had originally thought. I also came to realize that our therapeutic work together was in many ways a process of helping me be faithful to the Mennonite tradition. In fact, it was actually my own experience of therapy that shaped my emphasis on a tradition-sensitive approach to psychotherapy. Healing can be construed to be conversation between two or more people that represent in varying degrees a tradition(s). At least one objective in therapy is for the therapist to be faithful to his or her tradition in this conversation and for the client to move toward the ideals of his or her chosen tradition (Dueck, 2006b, 2007; Dueck & Reimer, 2003, 2009).

## LETTER

Dear Reader,

I am glad that you are considering psychology as an avenue of service. If you plan to engage mostly in research, may you be drawn in by curiosity, and if you wish to be an instrument of healing, I wish you wisdom. Amassing publications can become an end in itself, and therapy can be reduced to applying theories and effective techniques. In either endeavor, I encourage you to explore the vast differences between information and wisdom.

Perhaps you will become a leader. There are plenty of professionals who practice in the field, but maybe you will be the one to develop a vision for how to provide mental health services for those who do not have access to mental health insurance, or perhaps you will work with the World Health Organization to make mental health services available in underdeveloped countries. In any case, if you become a leader in the field, you will need to know that your discipline has a history, that knowledge emerges in a context, and that cultures develop their own vocabulary and grammar to understand mental illness and healing. Many of our theories of change are constructed with middle-class Western clients in mind.

Therapists burn out for many reasons; I hope you do not. I remember a therapist who was seeing more than forty clients a week—he wanted to retire early. I would not have wanted to be the last client of that therapist's week! To me, his caseload sounds like a recipe for burnout. See your therapeutic work as a ministry. To view your clients as individuals to whom you are asked to be faithful is to see your therapy as larger than your clients and to see yourself as part of the greater movement of God in history.

I encourage you to develop a holistic view of the self, one that encompasses the sciences and the humanities. In the past centuries, our understanding of the person has become positivist, truncated and reductionist. We have viewed the self as a self-contained being shaped by biological, psychological and social forces. The symbolic has been eclipsed. The language of the natural sciences has dominated our understanding of selfhood and of how persons change. There is a place for such a way of thinking and speaking, but there is also the temptation to forget that life itself is still a mystery. Those who are made in the image of God will remain inexplicable. Psychology as a science needs the corrective of the humanities. C. P. Snow (1959) made an articulate case for remembering both traditions and that our cultures would be impoverished if one were slighted. That applies to our discipline of psychology as well. So my encouragement to you is to enjoy the arts or learn an artistic skill. There are times when therapy is more like jazz than it is following a theory or a manual.

As a religious therapist, you will no doubt be warned not to impose your values on your clients. Actually, the issue is not *whether* you bring your values into therapy. You will—as do all therapists. More importantly, the issue is this: In the therapy room, will you create an environment in which the client will feel the freedom to speak in his or her religious mother tongue? Many clients come to therapy and leave behind their native tongue, instead using the language they think the therapist implicitly expects, that is, psychological. Will you be able to create a therapeutic context in which clients feel the freedom to use "God-talk," to interpret their current quandary in religious language or to describe their hopes in terms of their trust in God's faithfulness? If so, you will be honoring the religious tradition that your clients bring to therapy.

Remember that your clients are not bundles of symptoms but instead are made in the image of our invisible God; as such, they seek meaning and purpose in their lives. In some cases without even knowing it, they are invited to mature in the image of Jesus. Therapy then becomes as much about wisdom and ethical maturity as it is about pathology. Narcissism is about ethics. War trauma is more than the insipid label of PTSD; it is a consequence of those military and political leaders who have forgotten that we are to love our enemies.

I encourage you to love the church, the community of believers, with all its shortcomings and imperfections. As therapists we represent the church in the world. This is our community of accountability, of profound fellowship and of acceptance. Beware of making your clients your community. They cannot bear it, and you do well not to expect it. Better to find a community who loves you for where you are in your journey. We do not heal alone. We are partners of God, just as Adam and Eve were asked to name the flora and fauna of the garden. We are God's hands, and feet, and ears. Enlarge your world beyond the profession.

Blessings on the journey,
Al Dueck

## REFERENCES

Brett, D. (1988). *Annie stories*. New York: Workman Publishing.

Brown, W. S., Reimer, K., Dueck, A., Gorsuch, R., Strong, R., & Sidesinger, T. (2008). A particular peace: Psychometric properties of the Just Peacemaking Inventory. *Peace and Conflict: Journal of Peace Psychology, 14,* 75-92.

Carroll, J. (2001). *Constantine's sword: The church and the Jews: A history*. Boston: Houghton Mifflin.

Catholic Church & Franciscans. (1965). *Book of hours*. New Canaan, CT: Byzantine Franciscans.

Chagall, M. (1938). White crucifixion [Painting]. The Art Institute of Chicago.

Dueck, A. C. (1977). Education for justice. *Direction, 6,* 12-20.

Dueck, A. C. (1982). Prolegomena to Mennonite approaches in mental health services. *Mennonite Quarterly Review, 56,* 64-81.

Dueck, A. C. (1988). Psychology and Mennonite self-understanding. In C. Redekop & S. Steiner (Eds.), *Mennonite identity* (pp. 203-24). Lanham, MD: University Press of America.

Dueck, A. C. (1989). Story, community and ritual: Anabaptist themes and mental health. *Mennonite Quarterly Review, 63,* 77-91.

Dueck, A. C. (1992a). Congregational care needs and resources survey: A summary. *Direction, 21,* 26-40.

Dueck, A. C. (1992b). Metaphors, models, paradigms and stories in family therapy. In H. Vande Kemp (Ed.), *Family therapy: Christian perspectives* (pp. 175-207). Grand Rapids, MI: Baker.

Dueck, A. C. (1993). My many selves. In C. Lee (Ed.), *Storying ourselves: A narrative perspective on Christians in psychology* (pp. 237-60). Grand Rapids, MI: Baker.

Dueck, A. C. (1995). *Between Athens and Jerusalem: Ethical perspectives on culture, religion and psychotherapy.* Grand Rapids, MI: Baker.

Dueck, A. C. (2002a). Anabaptism and psychology: From above and below. In D. Zercher-Mast (Ed.), *Minding the church* (pp. 111-25). Telford, PA: Pandora Press.

Dueck, A. C. (2002b). Babel, Esperanto, shibboleths, and Pentecost: Can we talk? *Journal of Psychology and Christianity, 21,* 72-80.

Dueck, A. C. (2006a). Member care. In J. R. Kraybill, W. Sawatzky, and C. Van Engen (Eds.), *Evangelical, ecumenical and Anabaptist missiologies in conversation: Essays in honor of Wilbert R. Shenk* (pp. 257-66). New York: Orbis.

Dueck, A. C. (2006b). Thick patients, thin therapy and a Prozac god. *Theology, News and Notes,* 4-6.

Dueck, A. C. (2007). Anabaptism and psychology: Personal reflections. In D. Schipani (Ed.), *Mennonite perspectives on pastoral counseling* (pp. 46-58). Elkhart, IN: Institute of Mennonite Studies.

Dueck, A. C. (2008). Worship as transformed lives. In A. Abernethy (Ed.), *Worship that changes lives: Multidisciplinary and congregational perspectives on spiritual transformation* (pp. 348-68). Grand Rapids, MI: Baker.

Dueck, A. C., Becker, B., Goodman, D., & Jones, P. (2005). Violent religions: Monologue or dialogue? *PsycCRITIQUES, 50*(7), No Pagination Specified. DOI: 10.1037/040056.

Dueck, A. C., & Goodman, D. (2007). Substitution and the trace of the Other: Levinasian implications for psychotherapy. *Pastoral Psychology, 55,* 601-17.

Dueck, A. C., & Herrera, A. (1999). Communal identity and the Christian therapist. *Marriage & Family: A Christian Journal, 2,* 369-79.

Dueck, A. C., Langdal, J. P., Goodman, D. M., & Ghali, A. A. (2009). Prophetic words for psychologists: Particularity, ethics and peace. *Pastoral Psychology, 58,* 289-301.

Dueck, A. C., & Lee, C. (Eds.). (2005). *Why psychology needs theology: A radical-reformation perspective.* Grand Rapids, MI: Eerdmans.

Dueck, A. C., & Parsons, T. (2007). Ethics, alterity, and psychotherapy: A Levinasian perspective. *Pastoral Psychology, 55,* 271-82.

Dueck, A. C., & Reimer, K. (2003). Retrieving the virtues in psychotherapy: Thick and thin discourse. *American Behavioral Scientist, 47,* 427-41.

Dueck, A. C., & Reimer, K. (2007). Religious discourse in psychotherapy. In

P. Wong, L. Wong, M. McDonald & D. Klaassen (Eds.), *The positive psychology of meaning and spirituality* (pp. 125-40). Abbottsford, BC: INPM Press.

Dueck, A. C., & Reimer, K. (2009). *A peaceable psychology: Christian therapy in a world of many cultures.* Grand Rapids, MI: Brazos Press.

Dueck, A., Reimer, K., Morgan, J., & Brown, S. (2009). Let peace flourish: Descriptive and applied research from the Conflict Transformation Study. In M. Abu-Nimer & D. Augsburger (Eds.), *Peace-building by, between, and beyond Muslims and evangelical Christians* (pp. 233-54). Lanham, MD: Lexington.

Dueck, A. C., & Taylor, G. (2003). Imaginative prayer. *Conversations, 2,* 57-63.

Dueck, A. C., Ting, S-K., & Cutiongco, R. (2007). Constantine, Babel, and "Yankee doodling": Whose indigeneity? Whose psychology? *Pastoral Psychology, 56,* 55-72.

Dueck, A. C., & Walling, S. (2007). Theological contributions of Bishop K. H. Ting to Christian/pastoral counseling. *Pastoral Psychology, 56,* 143-56.

Dyck, C. J. (1993). *An introduction to Mennonite history.* Scottdale, PA: Herald Press.

Frankl, V. E. (1959). *From death-camp to existentialism: A psychiatrist's path to a new therapy.* Boston: Beacon Press.

Gergen, K., Gulerce, A., Lock, A., & Misra, G. (1996). Psychological science in cultural context. *American Psychologist, 51,* 496-503.

Green, J., & Baker, M. (2000). *Recovering the scandal of the cross: Atonement in the New Testament & contemporary contexts.* Downers Grove, IL: InterVarsity Press.

Kimelman, R. (1985). Abraham Joshua Heschel: Our generation's teacher. *Religion and Intellectual Life, 2,* 9-18. Retrieved from www.crosscurrents .org/heschel.htm

Lamott, A. (1999). *Traveling mercies: Some thoughts on faith.* New York: Pantheon Books.

Levine, A.-J. (2006). *The misunderstood Jew: The church and the scandal of the Jewish Jesus.* San Francisco: HarperSanFrancisco.

Mwiti, G. K., & Dueck, A. C. (2006a). *Christian counseling: An African indigenous perspective.* Pasadena, CA: Fuller Seminary Press.

Mwiti, G. K. (Writer), & Dueck, A. C. (Writer). (2006b). *Christian counseling: An African indigenous perspective* [DVD Series]. (Available from Fuller

Theological Seminary, 180 N. Oakland Ave, Pasadena, CA 91182.)

Parsons, T., & Dueck, A. C. (2002). Formation of the moral self. *Journal of Psychology & Theology, 30,* 84-86.

Potok, C. (1972). *My name is Asher Lev.* New York: Random House.

Reimer, K., & Dueck, A. C. (2006). Inviting Soheil: Narrative and embrace in Christian caregiving. *Christian Scholar's Review, 35,* 205-20.

Reimer, K. S., Dueck, A., Neufeld, G., Steenwyk, S., & Sidesinger, T. (2010). Varieties of religious cognition: A computational approach to self-understanding in three monotheist contexts. *Zygon: Journal of Religion and Science, 45,* 75-90.

Reimer, K., Dueck, A. C., Morgan, J., & Kessel, D. (2008). A peaceable common: Collective wisdom from exemplar Muslim and Christian peacemakers. In A. Day (Ed.), *Religion and the individual* (pp. 79-94). Aldershot, UK: Ashgate.

Schleitheim Confession. (1527). Retrieved from www.crivoice.org/creed-schleitheim.html

Snow, C. P. (1959). *The two cultures.* New York: The New American Library.

Sorenson, R. L. (2004). How to anticipate predictions about integration's future trends. *Journal of Psychology & Theology, 32,* 181-89.

Stendahl, K. (1983). *Paul among the Jews and Gentiles: And other essays.* Philadelphia: Fortress Press.

Ulanov, A., & Dueck, A. C. (2007). *The living God and the living psyche: C. G. Jung's psychology and Christian faith.* Grand Rapids, MI: Eerdmans.

Vermes, G. (1973). *Jesus the Jew: A historian's reading of the Gospels.* London: Collins.

Wang, X. (2002). Theological thought of Zhi Mian—Understanding *Bishop Ding's Collected Writings* from the perspective of Zhi Mian psychology. *Nanjing Theological Review, 52,* 41-54.

Yalom, I. (2002). *The gift of therapy: An open letter to a new generation of therapists and their patients.* New York: HarperCollins.

Yoder, J. H. (1972). *The politics of Jesus: Vicit agnus noster.* Grand Rapids, MI: Eerdmans.

# 10

# Reluctant Integration

*J. Derek McNeil, Wheaton College*

**I** have been teaching, speaking and writing about integration for almost fifteen years, but it is only after saying yes to this project that I realized that I have never been asked to actually share the *development* of my thoughts, as they have emerged over the course of my life's journey. Moreover, I have never been asked to thoughtfully consider how my life journey has affected my thinking about Christianity and psychology, and conversely how that dialogue has impacted my life. In considering this task, I realized I could not share my own thinking without sharing something of my understanding of how to live. Now I say this with some trepidation, because I do not see my journey as particularly unique or eventful. However, I am at a unique moment in my journey. I have recently lost both parents, and their passing has served to push me forward in my journey, as I have become part of the older generation in my family. I have also felt pushed to offer something of my integration journey to those who are on their own journey. Hence, this project comes at a significant time of transition and change, where my need to offer something of value has outgrown my need to receive.

This powerful shift has reminded me of Joseph Campbell's (1949/2008) description of the "hero's return," in his classic book *The Hero with a Thousand Faces*. As a comparative mythologist, Campbell offered an analysis of different "hero myths," identifying three phases of the hero's journey: the Separation phase, the Initiation phase and the Return phase. In Campbell's framework, the Separation phase includes the movement of the hero away from home (or at least away from what is known) and into the mysteries of the journey. The Initiation phase includes the hero's entry into the outside world—with all its new possibilities but also with all its tests and trials. The Return phase includes the end of the quest, when the hero brings home all the gifts and wisdom he or she has gained while negotiating the challenges of his or her journey.

Campbell's (1949/2008) heroic figure is not a special person but is instead someone who has accepted the call to journey and has thus given oneself over to the transformational experience. Campbell described some heroic figures as willing and as selfless in the giving of themselves, but he described others as quite reluctant. The latter types of figures must be compelled to leave home, and then as their journey comes to an end, they must circumstantially be challenged to return home. However, if "reluctant heroes" are to complete their call, they must find their way home and tell their stories to those they wish to guide into the adventure of living life. In truth, I experience this project as something of that call to return. I consider it a unique honor to lend my voice and story alongside the others in this book, in the hope that those who find these pages will glean from their wisdom and join us on the journey.

## DEVELOPMENT

It has been a challenge not only to decide what stories to share in these few short pages but also to identify those themes that might have corporate value. I settled on two periods that I believe were essential to my direction and growth. I consider these two places vital settings in my life story, and they remain the principal shaping periods of my faith and my vocation. The first place I will call my "home village," which is an allegory for the space I grew up in with my parents and siblings. It was more than just the nuclear family; it was the world of my development that included friends, extended family, the church and the cultural neighborhood of my identity. This "home village" was the psychological context of my early orientation, and an appropriate metaphor to communicate the embedded nature of my development.

The second place that came to mind was Fuller Seminary. Fuller is a place that represents a developmental space of significant choices for me. To borrow some of Campbell's (1949/2008) terminology, it is my "separation" from home and my "call to adventure," a moving away from the familiar and entry into a world less known. These two symbolic places, "home village" and "Fuller Seminary," stand out because they represent pivotal moments in my development.

*Home village.* I grew up in the 1960s, the second child and first son of James and Ruth McNeil. My parents raised their three children in a working-class neighborhood in southwest Philadelphia. They moved to this house when I was a few months old, and they remained there until they both passed. My early years transpired amidst the dramatic social shifts of the civil rights movement, the Vietnam War, the rise of feminism and the sexual revolution. This is the world in which I saw my parent as actors—it was the world that influenced the worldview my parents translated to their children.

While all these movements made impressions on my family life, the civil rights movement was the most significant. I think that the magnitude of this impact was so great simply because racial barriers were chronic and debilitating, and they had to be managed every day. The shadow of "Jim Crow" was lifting, but persisting racial tensions and the residual social belief in black inferiority made for an insecure social environment.

I do not personally remember the wholly infectious nature of these times because of the buffering by my family village, but I was socialized to what could happen. My parents believed that it was their duty to inoculate us children against the debilitating experience of racialization. But with any vaccination process, the disease agent must be introduced to the body in order for the body to develop resistance to it. Such "inoculating" socializations helped me to resist many of the negative projections that young black boys experienced, but they also gave me a certain perception of the world. While I was told I could prevail, I also heard that I was an outsider in a system that did not value my participation.

This mingling of resilience and shame could also be identified in my mother's socialization. Her messages to me were a complex combination of both accommodation and resistance. On one hand she would preach good manners, respectful behavior and self-improvement, but on the other she would also model defiance, such as when I watched her confront anyone who disrespected her or her children. Raised in the American South, my mother had her share of experiences of subtle and overt forms of racism. Hence, she always viewed the world as somewhat unsafe, and therefore she prepared us to face adversity. Her stories of difficult experiences were told partly in order to create a vigilant posture in us, along with a motivation for us to work hard in school. Her ultimate strategy was to help us avoid hardship by succeeding in our education and thereby achieving social elevation. I recall her taking us places where there were few other children of color; she took us there to expose us to a different world. This world included going to concerts, recitals, museums and social events, many of which were beyond the experiences of other children in our neighborhood.

During one trip to a museum, when we were standing in line to go in, my mother pointed out a poor older black man who was selling peanuts. She said to me, "Do you want to grow up selling peanuts on the corner?" As she mimicked his slow drone "peanuts, peanuts, nice fresh roasted peanuts," I said "no" in such a way that it showed my own disdain at the possibility. "If not, then you're going to have to work harder in school." I felt embarrassment for this man, as my life lessons came at his devaluation. I also felt challenged to try harder, but even so, some part of me was wounded, because I saw myself in this man. I understood that this was my mother's way of pushing us, but at times, her lessons could feel quite harsh.

My mother was an immensely talented woman, capable of almost anything she put her mind to. She stimulated my interests in learning and in finding new answers to old questions. She always pushed to show us a world that was larger than our own immediate context. My mother's main weakness was her fear that her children would be unprepared if something were to happen to her. This was a reflection of her childhood losses and fears. My mother experienced the death of her own mother very early in life, and so she was infected with a fear of what could happen if the same were to occur for her.

My mother never finished high school, and at age seventeen she left

Knoxville, Tennessee, and went on the road, singing in a gospel group that traveled around with an itinerant preacher and church planter. This period was when my mother's determination was most evident in her story, as she went through a series of training experiences and regional moves in order to improve her life options. My first introduction to the integration conversation came from her determined push for learning and self-education. She was an avid bedtime reader, so there was always a treasure of books near her bedside. On occasion I would peruse her selections, sneaking off with one that caught my interest, while being careful not to take her current read. Her tastes would span widely, ranging from Christian religion and spirituality to light carpentry and upholstery, and then shifting to health and sexuality. Sometimes I would find a Watchman Nee, Martin Luther King, Dale Carnegie, Jay Adams, Tim LaHaye or Norman Vincent Peale book under her bed, and such books became my "pre-integration reading." During one of my searches, I found Carter and Narramore's (1979) seminal work, *The Integration of Psychology and Theology*. While I do not recall making sense of that book at the time, it was my introduction to the integrationist conversation. At the time I was more vocationally invested in architecture; psychology was only a curiosity.

If my mother was the life force in our family, my father was the steady rock. More soft-spoken, my father modeled a stubborn persistence of his own, as I watched him take care of his family within a context of limited opportunity. My father was a man who typified the generation of Americans that Tom Brokaw referred to as the "Greatest Generation." He was raised during the Depression and shaped by the Second World War. He believed in hard work, in dedication to his family, and in an enduring faith and reliance on God. After his struggle with cancer and subsequent death, I realized that I had never heard my father complain about his life—its struggles or its pains. Even so, my father still exhibited some signs of a man who was vocationally inhibited. He dealt with his vocational and status disappointments with a sort of distancing resignation, as well as an effort to pass his own dreams off onto the next generation. That is, in many ways we children were my father's vindication and hope. However, the backbone of my father's socialization was his religious worldview. For him, Christ was the source of our eventual social and spiritual triumphs. He modeled for us the fact that a deep faith in Christ would internally fortify us to deal with any social adversity and any challenge of limitations.

I do not know where my father's strength ultimately came from (as a quiet man, he honestly did not seem to share enough of his life with us), but so much of it was revealed in his wisdom. Ironically, my father always wondered whether his gifts were adequate or substantial enough for his children. Later he would tell me how much he was impressed by my education and by my knowledge of the world, while in comparison, he thought that he had little to offer.

In my life, my most impactful experience with my father came after I had left my home village. I had returned home from school for a holiday break, and I had begun to press my father for more of a relational connection. I was a student in the marriage and family program and was getting a fair amount of encouragement to work on improving the relationships within my family system, especially my relationship with my father. Consequently, one day on this particular vacation, my father and I spent about four to five hours in my old bedroom, talking together about my life. It was a closed-door session that changed both my life and my relationship with him. We became better friends and continued developing our relationship until he died.

My family's response to the world around them was decidedly Christian, but it was never one that was withdrawn from a social purpose. My family was conservative in our belief in and use of Scripture; we were traditional in our views of the church; and we were fully committed to a personal relationship with Jesus. But my parents were also deeply concerned about the devaluation and inequities that their children faced daily and would encounter in adulthood. Their desire for civil rights was not only a political statement but also a hunger for a spiritual movement that had social and interpersonal consequence. For my parents, the context and conditions of American apartheid and their identification with a biblical people (Israel) had shaped a different set of questions. As I reflect on this, I realize that for my parents, there was very little separation between what it meant be a Christian and what it meant to be personally and socially accountable. They taught us that one's personal faith has social and global consequence—that holiness promoted justice. Hence, I did not come to the integrative conversation with a blank slate. I had many inherited impressions and ideas from my home village.

*Fuller Seminary.* My arrival at Fuller Seminary in Pasadena, California, came through a series of uncanny circumstances—circumstances which I admit could only have been engineered by someone beyond my capacity. For a few years, I had been praying and fasting about the possibility of going to graduate school. I knew that I would have to go back if I was going to become a counselor or psychologist. However, I was unclear about the when and where, and I was even a little unsure about how to get into a program and to finance the experience. In the interim I was working for an organization, Youth for Christ/Youth Guidance with Tony Campolo in Philadelphia, and doing counseling with inmates in a prison. Both jobs had a ministry quality to them in that they each intermingled counseling with service. As I got to do some counseling, my itch to go to graduate school grew even stronger.

During a summer training with Youth Guidance, I met a couple who befriended me in Rockford, Illinois, and we shared a familiarity that belied the time spent together. This couple was leaving Youth for Christ to begin at Fuller Seminary, and they encouraged me to consider the possibility of going to graduate school there as well. The couple, Rick and Coral Gray, contacted me again once they had started their respective programs, still encouraging me to consider coming the following year. They sent an application, let me know about the available financial aid options, and said that I could live with them if I decided to come. I had never felt a door open so widely and with so little effort. And so, in the summer of 1982, I left my parent's home and arrived in Southern California, ready to begin my graduate training.

There are too many experiences and too few pages to offer a full telling of my Fuller story, but here I will try to capture some of the most meaningful experiences from that leg of my journey. When I came to California, I brought with me strong foundational beliefs in God— beliefs that had been nurtured in a "thick" community over the course of my early life. My time at Fuller took those beliefs and shaped them even further. What Fuller provided was a new community that was more globally encompassing, culturally diverse, theologically complex and psychologically challenging.

When I arrived at Fuller, I had a number of early ideas and questions that were in many ways naive, including ideas and questions about how to follow Jesus and how to be a "healer." During my time there, I was plunged into a world that was organized very differently from the one that I had come from. Fuller was a place that allowed me to explore my theology, but it also was a place that in many ways caused me to question my home village and what they had taught me to believe about the world and my faith. The most reverberating challenges were those that centered on core issues of identity—the ones that questioned who I was as a psychological being. I discovered that I was more wounded than I knew, more broken than I had acknowledged, more fearful than I had realized and more talented than I recognized. In addition, I had always been a person with a hunger to understand how things and people worked, but this space gave me the tools I needed to make sense of my own inner world.

Ironically, I began the formal conversation about integration with a mentality that was resistant to the idea that the disciplines of clinical psychology and theology could be fully integrated. In fact, I do not think that I had much interest in the integrationist dialogue until the latter part of my experience at Fuller. The integrative conversations we were having in class and in the Christian psychology community at large seemed to me as if they were pointed toward reassuring the field of theology that the church was a valid Christian venture and toward exhorting the field of psychology that a Christian identity was a valid self-organizing principle. Hence, I believe my initial reticence to join in on the dialogue was primarily because the conversation felt less relevant to the context I felt like I would eventually serve in, the hugely under-served African American community.

I wanted training in how to address the practical needs of people in the African American community. From my intellectual and cultural vantage point, at the time there were too many conflicting ideas and

core assumptions when it came to serving the people of that community. I saw points of intersection, but there was as of yet not a true union
of the fundamental assumptions regarding the material and immaterial
realities that faced them. I also felt as if our ongoing integrative conversations were culturally narrow, with the participants being either unable or unwilling to acknowledge the embedded nature of the dialogue,
as it related to diverse populations. I left Fuller with a number of these
reservations intact, but I must credit my years at the seminary as being
my essential, formal introduction into the integration conversation. My
years at Fuller also gave me the tools I needed to begin asking and answering some of my own integrative questions.

In short, looking back at my time at Fuller, I deeply valued the collective set of experiences I had there, both in the classroom and in the
outside community. Fuller was a place that nurtured a new life for me,
most significantly including a new marriage and my first child. Moreover, it gave me a sense of calling and provided me with a journey
through trials—a journey that ultimately forced me to put away child-
ish things.

One such experience came right at the end of my training. For me
that was a time of deep disillusionment and discouragement. I had just
graduated from the seminary and had been married for a year, but I was
really struggling to find a job. I had a few offers for part-time counseling positions, but none of them seemed quite right for me. I had haughty
notions about doing private practice with long-term clients, and of note,
I had all but lost my sense of mission. I also felt a need to impress and
support my new wife. I did not want to settle on just any job, but I also
needed to feed my family. I spent my days trying to get interviews and
my evenings worrying about finances. I wondered whether or not I had
wasted the past four years of my life. My relationship with God was
distracted by the many questions that God seemed so slow to answer. I
became frustrated with my circumstances and seemingly deflated future, and hence I became angrier and angrier with God. It was an immature and wounded perspective, but God heard my hurt, in spite of its
foolishness.

One morning about three a.m., I woke up suddenly, and I just knew that I had to get up and read my Bible. Reading the Bible was a comfort to me, so it was not unusual for me to read it, but to date, I had never felt such a strong compulsion to open it up and read it. I crawled out of bed and made it over to the living room of the small, one-bedroom apartment that my wife and I shared as newlyweds. I sat in a rocking chair, turned on the light, and put the Bible on my lap. I then did something that, as a seminary student, I am still a little embarrassed to confess. I closed my eyes, opened the "good book," and put my finger down onto the page I had opened to. My finger landed on Isaiah 49, where the prophet is complaining about his laboring in vain and about the lack of reward. In my mind God's immediate response was to chide: "Is it too small a thing for you to be my servant?" (v. 6). And then, God's subsequent response was a promise that he would use the prophet to restore his people (vv. 6-7). I was instantly disarmed by how immediate God's words were to me, and I was deeply remorseful for my complaining. There are moments when things come together in an almost unexplainable fashion. I needed to be reminded that God had a "call on my life" and that my efforts were not unseen and unheard. As I read these words of Scripture over and over again in giddy disbelief, they seemed surreal, but they also stung me very deeply. Strangely, I felt profoundly held by my Father, like he was holding me there, as a loved son who was worthy of scolding. I sat there and cried aloud.

I tell this story to highlight how important a sense of "calling" is to one's orientation to work and to life. In a culture that suggests we are of little value if we are unknown and ordinary, we are increasingly struggling to find ways to be special (i.e., famous). The desire to be known is innately human, and at the moment I just described, there was no greater knower of me than God my Father. In this moment, I needed to hear that what I had worked so hard for was not in vain and that what I had hoped so strongly for was not a fantasy. Ultimately, I believe that all of us need some sense of our call, a reason to begin to be and to remain resilient on our journeys. We need a deeply held conviction that our life's fullness is found in serving a God-given purpose that is larger than ourselves.

## STRUGGLES

I have had a few challenges in my life, but perhaps the biggest is that most of my life, I have struggled a lot with fully trusting people in authority. (I remember one time a Sunday school teacher called me a "rebel without a cause.") Beyond the spiritual nature of this struggle, I believe that my conflicts over the issue of submission were shaped by at least three different things: a self-protective defensive style, being witness to my father's pain and my identity as an African American man. God has been very gracious to me in this struggle, as over and over again in my life he has said to me in so many ways: "Trust me, son. Trust me."

Along with God's grace impressing itself upon me in this area, there were two Bible stories that challenged my beliefs about how God worked. The first was the story of the centurion who asked Jesus to come to his house to heal his servant (Matthew 8:5-13). Jesus was greatly impressed with this man's faith, but he was also impressed with the man's understanding of what it means to be under authority. The centurion maintained that Jesus did not even need to come to his house; all he needed to do was "just say the word" (v. 8). As a man who was under authority, the centurion understood how authority works (v. 9). He also seemed to recognize that Jesus was under authority—the authority of the kingdom of God—and that the kingdom of God worked via mechanisms of authority.

I was fascinated that Jesus called this knowledge great faith. I had always thought of faith as belief in the idea of Jesus as the Christ. This centurion believed in the Jesus, but more powerfully, in the authorization that Jesus was under. In this biblical narrative, authority was not oppressive, but empowering, and conversely the rebellion that I had embraced as powerful was spiritually debilitating.

Recognizing this truth, I had to acknowledge that my resistant posture toward people in authority was also resistant posture toward the reign of God. This obviously created some discomfort for me, and it led me on a search in which I tried to gain a deeper understanding of authority and obedience. I eventually came to the story of Jesus' desert trial (Luke 4:1-13), and I began to reconsider it in light of my questions about authority.

In reading this passage at that time, I read about how Jesus was led into the desert by the Spirit, and after a series of tests, he exited with a new expression of the power of God. In reading this passage previously, I had downplayed the humanity of Jesus and had seen Jesus in his divinity facing the temptations of Satan. I had not considered that the desert was the place where Jesus could have failed in his mission. However, the more seriously I considered the issue of authority, the more seriously I considered the issue of Jesus' humanity. In the desert, Jesus was being tempted to assert his will above God's will—his authority above God's authority. At the core of all three temptations of Jesus was the temptation to reject the authority of God and to come under the authority of Satan. Even when under duress, Jesus passed the tests that most of us fail: he resisted the temptation to use his power to feed himself; he resisted the temptation to pursue his destiny without God's authorization; and he resisted the temptation to pridefully posture himself in a self-promoting quest for significance. But reading about Jesus' temptations at this time in my life, what captured me the most was his willingness to obediently follow the Spirit into a place of deep challenge and duress.

More recently, I have found myself again in the desert, facing difficult challenges and choices, but this time, I have also been more hopeful in God's desire to meet me there and lead me through it.

## MENTORING

I remain convinced that mentoring is our greatest resource—it is the absolutely central tool for both shaping and being shaped. However, that said, taking advantage of the mentoring around me was initially quite difficult for me. There were times when I wanted more, but I did not want to risk the disappointment. I have already shared about my struggles with trust, along with the initial difficulties I had letting others care for me, but in my integration journey, God has used several guides who have helped to facilitate the healing of some of these wounds. God has continually placed people in my path who have loved my heart enough to share their wisdom and to offer guidance. Mentoring is undoubtedly the most powerful tool that God has used to touch me and speak to me in a language that I could hear. Because they have collectively influenced my life so greatly, I am compelled to name a few of my mentors; along with my parents, my mentors have been Irene Knox, Mary Brown, William Grier, Lyle Foster, Dr. C. Milton Grannum, Dr. Martha Shallitta, Miriam and Alwyn Dennis, Dr. Anthony Campolo, Dr. Betsy Morgan, Dr. Dennis Guernsey, Dr. Judy Balswick, Dr. Bill Pannell, Dr. Gunhild Hagestad, Dr. Bob Suggs, Dr. Phil Bowman, Dr. Winston Gooden and Rev. Dr. Richard Chiles. I cannot thank these people enough for their investment in me—for leaving their imprint on me, passing their legacy on to me and speaking their blessings over me.

Intellectually, there are two mentors whom I have only encountered through their writings, Watchman Nee and Howard Thurman. Watchmen Nee was the first Christian theologian in whom I found a deep resonance. Living from 1903 to 1972, Nee was a Chinese Christian author who wrote prolifically during the early twentieth century and then spent the last twenty years of his life in prison, falsely accused, imprisoned and persecuted by the Communist party (Kulp, 1998). During my high school and college years I tried to read as much of Nee's writings as I could. His works challenged both my head and my heart, and they offered me a theological perspective beyond what I was receiving at my home church. Indeed his writings were foundational to many of the ideas that I have now made my own.

The other mentor who influenced me via his writings was Dr. Howard Thurman. Thurman was an African American theologian and philosopher who, through Martin Luther King Jr., greatly influenced the spiritual tenor of the civil rights movement. The influence of Thurman's writings came later on in my journey, at a time when I was searching for heroic thinkers whom I could relate to culturally. In Thurman's tones and shades, I have found a voice that both soothes and challenges. There is also a maturity in this theologian in that he both understood and modeled for us that we must engage the world and not flee from it. He showed us that we must engage the world with a depth of spirit and an eye for justice. As I do my own work to build a philosophy that resonates with head and heart, I have drawn from Thurman's thinking and perspectives. More importantly, at those times when my view of the world differs from my colleagues, I have discovered that his story allows me to feel less alone.

## SPIRITUAL DISCIPLINES

The disciplines for my spirit that have consistently remained with me have been those that have emerged out of my journey itself, the tools that have helped me deal with important moments of challenge and decision in my life. The three spiritual disciplines that have become most salient in my story are fasting, praise/prayer and sabbath. I was introduced to fasting as a senior in college, trying to hear God in my decision about a woman I felt in love with at the time. As she saw how much I was struggling to do the right thing, my best friend's mother, Miriam Dennis, took me aside and inquired about my spiritual practices. She asked if I had ever fasted before, and she encouraged me to pick a day to fast once a week, until I heard an answer from God in my heart. This was the first time my religious practices did not simply involve being obedient to what I thought I should do. Long after I decided the particular romantic relationship in question was not the one I was to pursue, I continued to fast every Thursday. Thus, fasting became my primary spiritual discipline through graduate school, early marriage, childbirth and early employment. Even to this day, I still fast—but not weekly.

The spiritual discipline of praise and prayer came more in focus during my early years of marriage, as I learned the challenge of joining another for life. When my wife Brenda and I married, I was a graduate student at Fuller Seminary, and the first few years of our marriage were about finishing school and transitioning into our professional roles. After graduation I worked at a residential treatment facility during the day, while I worked with Dr. Winston Gooden during the evening, as we tried to build a clinical practice together.

Naturally, the years immediately following graduate school were a time that required a fair degree of financial constraint and budgetary creativity. Brenda and I had been married a couple of years when her car broke down, and so we had to share one vehicle. We decided to try to get a second vehicle, because sharing one was not working out very well. However, the process of getting a second vehicle was not as easy as I hoped, and I became frustrated and disappointed. Brenda managed my grumpiness and maintained her firm hold on hope.

One morning after praying, Brenda came to me and said she felt like God had given her a "word" for us regarding our car situation. First, he had told her that she was to encourage me, and second, he had told her that together we were supposed to "praise him for it," meaning the car. I was my usual reticent self, but Brenda's faith was strong, and I wanted to believe, so we prayed and praised God together that morning. After praising God with Brenda, I felt lifted up—and a little more open to seeing what might happen. Brenda stayed active, calling our creditors and trying to determine whether we had been late on any payments.

A couple of days later, she called the credit union, the holders of the title on our other car. The woman she reached conveyed that everything was fine but asked why she was inquiring. Brenda disclosed that we were trying to lease a car and then explained some of the difficulties we were having. The woman said, "Well, you can lease with us." We came to find out that on the same day that Brenda and I had prayed and praised together, the credit union had entered into a new relationship with an auto-leasing company. We were invited to lease a car through the credit union, amazingly as the first leasers in the new program they had just started. I was stunned, and yet again, I was reminded of God's desire to meet our needs. Now I recognize that God's message to us about the car was less important to my journey than his message to me that I could trust him to do what is beyond my capacity.

The significance of the sabbath has only recently become important in my life. Importantly, my understanding of sabbath had more to do with Sundays and church than it has to do with resting in God. A few years ago, a good friend called my home and left a message with my wife, saying that he really needed to talk with me. This friend had just come back from ministry in South Africa. I have to admit that I was incredibly curious as to what my friend had to talk with me about, but honestly I was also somewhat taken aback.

My usual interactions with this friend were more intellectually playful—two scholarly soulmates, simply enjoying the fun of talking theology, psychology, philosophy and current events with one another. This time, the message he gave my wife seemed serious, and I simply could not figure out what it was that was so gravely urgent that he needed to share it with me. It was probably a week or so before we actually spoke on the phone. When I finally reached him, he began the conversation in an apologetic fashion—but still quite pastorally. He admitted that he felt some awkwardness in talking with me in this way, since he was not my pastor and we had never had this type of dynamic emerge in our relationship before. However, that said, he felt strongly that God had given him a "word" for me; in fact, the term he used to describe it was an "epiphany."

My friend relayed to me that this one-word epiphany was very simply the word *sabbath*. He went on to explain how he was in a period of prayer and meditation on his trip, and I suddenly came strongly to mind, along with the word *sabbath*. My friend said that he was sending me a book on the sabbath, and he recommended a few others on top of that one. He did not linger on the phone, and the brevity of his message seemed contrary to the urgency of his trying to connect with me to transmit it.

All of this felt quite mysterious and unusual for him, and I admittedly had quite mixed feelings of my own about it. I frankly did not know if I accepted the idea that one could have an epiphany for someone else, but he was a good friend and I trusted him. What is more, I just could not seem to brush off the demeanor that my friend had had in our conversation—or the word he actually delivered. At that time in my life, I was teaching at Wheaton, but I was feeling very dry and very numb. Finally embracing God's indirectly delivered message to me about the sabbath was again a reminder of God's ability to do what I could not; it was also yet another wonderful reminder of my ultimate dependence on him.

## THERAPY

I spent most of my early clinical life trying to determine how "Christian" I needed to be in the therapy context and how much I wanted to focus on the spiritual life of my clients. As someone who trains clinicians, I often see such questions at the heart of dialogue about integration. How might I serve Christ in the therapy, and should I or when should I proclaim the good news to my clients? These conversations often revolve around methods and strategies, such as how might we use prayer, meditation or spiritual formation practices to better serve our clients' holistic needs.

Occasionally, there will also be an earnest student who believes strongly that our first duty as Christians is to share about Jesus and that therapy is a good vehicle or tool to do so. Typically, we try to downplay this type of approach to therapy by recommending the utilization of a sort of "delegate posture." We suggest that clinicians learn to be available to respond to the spiritual needs of a client but that in their clinical work, they should not operate from a preplanned agenda.

More recently I have come to rethink this posture, but more importantly the assumptions underneath. Most of my focus has been on the methods of integration, whether it was clinical or philosophical, or faith and praxis. I believe the method focus is shaped by the metaphor of "integration," which cues us to think of bringing two or more things together into a unity. It makes us less available to talk about the discontinuity of the enterprise, and we have fewer conversations about our mission as compared to our methods. In clinical work, I am not advocating that we focus exclusively on getting people "saved," but we do need a more thoughtful biblical and theological exploration of what our mission might be. Maybe it would be helpful to briefly look again at the text in the St. Luke passage (4:1-36), where Jesus comes out of the desert and returns to Galilee and then Nazareth.

Returning from the desert, Jesus eventually returned to his home village of Nazareth (Luke 4:16). Luke described how Jesus went to the synagogue on the sabbath, "as was his custom" (v. 16). Once there, Jesus was given the scroll of Isaiah's prophecy, at which time he opened up the scroll and read the mission statement of the Messiah:

> The Spirit of the Lord is on me,
>   because he has anointed me
>   to preach good news to the poor.

He has sent me to proclaim freedom for the prisoners
 and recovery of sight for the blind,
to release the oppressed,
 to proclaim the year of the Lord's favor.
 (Luke 4:18-19; cf. Isaiah 61:1-2)

When I read this passage, two things are cued up for me: the first is the narrow way that is defined as our life's mission, and the second is how central that mission is to our methods.

As evangelicals we are prone to narrowing the messianic mission to getting people to accept Jesus as their savior. This may be the essence, but not the whole mission. Jesus identifies himself as the anointed one who is changing the age, and it can be seen in his acts toward the poor, the prisoner, the blind, the oppressed and those waiting for jubilee. We have been vulnerable to making these statements spiritualized symbols of Jesus' divinity, and not acknowledging them as aspects of his mission. If we are his followers should we not also be declaring the change of the age, and would it not be in our telling to the poor news that is good, proclaiming liberation for those in prison or imprisoned, declaring sight for the blind, binding up the broken hearts and proclaiming the age of God's grace?

For us as Christian psychologists and counselors, it would seem that our mission especially centers on helping to bind the brokenhearted, as a sign of an age that is both now and not yet. Such a perspective may shift our focus from simply sharing the good news to pursuing and holding the most broken people in our world, partly as a way of proclaiming the reality of the good news. In short, my hope is that in our integrative training efforts, we model and teach our students to consider what it means to be more missional—that is, to be more connected to what God is doing in the earth. As followers of Jesus, if we can accept his articulated mission as our own, how might that impact our integrative methods?

## LETTER

Dear Friends,

I was having trouble writing this last section, so I asked one of my students what I should do. She said, "Do what you do with us; tell them where you are." I thought it a good suggestion, so I will briefly say where I am after this experience, and then I will offer three things that I hope you will consider as you continue on your own integration journey.

As I stated earlier, after I began this writing project, both of my parents passed. Consequently, the past several months have been a wounding time of transition for me, a moment when I have felt forced to face the past in order that I might look ahead. The losses have been tremendous in their intensity, and I understand more deeply now when people talk about being "orphaned" in adulthood. However, it has also been a time of gratitude and of celebration. My parents were ninety years old, so they lived long and productive lives, and they left our family a wonderful legacy of hope and purpose. I had the opportunity to share a few words at both of their funerals, and at my mother's, I told the audience that she had raised me in such a way that "I no longer needed her." I said: "I miss both my parents deeply, but thankfully, because of their great parenting, I no longer need them to go on living." That was one of their greatest, most impactful gifts to us children. I am sure that I indulged a bit in telling some of my parents' story in my own, but their intense desire to leave a legacy has certainly been impressed upon me as I have written these stories down for you.

The next thought I wish to share with you is this: There are moments when we must reach back in order to move forward. *Sankofa* is a Ghanaian word that means reaching back into the past in order to retrieve what is good for the future. Hence, I have three requests of you as you reach back in order to move forward. The first is that you not forget the biblical narratives and the biblical text, including its essential position in our integration conversation. Increasingly, my students have less and less interest in the narratives of the Bible, and thus in their integrative conversations and writings, they are left with the cliché use of Bible verses. And yet, the biblical narratives remain rich and vibrant. They tell a fascinating and substantive integrative story of God's engagement with humanity. Without these narratives, biblically based propositions often just seem empty and rote. The text of the Bible must also be engaged with new interpretive eyes, giving consideration both to its sacredness and to our own context. Moreover, when interpreting the biblical text, we must do a better job in recognizing the significance of the contexts within which we are embedded; otherwise, we might become unhelpful to those from other communities—communities that more than likely have different questions and different perspectives.

The second "reaching back" request I have for you is related to the first: I urge you to remember a theology of the Holy Spirit (pneumatology). Having been adopted into the evangelical family, I find little discussion of the Holy Spirit in our integrative conversations. I recognize that the mere suggestion of remembering the Holy Spirit might send chills up a theologian's spine, but without considering the Spirit, how do we consider God's activity in human affairs? It is the Holy Spirit who quickens, inspires, empowers, mediates and brings us into all truth (John 14:26; 16:12-15). It could be argued that the Holy Spirit is found in the interface between the material and immaterial. At the very least, it is clear to me that the Spirit is essential for conversations about faith and praxis.

Lastly, I wrote this chapter with a challenge in the back of my mind, one that was as much for me (the writer) as it was for you (the reader). My hope was to persuade you to consider your own "heroic integration journey." Joseph Campbell's (1949/2008) heroic figure is called away from home to take a transformational journey. The hero's journey includes a "road of trials," places of struggle that reveal the hero's wounds and his or her great potential. These parts of the journey entail facing the challenging legacy of mother and father, as well as embracing the gifts and giftedness of one's calling. They also necessitate finding the Spirit, the source of our resolution and unity, and facing death and the discontinuities of living.

However, this heroic journey is not just about identity and self-discovery; it is also about service to a community. Consequently, while I believe that all integration is personal, it is also contextual/communal, happening in a historical space in which there are certain questions that we are all trying to answer and certain realities that we are all trying to live with. Hence, each hero will face his or her own personal struggles, but his or her integrative journey will take place within the context of a shifting global Christian community and an increasingly data-driven, eclectic psychological community. This complex setting will raise a host of old and new questions, each of which must be engaged. You may feel reluctant, as I did, for fear you that do not have an adequate voice or do not have a part to play, but each generation always needs its heroes and heroines to say yes. Taking your heroic integration journey is more than just a philosophical exercise—it is to be used by God to do the thing that you were born to do.

## REFERENCES

Campbell, J. (2008). *The hero with a thousand faces*. Novato, CA: New World Library. (Original work published 1949)

Carter, J. D., & Narramore, B. (1979). *The integration of psychology and theology*. Grand Rapids, MI: Zondervan.

Kulp, S. (Ed.). (1998). *Secrets to spiritual power: From the writings of Watchman Nee*. New Kensington, PA: Whitaker House.

# 11

# Faithful Skepticism/ Curious Faith

*William L. Hathaway, Regent University*

## DEVELOPMENT

The fifth of six children, I was born into a hardworking, Midwestern blue-collar family at the end of the 1950s. In the small Michigan town where I spent the first nineteen years of my life, there was a high level of consistency in our simple life. We lived in the same house for the first eight years of my life, and then we moved about a half mile away, to a home that has remained my parents' home ever since. From the top of Clay Cliff nearby, one could view my small hometown, with its state technical college.

Located about a quarter mile from my family home, Clay Cliff was nestled back in the woods, with one of the ubiquitous Michigan creeks running below it. The wooded sides of the cliff led up to small, elevated areas that formed a plateau above the cliff. The soft clay cliff faced the town and extended all the way to the creek below. The area around Clay Cliff was the backdrop for countless childhood adventures and explorations. There were games of Capture the Flag in the woods, lessons in various types of water sports in a dammed-up creek pool, explorations of a rusty old Model-A Ford in the secluded woods, mini-geological expeditions for Scouting merit badges and frequent encounters with deer or other wildlife.

Looking back, it seems as though I had two different childhoods. My early childhood years were spent as the second youngest of a relatively large family. I remember the busyness of living in a home that housed six children. My earliest memories are of when my four older siblings were in their final years of living at home. In terms of birth-order effects, I felt a bit like a youngest child during these early years. My parents had already been through this childrearing process four times before me, and it seemed that the family was always around to help keep an eye on me. The net result was that I had a great deal of freedom to explore my neighborhood. Fueled by my healthy curiosity, that is exactly what I spent much of my time doing.

In those early years, my friends were the people who would later on become the high school jocks. This seemed only natural, since my father had been a local baseball star in his youth and had always been a sports fanatic. Once we moved to our new home across town, things changed. Soon thereafter, my older siblings moved out, leaving me the oldest child in the home, with my sister being five years my junior. The neighborhood I moved into had fewer kids my age, so I spent those years turning to other interests. I developed a friendship with a neighbor who was not as into sports. I became fascinated with science. In my freshman year of high school, I joined the local college astronomy club and spent hours reading science texts at the local college library. My previous explorations of my small community now gave way to increasing explorations of my mind's horizons.

A curious, adventuresome nature that had been combined with a substantial amount of freedom might have led to trouble for a young person like myself, living in a college town in the late 1960s and early 1970s. But I had witnessed the problems some of my older siblings had faced when they had gone down the partying route, and I did not have an interest in repeating the same pattern. My older brother entered the army and was sent to Vietnam. My father had served in the Second World War in Burma. He was a scoutmaster of a long-running Boy Scout troop in Michigan—one that had attracted a number of veterans to serve in various volunteer roles. Throughout my grade school years, I remember being taken along with the scoutmasters on the seasonal troop campouts. The discussion around those scoutmaster campfires often turned to their military experiences. Even when it didn't, there was a sense of honor present whenever a person's service came up.

But Vietnam seemed different. I remember watching the nightly news with concern, as they often showed quite graphic footage of the war. I remember my mother frequently sending care packages to my brother who was serving, and I had a sense that she often worried about him. During that time in history, the sober reality of thinking about my brother serving in Vietnam seemed like such a stark contrast to the relatively safe setting of my hometown. Existential thoughts were very much on my mind at the time. Why is life so fragile? Why is there so much suffering? What is the point of it all? Eventually, my brother returned home from war, and life moved on.

In my mid-teenage years, these existential thoughts returned and intensified. My family regularly attended a Protestant church. My mother was a first-generation immigrant daughter whose parents were from Italy and Switzerland; thus Catholicism seemed to be just an assumed part of the identity on the maternal side of my family. Throughout my childhood, I frequently saw my maternal grandfather, along with many other relatives from my large, Catholic extended family.

But my mother had left her Catholic faith when she met and married my father. The pastor at our family's Protestant church had been a student of Paul Tillich. He was very good at raising thought-provoking moral and existential questions, but he never seemed to provide any clear answers to those questions—at least not to my satisfaction. Thus, when I started to wonder more about these things as a teenager, it did not occur to me to expect direction from the church.

When I was a young child attending my church's vacation Bible school classes, I do remember feeling connected to something spiritual. In those classes, Bible stories were taught to us without the sort of "demythologizing interpretations" that would come later in my religious inculcation. But by the time I went through the church's confirmation class a few years later, I had learned that we should not take such stories literally. In fact, I knew that the church had professed atheists singing in the choir, and no particular set of beliefs seemed normative for the congregants to uphold, despite our frequent recitation of classic Christian creeds in the liturgy. I had a number of friends in the youth group whom I had known for my entire life. Yet these warm memories aside, I did not think of my church as a place where I could go to get spiritual answers.

My early teenage years arrived as discussion of the dawning of the "age of Aquarius" was peaking among the local college population. Fad trends, combined with reawakened existential concerns, catalyzed my first deliberate spiritual quest. I read several New Age texts and became drawn to Taoism. I also started reading some classical philosophy. By this time, I was a member of the scout troop my father had led.

The new scoutmaster was a chair of the university psychology department. He attended my family church but identified himself to me as an agnostic. During my years in the scout troop, I had several conversations with him about these themes, and in fact, many of our conversations are what led me to become interested in psychology. While psychology, Eastern philosophy and science all seemed to provide important pieces of the spiritual puzzle I was trying to solve, I still did not believe that I could see the big picture with any sort of clarity and confidence. Something still seemed to be missing, and without it, the various spiritual and existential insights I was able to garner still seemed hollow.

I believe now that I was looking for some transcendent or ultimate reality that would give meaning and context to both my life and the world in general. My family and my home church community had taught me a number of prosocial civic values. My participation in scouting only amplified these and added to them lessons in developing an environmental consciousness. But I concurrently developed a nagging sense that if the picture were to become complete, something more was needed. I wondered: If we are the product of a blind, impersonal naturalistic process, why should any of these values really matter?

My beliefs were in flux, and I was willing to consider any worldview that would provide me with suitable answers to the questions I was asking. And yet even in this unanchored state, I retained the skeptical impulse that my home church had cultivated in me. While I could recognize positive things about a number of the perspectives I was exploring, I was not interested in accepting a viewpoint just because it felt good. I wanted to know what was true and then let the chips fall where they may. I was not at all convinced that this sort of approach would lead to a positive view of the world; in fact, I was quite aware of the fact that this journey could possibly end in cynical despair.

During my sophomore year in high school, I developed a friendship with some other students from my neighborhood. These students were evangelical Christians. One was particularly confident in his personal beliefs, so much so that he felt very comfortable arguing for them. I had encountered other conservative Christians before then, but the thought had never occurred to me that such a belief system might be the sort of thing that someone could rationally investigate. My new friend presented his Christian beliefs using the classic apologetic method of logical question and answer.

This friend and I went through several months of intense discussions. I started reading everything that I could find that was related to Christian apologetics, such as writings by Francis Schaeffer and C. S. Lewis. I discovered an entire world of Christian perspectives that I did not know even existed. I also started to remember the old sense of spiritual reality that I had experienced during my vacation Bible school days. I launched into reading the Bible, along with everything that I could find about it. I started attending my friend's Baptist youth group and my local college's InterVarsity Christian Fellowship meetings.

After several months, I realized that I had gradually shifted from viewing Christianity as a source of questions to viewing it as a source of answers. Though I never had any sort of event that served as an culminating conversion experience for me, I do remember a specific time of praying for salvation. For me, my conversion was more like a gradual awakening that occurred over the course of several months. By the summer of my sixteenth year, I had come to view myself as a born-again Christian. My spiritual longings were replaced by a sense of spiritual and existential fulfillment.

My Christian rebirth did not dampen my sense of wonder and curiosity about either spiritual things or about the world around me. My parents were a bit uncomfortable with my newfound conservative religious zeal, but they did not object to my involvement in other Christian churches, as long as I agreed to continue attending the family church.

It was now the mid-1970s, and the Jesus movement had reached our community. Something of a mini-revival broke out on our local college campus, and all the Christian groups started meeting together, to have all-campus worship services.

At these all-campus worship services, the participants were quite diverse. They included Pentecostal groups, Christian Reformed groups, the Black Gospel Club, the Catholic campus ministry, InterVarsity and Campus Crusade. Having grown up in a socially progressive society during the peak of the civil rights era, it was quite remarkable to see close social bonds being formed across racial, socioeconomic and other common dividing lines. This was the sort of diverse community that members of my liberal church had spoken of desiring, and yet I first saw it become reality among these Bible-believing Christians. This experience seemed like nothing short of a vindication of my newfound faith, which had taken root in me earlier that year.

I found other vindications of my faith as well. Internally, I found a sense of joy and contentment that I had not known previously. It was a strange sort of contentment. While I felt that I now had what was previously missing in my spiritual and other life quests, I paradoxically felt a greater appetite for more spiritual reality. If this biblical worldview was *really true* then it would mean that I would need to be even more careful sorting out fact from fiction. In short, my new belief in a real truth became the catalyst for deepening my commitment to a skeptical attitude. In addition to reading Christian literature, I sought out writings by atheist philosophers and higher critics. I discussed my evolving convictions with my family church pastor as well as with people of other faiths. In these discussions, thoughtful objections and alternative perspectives were raised, but my Christian beliefs consistently kept winning out.

This period of time in our community was also characterized by a resurgent interest in biblical prophecy about history and the future. My eschatological explorations heightened my curiosity about a new frontier that I was just beginning to explore: Christian doctrine. Essentially, they led me to develop a passion for exploring Christian doctrine—a passion that has stayed with me to this day. To some extent, the questioning and reflective nature of my liberal church background was present in my approach to studying doctrine. I did not believe anything simply because a particular group believed it; instead, I always felt compelled to check out the belief for myself. What differed from my pre-evangelical spiritual search were the criteria I was relying on to determine the veracity of a belief. Reason and evidence continued to be vitally important for me, but now I added a new standard of verification: the belief must square with Scripture. I carefully considered the opinions of a number of evangelical pastors in our small community, as I spent hours in their offices asking them about their beliefs. In the end, my decision regarding any topic started to rest most fundamentally on what seemed to agree the most with Scripture.

My theological explorations were also aided by a new Christian bookstore. A retired Air Force colonel had moved into our community and opened a Logos bookstore. The colonel attended a local Assembly of God church and was charismatic. By temperament, he was a quiet, reflective, and disciplined man. He lived off of his military retirement and ran the bookstore as a ministry. I had become aware of the uneven quality of Christian scholarship and publications. Some Christian bookstores would carry anything that sold, even if it seemed to be of questionable theological quality. This man was different. While the books he stocked did not have to reflect his personal viewpoints, he held them to a high standard. I spent many hours in the bookstore, buying those books I could afford and reading many others. My interests covered a broad range of topics, so I read whatever I could in the colonel's small but carefully selected inventory of books.

It was in this bookstore that I discovered the emerging literature on the integration of psychology and theology. Among others, there was Carter and Narramore's (1979) *Integration of Psychology and Theology*, Evans's (1977) *Preserving the Person*, McKay's (1974) *The Clockwork Image* and Cosgrove's (1977) *The Essence of Human Nature*. The integrationist literature added to my nascent evangelical faith a belief that I could critically incorporate what was true and valuable in psychology into a biblically faithful worldview. I did not know it at the time, but the experience of reading all these integrationist works also set the stage for what would become for me a vocation in psychology—one that is in fact dominated by an integrative ethos.

A few other experiences also strengthened my passion for integration. For example, I had become familiar with the contemporary Christian music movement. The mission of this movement was such a simple thing, but it had such profound implications—expressing perennial Christian truths through contemporary forms of music and artistic expression. Some friends in a Free Methodist youth group invited me to go to a Christian music festival called Ichthus, held at Asbury College. I was not quite prepared for the experience. It was truly remarkable to see fields that were packed full of thousands of young people who were joining together in worship. For several years after that time, I became involved in promoting Christian concerts—so much so that I thought that this would probably be my life path.

This vocational sense led me to attend a state conference for contemporary Christian ministries. At that meeting, several prominent ministry leaders—Christians who had started out as part of the Jesus movement—expressed regrets that they had not received formal college educations. Although these ministry leaders still seemed quite effective to me, they claimed that their lack of educational training had made it more difficult for them to have credibility and thus had created impediments for their ministry. They recommended that anyone interested in doing Christian ministry should obtain a college degree. This was a huge concession for the leaders of the paradoxically culture-embracing and countercultural Jesus movement—inspired leaders for whom the "simple truth" of the Bible was frequently touted as an antidote to the destructive "worldly wisdom" of the establishment.

I had been on this journey with a tight-knit group of friends. We worked, worshiped and played together throughout my early Christian journey. This group had a relatively stable core, but some folks would enter the group periodically, and some would leave. In this friend group, we talked constantly about the big and small questions of the faith, with each of us bringing a slightly different skill set to the discussion, just as each of us felt comfortable challenging one another's points of view.

In addition, there were a number of folks who served as part of our extended Christian family. Over the years, I came to deeply appreciate the role these background people played in my life. Of course, these same individuals were foreground people in the lives of other persons, but they were background for me, because I only interacted with them sporadically—or only for brief moments. For example, these background people included the ushers I saw every week at church or the coworker from a Christian camp whom I would occasionally encounter. For me God often used such persons to either challenge me about things I was overlooking or to bring encouragement.

One of the individuals who entered our Christian circle was a young woman named Viva. She had grown up in a military family and moved around quite a bit. She was also a new convert and was drawn to contemporary Christian ministry. As a new Christian, Viva had struggled to find acceptance among the Christian youth who had known her in her high school previously. She had become a Christian through the influence of the roommate she had during a summer staff job at Michigan's Mackinac Island, a tourist site. This roommate was working on Mackinac Island as part of a summer tent-making mission, arranged by InterVarsity. Viva's conversion to Christianity was indeed radical and classic.

Concurrent with her senior year of high school, Viva started a technical degree program at the college in my hometown. I met her at local college-ministry functions. She entered our group of friends, first as a background person in our social group, but then increasingly as a part of the foreground. Over the next few years, as we journeyed together through a number of life events, our relationship changed, and we fell in love. We had some obvious differences. She was a tremendous extrovert, and I was a pronounced introvert; I liked private contemplation, and she preferred social engagement. But on ministry passions, common beliefs and spiritual fervor we both shared a kindred bond. I asked her to marry me, and thankfully she accepted. Viva had finished her associate's degree in technical illustration, and heeding the counsel of folks in our contemporary Christian ministry, we agreed to start our new married life together. So we moved to Upland, Indiana, in order for me to attend Taylor University.

## MENTORING

I have already mentioned the key influence of a number of people that God brought into my life throughout my early years. These mentoring influences became more central to my development as I entered college. I pursued a double major that was tailored to my integrative interests. I majored in psychology and took as many courses as I could from the faculty who worked in the area of integration. In particular, Mark Cosgrove was a major influence on me at this time in my life. Dr. Cosgrove had become a Christian while finishing his doctorate in experimental psychology at Purdue, a rare event for academicians at that stage of life or in that degree path. After his conversion, Dr. Cosgrove had spent several years working with Probe Ministries, traveling around to secular college campuses, talking about integration and doing a sort of psychological apologetic for the Christian faith. I learned many things from Dr. Cosgrove, but he particularly taught me a lot about worldview integration.

At Taylor, I also completed a second major in the philosophy of religion. This was a designed major that consisted of biblical, theological and philosophical emphases and took a historical survey approach. I came to appreciate philosophy as the missing link in the integrationist literature. In other words, I came to view integration as the unifying of distinct perspectives and disciplinary frameworks using conceptual tools that are best developed in philosophy. Since then, philosophy has been for me the overarching rubric that has unified the academic disciplines, even as it has served as the *handmaiden* to theology during much of Christian history. I owe an inestimable debt to the faculty members at Taylor who mentored me in these areas. Two of these, my primary philosophy professor, Dr. Win Corduan, and my Bible professor, Dr. Larry Helyer, patiently endured many hallway and office-hour discussions that went above and beyond the call of duty. The Taylor experience consolidated my Christian identity, prepared me for parachurch and church ministry work, helped launch my integrative work, and gave me the

Christian worldview foundations that I needed to persevere in my Christian faith during my subsequent work in secular contexts.

I designed my undergraduate studies not so much with a specific career path in mind but rather in view of learning things that I thought were important for integrating psychology with a Christian worldview based on what I had heard and read from Christian psychologists who had been pursuing this goal. Toward the end of my studies, I heard about a new graduate program in "applied philosophy" at Bowling Green State University (BGSU) in neighboring Ohio. This new program was attempting to reverse some of the disciplinary fragmentation that has been accelerating in recent centuries. In particular, by emphasizing a specific application of philosophy to applied concerns, it was trying to reverse the way that philosophy had become detached from the practical concerns of other disciplines.

During my last year at Taylor, my wife and I had our first child, Joshua. The three of us relocated to Ohio, where I entered the graduate philosophy program at BGSU. The innovative nature of the program allowed me to tailor my studies to my own personal interests. As an applied philosophy graduate student, I completed a nine-month internship at a community mental health center. I also discovered that a professor in the clinical psychology program, Dr. Kenneth Pargament, had developed a research niche in which he was exploring religion and coping. This type of research focus was quite rare for a secular school in that period. I connected with Ken, and he invited me to participate in his research team. He also agreed to serve on my applied philosophy master's thesis committee, since my thesis addressed ethical issues that frequently arise in the course of collaboration between religious and community mental health organizations.

Ken is a Jewish psychologist who has become one of the most respected contributors to the field's resurgent interest in psychology of religion. The psychology of religion does not presuppose the truth on any religious beliefs but simply takes religious phenomena as variables to be explored through the methods of psychological science. I was prepared to take this secular work in the psychology of religion with a grain of salt, since I believed there were religious truths that could and should properly inform my worldview as a psychologist at a presumptive level. I was not sure what the value of psychology of religion work would be if it did not proceed primarily by unpacking theological truths. But as I studied with Ken, I became increasingly aware that the variables he explored did not have a simple connection to the theological tenets that I remained confident about.

We looked, for instance, at how people relied on their faith to deal with life's problems. It became clear that believers within the same faith tradition often appropriated their faith in psychologically divergent ways, based on idiosyncratic understandings of their spiritual beliefs. Most importantly, our research group identified three styles of religious coping, which differed based on the relative active-versus-passive posture that the individual attributed to God and to the self as he or she was navigating the coping process. The three styles of religious coping we identified were collaborative (both God and the person are active partners), deferring (the person is passive, relying on God to solve their problems) and self-directing (a sort of deist approach in which God is viewed as passive, leaving it up to the person to solve his or her own problems). We developed scales to assess these three styles, and these scales performed quite well psychometrically. We also found considerable variability in how people responded on these scales, whether they were administered in either liberal or conservative churches. It dawned on me that there was something more to this psychology of religion stuff than just theological squeamishness on the part of the researchers.

After finishing the philosophy program, I decided not to go to a Christian graduate program. I had not originally intended to stay at BGSU for my doctoral clinical psychology degree but felt called to stay to work with Ken. Ken was an incredibly generous and invested mentor. He was always highly respectful of my beliefs but at the same time unafraid to challenge my thinking.

## STRUGGLES

My entire Christian history has been marked by a search for spiritual reality. After all these years, I remain convinced that the basic tenets of the Christian faith are true and that a personal relationship with Jesus

Christ uniquely provides the supreme fulfillment of our deepest spiritual longings. Yet I also have remained very much aware of my own fallibility and the fact that there are real points of tension for the Christian faith that arise from an open and honest encounter with life. I had seen a young child die in a tragic accident, a Christian leader that was widely respected have an affair devastating multiple families, and toxic forms of Christian life displayed in many ways. I had also continued to meet people of fundamentally different worldviews who appeared to be of strong character and impressive moral and spiritual sensitivities. Although I did not find my faith eroding from such experiences, doubts naturally arose. How do I know this belief is true given such experiences?

Shortly after transferring to the doctoral program in psychology, I learned that the renowned British atheist Antony Flew was a visiting scholar at the university. I sought out Professor Flew, and he agreed to oversee an independent study in which we read through Richard Swinburne's (1977, 1979, 1982) defense of theism, which Tony considered to be the best of the then-current defenses of theism. We would meet each week in order to discuss sections of Swinburne's texts.

I approached this opportunity with the realization that if anyone could dispel my Christian beliefs, it would likely be Tony. I did not want to retain my beliefs should they prove false. Skeptical inquiry had led me to my Christian convictions, and because I believed Christian truth claims were objectively true, I had confidence that reason would not be an enemy of faith. There were of course moments of tension and doubt in these and my other explorations. Skeptics, particularly of the New Atheist variety, are often quick to point out problems for traditional Christian belief as though these in and of themselves are sufficient to bring the faith down. The missing part of the equation is to look at the relative evidence also considering the weaknesses in the alternative live options available to us. I still find that there are many things that I don't understand about my Christian faith, but I have sufficient grounds to hold it to be true and still see it as comparing favorably to all of the alternative worldviews I have encountered.

I was gratified to hear in 2004 that Professor Flew had become a theist. While Flew at present does not adhere to any religious convention, and his beliefs may be more accurately described as deist rather than theist, this worldview shift is nonetheless a dramatic change for him. The story of that change is recounted in Flew and Varghese's (2007) text, *There Is a God.* A number of Flew's former atheist allies have uncharitably chalked his new belief up to either senility or angst, allegedly due to his approaching the end of his life. Some have even suggested that Varghese wrote the text and Flew was being manipulated.

Even so, as I read through this text, I recognized continuities between the arguments presented and my discussions with Tony back in the 1980s. For example, the book recounts an exchange with Swinburne that transpired at BGSU in the 1980s. I had arranged the event, which was not taped and only involved a small group of university attendees. I have no doubt that the details describing this event came from Flew. I had the opportunity to speak with him by phone shortly after his text was released. I recognized in our conversation the same careful desire to "go where reason leads" that characterized him all those years ago. He was also quick to point out that he still does not believe in the immortality of the soul, so his change in conviction is not motivated out of some late-life desperate attempt to appease a maker.

I continue to struggle with tension points in my Christian belief. These include struggles related to the life of the mind. A similar pattern seems to repeat itself. I encounter issues that do not seem to fit my prior Christian conceptions. I prayerfully explore the topic and look for some way to make sense of the thing that does not fit. At times, this has resulted in my rethinking some aspect of my conception, but usually it means adding in some additional notions or perspectives that complement and flesh out my Christian beliefs.

As I have moved out of college years and into family life, I have found that the greater challenges to my spiritual life come not from the contending with contemporary philosophical atheism or other grand challenges but rather from dealing with the routine cares of life. As a father (now grandfather) and husband, countless mundane cares arise over the course of the days, weeks and years. One has bills to pay, tasks to perform and deadlines to meet. These trappings of grown-up life don't diminish but accelerate. I suspect that dealing with theses daily hassles or "worries of this life" (Matthew 13:22) present the greatest challenge to my spiritual fruitfulness at this season of my life.

## SPIRITUAL DISCIPLINES

I have tried to keep myself spiritually centered over the years by maintaining some basic spiritual disciplines. In terms of personal strategies, I have derived much sustenance from Bible reading, prayer, listening to Christian music, practicing God's presence and Christian meditation. I have sometimes heard Christians argue that they do not need to participate in a formal Christian fellowship or church because they get their fellowship informally from Christian friends and they have too many discouraging experiences in churches. But I have found it vitally important to be anchored in a local church even when I have not always found that experience to live up to the Christian ideal. Committed participation in the corporate forms of Christian life serve a wide variety of faith-strengthening functions such as reinforcing perennial Christian beliefs and values, providing a context for mutual accountability in the Christian life, delivering encouragement and exhortation, or providing opportunities to practice obedience to Scriptural mandates regarding our role within the body of Christ.

This discipline and other disciplines became even more reinforced for me after the birth of our daughter, Christina, during my first year in the doctoral program in psychology. Over the next few years, my wife and I realized that we would be in this limbo period of being a college student family for some time. We recognized that we could not wait on building routines in our family life until some ethereal post-college time when we would have *grown up* as a family. So we worked to build more deliberate spiritual routines in our family life. We added devotional times with our kids to our personal devotional routine but we relied more directly on the teachable-moment strategy that was central to ministry format at a Christian camp with which we have long been involved. The teachable-moment strategy actively looks for ways to use everyday events to illustrate biblical themes while the events are fresh in a person's consciousness. In addition to remaining active in church, we sought out home groups with other couples at similar stage of family life, started a yearly Christmas communion fellowship at our home—a tradition that we continue to this day—and maintained contact with our extended Christian family. We remained active in ministry of various sorts and emphasized participation in Christian service for each member of our family. So there were mission trips with youth groups, participation on global serving teams to help pull off Christian events oversees, helping with food pantries and the like.

All of these familiar accouterments of an evangelical spirituality have played their role in keeping my faith alive since my teenage conversion. Yet I want to return full circle to an approach to the spirituality that was prevalent in the origin of that faith. This is the discipline of study. I was drawn to Christian belief through a process of reflection and dialogue. I have found that my faith is continuously strengthened and reaffirmed through the same. It is by reflecting back on the ways God has met me in this process that I have found my richest sustaining resources to persevere through both life's calamities and wearisome hassles.

## CLINICAL PRACTICE/THERAPY

After completing graduate school, I served as an Air Force psychologist for several years. An early-career military psychologist tends to be a generalist, so I found myself engaged in a wide variety of interesting clinical work. I arrived at Shaw Air Force base, my first post-internship assignment, eleven days after the base had deployed for Desert Shield. I was initially the only mental health professional left at the base, and I reopened the office to numerous spouses who were experiencing pain and crisis regarding the deployment. During the next six years, I remained in a primary mobility slot, always prepared to be deployed.

I worked with many individuals who had been in combat or other life-threatening situations and had witnessed much tragedy. This type of clientele kept me ever-mindful of those existential issues that had been a recurrent theme in my familial, personal and spiritual journeys. Many people in the military contend with existential issues by turning to a spiritual faith. Consequently, it was common for religious/spiritual discussions to become a part of the therapy process. Importantly, I was also ever-mindful that my role was as a psychologist and not a chaplain. There is a wide spectrum of spiritual and nonreligious worldviews represented in the military, but I found that God had prepared me to connect with folks from many different backgrounds. A few years ago, I wrote about some of these cases (Hathaway, 2006).

Toward the end of my military service, I was stationed in Germany. While there, Stan Jones (a Christian psychologist from Wheaton College) came to visit. Stan came to a Sunday school class that I was teaching at our local church in Germany. Once he was introduced, someone in the class asked about how we do psychology as Christians. After some brief discussion about integration, this same individual followed up by asking how I could bring Christianity into my work since I was a "government psychologist." I reflected back on my experiences in the military and in other practice contexts, expressing how I could not imagine that I would have practiced any differently in an explicitly Christian practice, as compared with how I had practiced to date in a military setting. I explained that whenever it was clinically relevant, I had no problem exploring Christian beliefs, experiences or coping resources explicitly in the secular settings I had been working in to date. I also described how, in fact, military clinicians had frequently asked me to provide in-service training on how to address religious/spiritual issues in treatment.

In short, I always felt free to follow my clinical judgment and practice in ways that were congruent with the full range of my worldview. I did not approach my sessions looking for a way to proselytize my clients or to introject my Christian beliefs explicitly into our discussions. I had been taught that such imposition would run counter to my professional role and ethics. I retain this professional self-understanding as a psychologist who has now worked in a Christian doctoral training program for over a decade.

Having learned to function as a Christian working in secular contexts, I assumed I would continue on to have a career in secular settings. I left the military to complete a postdoctoral fellowship in clinical child psychology at the University of Massachusetts Medical Center, in the Attention-Deficit/Hyperactivity Disorder Clinic with Russell Barkley. Russ is a graduate of BGSU's clinical psychology program, and he has become well known for his cutting-edge work in the area of ADHD. Like my earlier experiences with Ken Pargament and other mentors, I found Russ to be a highly generous and supportive mentor, and since my fellowship ended, he has continued to be an important source of advice and perspective for me. Next I accepted an administrative faculty position at Regent University, which at the time was a new Christian-integrative doctoral psychology program, housed in a relatively new Christian-integrative university. It has been a true blessing to watch this program develop, to become a part of the remarkable team of Christian psychologists who staff the program and to have the privilege to work with the students who have come through it.

My work at Regent has allowed the separate streams of my life history to come together. I teach a survey course in Christian history and doctrine, going through the Bible and various other Christian texts with our doctoral psychology students. As program director, I also work with other faculty members in our department as we collaborate on how to shape the integrative mission and operation of our program. Further, I have supervised student trainees in our program, while they treated clients in our campus training clinic. While the clinic does not just serve Christian clients, it is a Christian practice context and we frequently utilize explicit integrative techniques or protocols at the clinic. In every case, screening assessments explore whether spiritual concerns are present or relevant to the client's clinical issues.

My time at Regent has also led me to become increasingly active in various roles within the profession of psychology. I served on the Board of Psychology for the state of Virginia and in leadership roles within the Psychology of Religion division of the American Psychological Association. These professional service roles have made me much more attentive to role-related issues that are relevant to the tasks of integration. The practice of psychology involves voluntary acceptance of a role that is regulated by various governmental bodies of professional colleagues. A Christian who enters the profession is making a fiduciary commitment to practice in ways that are reliably congruent with that role. As a result of this commitment, integration becomes not just a theoretical or even a technical issue—it becomes a sociopolitical issue. Integration raises ancient themes concerning the proper role for Christians to adopt when working in civic-service positions. There are many nuances to this topic, but I certainly think that anyone would be hard-pressed to justify accepting such a role in bad faith, deliberately knowing they were not going to comply with professional standards of practice.

Unfortunately, I have sometimes seen Christian counselors who have claimed that their faith affords justification for them to neglect standard treatments in favor of spiritual interventions that have questionable effectiveness. Or, I have heard Christian clinicians boast of their efforts to proselytize clients over the course of therapy. I have encountered secular professionals who view Christian counseling as quackery, partly as a result of encountering or hearing about such practitioners. I would hope that Christian psychologists, resourced by the treasure of divine revelation and of the Christian faith, would be known for excellence in all they do. This would seem to me to be an important precondition for our redemptive engagement with contemporary psychology. Thankfully, there are many Christian psychologists who have risen to this high calling, functioning as both faithful Christians and exemplary members of the profession of psychology. I yearn for all who pursue their own integration journey to follow those traveling this latter path.

## LETTER

Dear Reader,

It is hard for me to believe that I have been on this career path of integrating Christianity and psychology for three decades now. I am still well aware that there is so much more for me to figure out and live out. In terms of how my integration journey relates to yours, I would encourage you to embrace the discipline of study, not as an onerous task but rather as a spiritual-formation tool. I started out on this journey with a robust sense of curiosity, which fueled my resolute search for answers. I eventually found that reverential study provided me with a tool that I could use to begin to decipher the mysteries of the human condition, following the clues that God had made accessible to our knowing faculties.

And yet I also found out that this search for answers is not just a game of Trivial Pursuit. The answers to spiritual and existential riddles relate to the most profound passions, struggles and needs that face humanity. With that recognition in mind, I encourage you to study deeply, study broadly and study relationally—in dialogue with a faithful community of Christian peers. Pay attention to relevant side disciplines. Pay attention to what is going on in biblical studies and Christian thought as well as in psychology. At the same time, note trends in popular culture, and keep an eye open to whatever truth God may be bringing your way. Sometimes God uses very surprising sources to teach us the most profound things. Never be afraid to squarely face the hard truths of life or to confidently engage with those of differing convictions; always remember that we serve the *real* God—the One who is the Creator and Sustainer of all.

Study is important, and it is a spiritual discipline, but it only has value if it contributes to the development of Christ in us. Network with other faithful Christians in your profession. Remain active in a Christian fellowship community, and press on in your Christian journey. Treasure your family and friends. Strive to be faithful in all that God calls you to, and wisely pursue the kind of balance in your commitments that would facilitate such faithfulness. Remember that you will not have time for this sort of deliberate growth if you do not make it a priority. Christian integration in psychology is, after all, just an aspect of Christian discipleship for those who want to recognize Christ as Lord of all of their life. If Christ abides at the center of our science and practice, then our work becomes a sacred encounter where we can be ministers of God's grace to people at critical points in life. I have been humbled by witnessing this play out in countless unexpected ways, and I invite you to celebrate with me this remarkable privilege God has given us as Christian professionals.

## REFERENCES

Carter, J. D., & Narramore, S. B. (1979). *The integration of psychology and theology.* Grand Rapids, MI: Zondervan.

Cosgrove, M. P. (1977). *The essence of human nature.* Grand Rapids, MI: Zondervan.

Evans, S. (1977). *Preserving the person: A look at the human sciences.* Downers Grove, IL: InterVarsity Press.

Flew, A., & Varghese, R. A. (2007). *There is a God: How the world's most notorious atheist changed his mind.* New York: HarperCollins.

Hathaway, W. L. (2006). Religious diversity in a military clinic: Four cases. *Military Psychology, 18,* 247-57.

MacKay, D. M. (1974). *The clockwork image: A Christian perspective on science.* Downers Grove, IL: InterVarsity Press.

Swinburne, R. (1977). *The coherence of theism.* New York: Oxford University Press.

Swinburne, R. (1979). *The existence of God.* New York: Oxford University Press.

Swinburne, R. (1981). *Faith and reason.* New York: Oxford University Press.

# 12

# Setting One's Face Toward Jerusalem

## A Personal Integration Journey

### Linda M. Wagener, Fuller Theological Seminary

*When the days drew near for him to be taken up,*

*he set his face to go to Jerusalem. (Luke 9:51 NRSV)*

In the New Revised Standard Version of Luke 9:51, I love the phrase that is used to describe the determination, the discipline and the fidelity that Jesus needed to follow his earthly purpose. In the days just before the moment that is described in this passage, Jesus' attention was drawn to many, he had been healing the sick, raising the dead, teaching and feeding the multitudes and preparing his disciples for their future ministry. And then, according to Luke's description, "he set his face to go to Jerusalem." Here was Jesus, fully human, knowing absolutely what he was going to face in Jerusalem. In Luke 9:22 (NIV) we read, "And he said, 'The Son of Man must suffer many things and be rejected by the elders, the chief priests and teachers of the law, and he must be killed and on the third day be raised to life.'" Yet he turned from the multitude of followers, from the many who were yet unhealed, from his disciples who still did not understand, and "he set his face to go to Jerusalem." In this single line of text we see the whole of human history turning on the faithful

Son's steadfast resolution to be obedient to his Father's will.

More than 2000 years later we can point to this passage in Luke and emotionally enter into the moment Jesus began his walk toward the cross. The narrative that follows this passage emphasizes the absolutely inevitable nature of the task that is before him. And this is a lesson also for us. A clear sense of our Father's will gives us discernment, and it gives us the will to face adversity, pain and suffering. Without that sense of purpose, we can become disoriented, unclear about our path. When there are too many demands on our time, our energy and our resources, we, like Jesus, must resolve to set our faces toward Jerusalem.

## DEVELOPMENT

If only I could claim that I have had that same clarity of purpose in my role as a psychologist who is also a Christian. Though I grew up in a Christian family and had a personal encounter with the living God at the age of twelve, I confess that until I had completed my doctoral training and was searching for my first job, it had not occurred to me that psychology was a field that had anything but the vaguest relevance to my faith. Within the field of psychology, I was initially drawn to the field of human development, and later I was drawn to the field of clinical psychology, simply because I found it intellectually fascinating. Humans are complicated and compelling creatures, and I thought that figuring them out would be a subject that would never get boring.

I wish I could say that I went into psychology because I wanted to help people. I enjoyed clinical work and found it rewarding to see my clients improve in their functioning; however, truth be told, I had no intention of becoming a practitioner. What I really wanted to do was think about what it meant to be human and about how it was that we could engineer community- and family-based conditions that would encourage positive and healthy youth development.

The split between my professional identity and my faith identity was reinforced along the way by the education that I received in secular schools. My mentors were not apparent believers. They were secular humanists, and many had fairly explicitly rejected religion as a superstitious and primitive system of belief, manufactured by people in order to preserve a sense of safety and well-being in the face of the threat of existential nihilism. The educational culture that shaped me relied on the scientific method as the primary way to determine truth in research. (Though, interestingly, hermeneutical inquiry was appropriate to the orientation of psychodynamic psychotherapy that was preferred in my graduate training.) In short, my faith became private and irrelevant to my intellectual life. As my professional identity and activities grew, my faith became less and less important to anything I did in daily life. At best, it was relegated to Sunday morning service attendance. At worst, it became something that was fondly associated with nostalgic traditions of childhood. Yet I still believed that I belonged to God, and in some way, I recognized that God had placed a claim on my life. In those days I would have described my faith identity as a general commitment to be ethical and loving, as well as to care for the underserved.

I now realize that my faith has everything to do with answering the core questions that I was asking. Theology, particularly theological anthropology, was exploring the meaning and purpose of human life long before the field of psychology was birthed. I first learned that the integration of psychology and theology was an ongoing conversation and project of scholarly inquiry when I entered the job market and learned that Fuller Theological Seminary had a School of Psychology and an opening in the area of child clinical work. The Fuller faculty in both psychology and theology took a chance with me, feeling that I could learn the art of integration, in which they have patiently mentored me for these many years. I am immensely grateful that I have had the opportunity to work alongside men and women who have modeled integration for me, both through their professional and their personal lives. Through them I have learned that the intellectual pursuit of understanding human functioning is an activity that honors God. Because of them I have understood that in seeking to live a life as fully human, I can glorify God, even in my brokenness. In my own limited way, I am setting my face toward Jerusalem. As I understand it now, my professional purpose is, through integrative research and practice, to more fully realize what it means for human beings to flourish. The primary method I use to work toward this goal is classical psychological research in the scientific tradition. But importantly, I also engage in scholarly dialogue, teaching and writing, with students and with theologian and biblical-scholar partners. In these various interdisciplinary conversations, we collaboratively sharpen our understanding of human behavior, in the light of salvation history.

Importantly, neither scholarship nor Christian integration are individual pursuits. I believe one of the grave limitations of psychology, a discipline that has been almost exclusively developed from a modern Western framework, is its exaggerated championing of autonomous individuality and autonomous functioning. My own experience, as well as my professional understanding of human experience, is significantly different. It is only in relationships and in community that we develop. We are ultimately dependent on the work and wisdom of others, and at Fuller, I have been fortunate that I have been part of a group of generative people who are open with their ideas, their critique and their encouragement.

## MENTORING

I think of a mentor as someone who is in a position to help us discern our purpose; metaphorically, they are one who help to direct us toward Jerusalem. They identify our gifts and enable us to undertake projects in which we can make a significant contribution. The best mentors also help us to realistically assess and accept our limitations, as well as to shed the important in order to focus on the essential. They stand alongside us in adversity and help to direct us toward opportunities. Through their presence in our lives, we are able to do more than we ever could have done on our own. They provide scaffolding that allows us to reach higher than we otherwise would have imagined we could.

As I think through the long list of people whom I would count as mentors, I realize that they often filled complex roles in my life. Parents, teachers, friends and colleagues have generously given of themselves, mentoring me both directly and indirectly. I am also struck by the fact that many of my "mentors" were also no doubt thinking that I was their mentor. Students, clients and even my children have at times filled the role of mentor in my life.

There have been several mentors who transformed my sense of self by clarifying my aptitudes. For example, my fifth-grade teacher told my parents to find educational experiences that would challenge me intellectually and told me that I was capable of academic excellence. From that point on, I thought of myself as a good student and raised my expectations for my school performance. As an undergraduate in a large university, I was recruited to do research by a graduate student and a faculty member who each encouraged me to pursue doctoral work. Without their tap on the shoulder, I might never have considered graduate training.

Because of these formative experiences, I now deliberately look for opportunities to name the gifts I see in young people—such as the capacity for insight in an adolescent client, the inventive and poetic use of language in one of the high school girls from church, and my son's friend's ability to explain complex problems in simple language.

As a graduate student, the mentoring I received took a different shape. The faculty challenged the students to participate in intellectual dialogue at a professional level. They never held back from asking us to think through the most difficult philosophical problems. Their critiques were unrelenting but incisive and fair, and their encouragements were spare but precise and meaningful. Of the six students in my cohort, two were gone by the end of the first year. Those who remained were proven in battle, unafraid to engage in rigorous debate and eager to pursue their own big questions. One of the most meaningful experiences of my graduate training was a seminar that began as an exploration of evolution as a developmental theory and continued to meet for two years because of the high level of engagement. The role of the faculty person in that seminar was simply to egg us on. We chose the books, took turns leading the class, and sharpened our own ability to lead, teach and articulate our ideas. My dissertation chair, William Damon, now at Stanford University, has been an active conversation partner in my life now for three decades. It is a gift to have someone who has known me over so many of life's changes. His mentoring has extended well beyond the influence of my academic career. He has not only fundamentally shaped my understanding of human development but has also impacted who I am as a person.

Now on the other side of the faculty-student relationship, there is nothing that gives me greater satisfaction in my role as a mentor than to see my students morph into my colleagues. These relationships are often reciprocal, as my perception of the world is enlarged by gifted students. As just one example, Danielle Speakman introduced me to the complex questions of well-being that face the street kids she lived with, cared for and studied in Lima, Peru. She planted the seed that resulted in a project I undertook last summer, interviewing kids along Asia's Silk Road. We examined the processes of thriving and resiliency under the conditions of sweeping political, social and economic change that had fragmented the traditional systems that support human development.

I have already mentioned the debt I owe to my colleagues at Fuller who have helped me grow in my faith, even as they have also encouraged and supported me professionally. Without their influence on my lifelong learning, I cannot imagine that I would have had much to contribute. At Fuller we have worked deliberately to establish collaborative teams of faculty and students. This model is in contrast to the individual model of research and scholarship that is traditional in academia. Working directly with my colleagues Jim Furrow, Pam King, Rick Beaton, Al Dueck, Warren Brown and Winston Gooden has not only compensated for the gaps in my knowledge and skills but perhaps even more importantly, it has made work a whole lot more fun.

While it may seem counterintuitive to think of foundations as mentors, I am also blessed to have had the support of Thrive Foundation for Youth who through their influence and financial support have radically shaped the work that I do and who I have become. The vision of the founders of Thrive is to create a culture in which kids can thrive to become all that they were meant to be. This vision has greatly inspired me, professionally and personally. Because of their witness, in ways both subtle and overt, I have begun to see the world through the lens of positive development and growth toward full human potential. The Thrive Forum, an outgrowth of the foundation, has brought together like-minded scholars in order for us to ask deep questions about the qualities of families, communities and societies that are necessary to support the shaping of subsequent generations. It has been a rare luxury to set aside two days twice a year to go on a retreat together, simply to engage in deep discussions about the ideas that shape our research and scholarship. I owe a debt to each of the Thrive Forum participants—my colleagues, mentors and friends.

I place a very high value on mentoring and believe that both mentoring and being mentored is a unique relational experience that adds dimensionality to our human experience. I have mentioned above some of the characteristics of a good mentor, but I also believe that there are some attitudes and behaviors that characterize a good mentee. These include the following:

- Intimacy: we have to let ourselves be known.
- Openness: we have to allow ourselves to receive feedback.
- Pursuit: we have to sometimes ask for what we need.
- Patience: we need to create enduring relationships.
- Gratitude: we need to express our gratitude to those who give us the gift of their mentoring attention.

As mentor and mentee move more deeply and intimately into a relationship of real trust and confidence, they both benefit from the opportunity. New insights, self-acceptance, opportunities and creative solutions to problems are likely to be the fruit of such a relationship. Mentors do not always show up in our lives even though we might desire such a relationship. At times we have to seek out a mentor. While we may be shy about asking someone to take the time to invest in our lives, my experience with those who have been mentors convinces me that it is a position of honor and sacred trust. You must be willing to take your role as mentee seriously, to ask deep questions and to prepare thoughtfully for your time together. Under these circumstances, your mentor will likely be similarly invested in your relationship.

## STRUGGLES

The integration of psychology and theology, two distinct disciplines, is particularly challenging when you have only received training in one of them. Serving on the faculty of a seminary, I have had the good fortune of being exposed to theology, but my exposure has not in any way been thorough or systematic. I have continually had to confront the limits of my own understanding, even as I am dependent on my theologically trained colleagues to critique and extend my work.

The complexity of the task of integration is only heightened because the disciplines of psychology and theology share some common territory and ask some similar questions. For example, they each ask, how ought we to live? At the same time, psychologists and theologians rely on different professional languages; different methods of seeking truth and meaning; and different basic assumptions about human nature, purpose and capacities. I believe that ultimately, the conversation between the two disciplines enriches each discipline but leaves plenty of room for misunderstanding, particularly in areas where we operate from fundamentally different platforms. In what follows, I offer a very simplistic summary of just a few core concepts.

First of all, contemporary clinical psychology places a high value on empirical science, and it is built upon a medical model of human functioning, with a corresponding emphasis on symptoms, syndromes and treatments. Autonomous individual functioning is thought to be the ultimate goal of human development, and the individual person is thought to be the primary unit of analysis. An evolutionary understanding of the development of the human race raises function and adaptation above values as sources of meaning. The mainstream science of psychology seeks to uncover the principles that lead to improved human functioning as measured by the absence of symptoms and the presence of competencies such as work, healthy relationships and emotional well-being. Based in an enlightenment agenda, high value is placed on progress and rationality as a mean for bettering the human race.

On the other hand, theology takes as its starting point the revelatory work of God in creation and in Scripture. Theological methods are largely hermeneutical and are based in historical textual criticism and belief-system analysis. Because of the evidence of salvation history, little confidence is placed in the ability of humankind to improve itself. Hu-

mans are considered to be graced with unique dignity and respect because of their unique creation by God. Yet their lives gain meaning as
they enter into the people of God. Without God, humans can neither be
understood nor be saved from the deeply rooted conflicts that are inherent to their nature. The measure of a good life is to love God and to love
one another, even as we are loved. Values give meaning beyond adaptation, as is best exemplified in the sacrifice made by God when he entered
into human history to bring about a new creation. Thus sacrifice, humility, dependency, obedience and suffering are all important avenues of
development, not simply problems to be avoided or signs of immature
personalities. Mystery and encounter with the divine are often not rational, yet they are considered to be a legitimate aspect of formation.

While it would be comforting to find that there is a method of
resolving the discrepancies between theology and psychology, this is
not always the case. As I grow older, I am finding that I am growing
in my ability to tolerate ambiguity, to live in the space of unanswered
questions. As the oldest child in a large family, I admit that I grew up
as somewhat of a "know it all" (at least according to my four siblings!).
Once when I consulted one of my mentors about a new position of
leadership that I had assumed, he shocked me by saying, "of course,
you know you'll be wrong fifty percent of the time." Such a realization has added a dimension of maturity to my character. It has helped
me to become more comfortable admitting that I/we do not always
know the answer or even (heaven forbid!) that I/we could be wrong.
This extends to the theories and authorities of any human discipline,
including the disciplines of psychology and theology. Sometimes it is
enough to map the congruencies and the discontinuities. It is often
even better when we can propose a solution that takes the best of both
disciplines into consideration. What is never suitable is to belittle or
oversimplify the perspectives or arguments of any discipline whose
position differs from our own. In all of this, an attitude of humility,
along with a willingness to listen to the best wisdom that each tradition has to offer, leads to the most satisfying outcomes.

I recently had the opportunity to interview someone whom I considered to have led an exemplary life of service. His opening statement

went something like this, "It's hard to take the public accolades and descriptions of my life seriously, since I know that I have been so flawed. I know that I've lied, cheated and sinned." Similarly, it's often difficult to be in a position of authority on how to live life, since of course, I am also well aware of how often I have failed miserably to live by the standards that I believe God intends for us all. While I have no desire to catalog that list publicly, I do believe that it's helpful to remind ourselves and others that sin is a real and ever-present dimension of our daily lives. Suffering is also an aspect of our humanity that we cannot escape, and I have had my fair share of broken bodies and failed relationships. At this point in my life, I see that sinfulness and suffering are necessarily linked, though it is certainly not in some simplistic way. I have been witness to suffering that cannot be explained by the sinfulness of the victim, and I have certainly seen sinful behavior that has not led to suffering of the perpetrator. Yet in some way, I have seen that our suffering as well as our awareness of our sinfulness can shape us in ways that better prepares us to be participants in God's creation. It heightens our sensitivity, develops our empathy, reminds us of our dependency and vulnerability, and ultimately opens us up to God.

## SPIRITUAL DISCIPLINES

I admit that the words *spiritual* and *discipline* have not always sat so well together for me. And with my adolescence and young adulthood rooted deeply in the countercultural movements of the sixties and seventies, it is true that I have always been a bit of a wild child. Perhaps God has come to me in the ways that I have experienced, unbidden and unexpected, partly because of who I am. The adjectives that I would use to describe my spiritual life include surprising, unpredictable, overwhelming, emotional, profound and transforming. And search as I might, I have never been able to find anything in the patterns of my needs, or my prayers, or my church attendance that has been linked to these moments of numinous experience. In fact, it does not seem to be about me at all.

But perhaps oddly, I would also add that my spiritual life is thoroughly integrated into the mundane details of my daily life. For example, this morning during my run, I was aware of the beauty not only of the skies and mountains of Southern California but also of the perfect arch created by the very human engineers who built a bridge over the arroyo. How miraculous that God could knit together bone, flesh and blood into a creature that could experience God and creation. Moreover, human beings can enter into creation alongside God. The crafting of a fine wine and a good meal, participating in a loving relationship, building a home that is both beautiful and functional, composing a piece of music or creating a painting, articulating an idea that reveals something true; all these are experiences of the transcendent, and all are sacred in their own way.

In short, I have come to believe that God is revealed both in the transcendence of numinous experiences and in the fabric of everyday life. I have indeed grown to know, love, and experience God in the most of the ordinary warp and weave of my life. Nonetheless, there have also been times when God has broken through that same fabric of the expected, and I have experienced his love in ways that have no parallel in earthly dimensions.

## THERAPY

As a therapist, I have been deeply moved by the generosity and trust of my clients, as they have invited me into the deep currents of their lives. The opportunity to witness integration, as God moves and heals through daily lived experiences, has for me brought three-dimensional life to various ideas that have been born of research and scholarship. A case illustration may best demonstrate this process through example. Names and identifying information have of course been changed.

Bella's decision to attend seminary and enter ministry was the end result of a series of numinous experiences of deep and often frightening personal encounters with God. She was terrified of God and feared that God's touch would lead to her annihilation. She had a long history of emotional and psychological problems, including recurrent depression, suicidal ideation, eating disorders and fugue states. At the time, her current symptoms included depression, panic and dissociation. She was also very bright, loving, humorous, artistic and articulate, and she was very faithful to God and to her relationship partners. I was her fourth therapist.

I conceptualized my therapeutic work with Bella from an object relations perspective. For Bella, the developmental phase in which parents typically help the infant to transform the experience of organismic panic into signal anxiety had gone awry. Thus, throughout her life, she had experienced herself as fragmented, because she had never acquired a sense of self from an empathically protective and emotionally supportive "other." In our therapeutic journey together, my hope was to facilitate her development from an "annihilated" to an individuated self. Because we were aware of the ultimate brokenness and failure of all human relationships, including the therapeutic one, we worked to establish God as the omnipresent, faithful and loving "other" to Bella's self. In our work, we drew on the parallels between Bella's dependence on therapy with an over-idealized therapist and her relationship and understanding of God.

Bella considered therapy to be a sacred space, and I learned from her that it indeed can be so. God was the most real and influential presence in her life. In our work together, God's presence was immanent. Through God's Spirit and grace I was allowed to participate in Bella's ability to see God more clearly without the distortions that had accumulated through her painful life encounters. An example drawn from one of our sessions may illustrate this most clearly. I had been on vacation, and as was typical when we missed sessions, Bella had become fragmented. She came in; she was slack-jawed and her eyes were lifeless. When she began to speak, it went something like this:

> So raging mad I threw bottle but only hit wall turn on headphones as loud as possible to try to blow my brains out. The music is so banging loud it won't help can't stop violent feeling can't stop screaming crying can't stop it wish I did not hate so hard wish I could stop crying wish I did not have terror. Really should go and drown in ocean. Really should burn in car crash. Really should go to hell. Really should get rid of possessed thing. Really so sorry, really so lonely, maybe God can go way for to the pasture where no one be ruined and hated, where no one keep violent.

At a loss for how to get through to her, I quieted myself and felt God's presence. I asked Bella to close her eyes and imagine herself before God. I touched her forehead with the palm of my hand and told her God would come to her. For many minutes I watched as her tormented rage became the soft weeping of a small child. When I asked her to describe to me what she saw, she described how God had come to her as "rag woman." The two of them together were on their hands and knees scrubbing the dirt from the marble floor, in front of the altar of a large, empty cathedral. The next day I received an email from Bella in which she wrote:

> Last night was very disturbing, I got desperate and started grabbing and pawing, not able to clutch. Very slippery conditions. I called your machine because it feels to me like I am much less able to endure visitations from hell—even for a night or an hour. I lay on my pillow with my neck stretched, and soon I felt God come to me in that one spot and my whole face got very hot. Then I remembered that you had said that would happen. How did you know that? I wish that would always happen, because after that I do not remember anything until waking up. I slept for nine and a half hours. I slept into the very deep and rested. I woke up happy with only a rational memory about last night, not any feeling memory. I think that I cannot grasp God, but if I can quiet myself, I can maybe sometimes know God grasping me. Do you know Psalm 131?

>> My heart is not proud, O Lord,
>>     my eyes are not haughty;
>> I do not concern myself with great matters
>>     or things too wonderful for me.
>> But I have stilled and quieted my soul;
>>     like a weaned child with its mother,
>>     like a weaned child is my soul within me.

>> O Israel, put your hope in the Lord
>>     both now and forevermore.

> I wish to know that Psalm.

In that and in so many other sessions, I am learning that we are ultimately dependent upon God for our wholeness.

Over time, as a therapist I have made an effort to balance our discipline's inherent emphasis on pathology with an emphasis on human growth and potential, building on the positive resources in clients' lives. For me, this is an integrative task. There is something in the way that human beings are created that leads to our capacity to be resilient. No matter what we are subjected to in life, the most common outcome is that we will adapt. Individuals, families and communities have inherent resources that give them meaning, purpose, opportunity and support. Our task is not only to offer individualized professional services, but also to work within society to promote the development of resources that support the well-being of its citizens.

## LETTER

Dear Fellow Human:

Roughly translated, Irenaeus, the early church father, once wrote, "The glory of God is a human being fully alive." At this stage in my life, I am content to try to understand what it means to be fully human and to live in accordance with both the potential that is evoked in the understanding that we are created in God's image and the limitations that are inherent in our fall from that exalted state into our current state of brokenness.

A much wiser person than me has challenged me to think more about who it is I want to be and less about what it is I want to do. While I find it far easier to focus on doing, it is ultimately being that best captures God's intention for us. We are to be the people of God. We are to be salt and light to the world. We are to set our faces toward Jerusalem so that we can know and be shaped by the same God who fully entered into our human history. Every aspect of our humanity is relevant to God—our behaviors, cognitions, emotions and relationships. It is also important to always remember that both the work and the play of our lives are equal in their capacity to be pleasing to God.

Working in a Christian institution, I have seen how easy it is to be drawn into confusion about the boundaries between our work and God's. God's work to restore creation surpasses our collective human capacities, let alone our individual capacities. As best we can discern, we are called to align our lives with the vision of creation that is described in the Scriptures and that is understood through the theological traditions and practices of the church. Yet it would be a distortion to think that God requires us to do anything in particular to bring about his work of salvation, other than to love God and to love our neighbors, even as we love ourselves.

So I encourage you to ask yourself, What does it mean to be fully human? Who is it that I want to become? No matter what path you choose for yourself in your life, those questions will be relevant each and every day. In your work, your relationships, your communities and your society, are you being and becoming the person you wish for yourself to be and become?

Such a discernment process requires us to look both at who we are and at who we are not. We all yearn for wholeness, but because the world is a broken place, we are all subject to forces that often diminish or even distort our capacity to love and be loved. We are drawn to those areas of our lives where we feel competent, productive and rewarded. Yet often there are neglected, shadowy aspects of ourselves that remain underdeveloped or even malformed. It is far easier to avoid or deny these aspects of ourselves than it is to endure the anxiety required to claim them as our own. You will no doubt receive advice that you should enter into your own psychotherapy process. I would wholeheartedly agree.

Being a developmental psychologist, I have often asked myself why God chose to create us as fragile infants who have to spend nearly two decades in dependency on others for our survival. The parallels between the developmentally appropriate dependency that characterizes our relationship with our caregiver(s) and what should characterize our own relationship with God are readily apparent. To enter into a relationship with God, we must acknowledge our weakness, our brokenness, our complete dependence on him. Yet so much of our adult professional experience strives to deny or suppress those very characteristics. Our roles as clinicians require us to be the expert, the healer, the wise one. In order to combat this overwhelmingly powerful cultural force, we need to think about the processes and structures in our lives that will allow us to be incompetent and thus to depend completely on God. Toward this end, you may want to ask yourself the following questions and then proceed based on how you answer: What am I learning that is new? Where am I inadequate, dependent, clumsy and forced to lean on others?

Recently, a colleague and I were working with someone who was facing a critical choice in his life. The outcome of his decision was indeed weighty and would affect not only his life but those of everyone he loved and many more who were very dependent upon him. Just when the tension between the two choice points seemed to reach a peak, he sighed and said, "Whatever else I know, I know this: God is faithful and God will continue to be faithful whether I go left or whether I go right."

There is so much beauty and truth in that statement that it has continued to echo in my thoughts. I gladly pass it on to you, hoping that you will remember this truth: In the end, everything that must be done has already been completed.

# 13

# Integration and the Christian Imagination

*Cameron Lee, Fuller Theological Seminary*

**A** confessional approach to integration, I suppose, should begin with a confession. Thus, in the interest of full disclosure, here is mine: I am neither a psychologist nor a therapist. Though I originally trained as a marital and family therapist (MFT), it has been many years since I made the decision to walk away from pursuing the MFT license.

My reasons for this decision were primarily pragmatic. In 1986, I was beginning my full-time teaching career at Fuller Seminary, having been hired in the Marriage and Family department where I was still a doctoral candidate. My wife, Suha, and I had an infant son at home and a daughter on the way. I had a dissertation to finish, and I was gathering clinical hours in the evenings. But as any new faculty person will tell you, those evenings were desperately needed for lecture preparation.

Three years later, we had already moved twice. We finally had a home we could afford on an assistant professor's salary—thirty miles from campus. In Southern California, that means countless hours lost to commuting. Evenings became even more precious. I did not want to miss my children's toddlerhood, and simultaneously my job still needed attention. So in the push and pull of role demands, Daddy and professor won; psychotherapist lost. I closed the door on working as a clinician and have never looked back.

Not that I locked myself away in an ivory tower. As a family-life educator, I regularly teach workshops on marriage and parenting, mostly in church settings. I do premarital work with couples, with the occasional privilege of officiating at their weddings as well. I have an active teaching and preaching ministry in the congregation that licenses me as a minister. Indeed, several people seem to assume that I am on the church staff and hence address me as "pastor."

I am saying all this up front so that you will know how large a grain of salt to take as you read this chapter. In social constructionist terms, it is a matter of disclosing my *social location;* that is, the context from which I write and speak. My thoughts about integration have been formed in the crucible of a career that has attended more to education and ministry, rather than therapy. Thus, when I think of integration, ecclesiology is never far from my mind.

In the academy and in professional journals, integration often takes the form of exploring the relationship between domains of knowledge or fields of study. Sometimes the emphasis is on the relationship between specific theories or constructs. But the larger existential issue, I believe, is one of identity. Put differently, I view integration as ultimately a matter of personal *integrity*.

By this, I do not merely mean ethical professional behavior, since in practice, professional ethics is often more a matter of codes than it is of character. Rather, as I use it here, the term *integrity* refers to a state of being whole or undivided, as in the related word *integer.* Part of the problem to which "integration" is proposed as a solution is a fracturing of our narrative imagination, a lingering effect of modernity that has become firmly ensconced in the postmodern worldview. Graduate school tends to exacerbate the problem by pushing students toward increasingly specialized, domain-specific knowledge. Integration as integrity entails the cultivation of a coherent narrative imagination. I take that as a challenge for all Christians, not just those training in the psychological and helping professions.

This definition will probably make more sense within the context of my own journey. And please note that I regard the metaphor of a journey circumspectly, lest I fool myself into thinking that I know the destination better than I really do. In my mind, we believers are a bit like the post-exodus Israelites, heading into the unknown without a map, on the basis of a promise whose scope we have not yet grasped. Therefore, of necessity, our journey must be a humble one.

## DEVELOPMENT

I did not grow up as a Christian. At most, church was something our family did twice a year—on Easter and Christmas—in order to appease my grandparents. My sister and I would have to dress in uncomfortable clothing and sit forever on hard wooden pews, listening to songs and sermons we did not understand. We were given coins to put into the velvet-lined offering plate, but we had no idea what the money was for. (Frankly, at the time, I could always think of better things to do with a quarter!) For my sister and me, when it came to church, the only thing to look forward to was the promise of punch and cookies in the vestibule.

I did have a brush or two with the Bible growing up, without any life-changing consequences. My grandmother had given me a pocket-sized New Testament. However, its King James English was too mysterious for me to persevere beyond the first few chapters of Matthew. Another time, a friend in high school invited me to a Bible study. I went once, but that was all.

It was not until college that God caught up with me. Nothing dramatic—no Damascus road experience. It was my first day at the University of California, Berkeley. To register for classes, you had to go from building to building and stand in line. The art class I wanted was closed, so I plopped down on a bench, feeling a little lost.

And I must have *looked* lost. Two clean-cut men in rugby shirts approached me with a religious survey. The last question on the survey asked if I would be interested in a personal relationship with God. Bored and not wanting to seem narrow-minded, I said yes. They showed me a tract. Five minutes later, I read aloud the prayer that invited Jesus into my life.

Soon after, I started meeting with the ministry staff member who had led me through that prayer. I was assigned booklets and study guides to read, each of which we would later discuss. When I told my parents that I wanted to start going to Wednesday-night Bible studies, they were worried that I had gotten sucked into some kind of cult. But my parents eventually relented, and I became a regular attendee at those Wednesday meetings.

Such was my introduction to the Christian faith, plunged into an evangelical campus subculture with precious little preparation. Against that background, I have at times envied some of my colleagues for their deeply rooted denominational identities. They consciously stand in the midst of generations of churchly tradition. There is something about that kind of historical continuity that seems to lend integrity to one's spiritual narrative.

By contrast, I feel almost spiritually homeless at times. My spiritual story seems somewhat incoherent in this regard. My father's family was nominally Buddhist. My mother's family was Chinese Methodist, though Grandpa was also a Freemason, while Grandma gave thousands to her favorite televangelists. I was the first Christian convert in my family, and I was later baptized in the Evangelical Covenant Church, a denomination of Swedish origin. I currently worship and teach in an American Baptist congregation that does not have the word "Baptist" in its name and whose identity is patterned after the so-called seeker-sensitive model, which is itself under reconstruction.

In other words, my spiritual pedigree is "mutt." I suspect, however, that my story is an increasingly common one. The postdenominational pluralism of much of American Christianity is creating a new tradition of traditionlessness. In the current American cultural milieu, freedom of religion is less a matter of theological conviction than it is a lifestyle choice. I believe this sort of spiritual climate creates its own challenges for the task of integration.

My conversion came at a time when I had no clear idea of my future direction. When I finally declared a major at the end of my sophomore year, I chose Mathematics for Teachers, even though I had no intention of being a math teacher. I simply did not know what else to choose. During my bachelor's education, I took only one introductory course in psychology. It was not until my senior year in college that I actually decided to pursue graduate training in therapy. I had to make up the psychology prerequisites in night school, after Suha and I married in 1978. Then in

1980, I applied to Fuller and was accepted. On our second anniversary, we packed up our belongings and moved to Southern California.

The plan was to spend two years in Pasadena, complete a master of arts degree, and then return to northern California. But two years became three as I switched to the master of divinity. And three became seven as I went on to the Ph.D. In 1986, Fuller hired me on as a full-time professor, several months before completing my doctorate, and I have been there ever since. Suha and I never made it back north.

During my training, particularly in my practicum, I often felt deeply ambivalent about becoming a therapist. In family-systems terms, I had been triangled into my parents' conflicts as a child, and I had never really worked through the feelings attached to this triangulation. In fact, the therapist who briefly worked with my parents actually suggested that I might make a good marriage counselor (family dynamics was *not* his area of expertise), noting my occasional role as their mediator. It took some training before I realized why this piece of advice was not as wise as it seemed at first.

I remember the moment when my ambivalence over becoming a therapist resolved itself and when my vocational call seemed clearest. I was the teaching assistant for a seminary course. One day, sitting in the back of the classroom, I suddenly just knew: I was to be a teacher, *not* a therapist. As cliché as it sounds, it was like a light bulb had been switched on. I continued to collect clinical hours, and it would be a few more years before I would relinquish the pursuit of becoming a therapist altogether. I have never regretted that decision. Still, there are moments when, as a nonclinician teaching in a clinical program, that sense of homelessness catches up with me again. Even after more than two decades of teaching in the same institution, I still at times find myself wondering, *Is this where I really belong?*

Perhaps it will always be that way. I content myself with believing that my restlessness is at least partly symptomatic of the eschatological longing that Paul describes in Romans 8. Until God completes his work of redemption, we must live with the sense that things are not yet as they should be. That too is part of my story—or more to the point, part of the grand story to which we belong together.

## MENTORING

Writing this chapter has given me a fresh opportunity to appreciate how God has shaped my career through the attentive care of others. My earliest mentor was Del Olsen, the director of the Baptist Student Union (BSU) during my time at Berkeley. When Suha and I met at the end of our freshman year, she had already been attending BSU meetings, and she drew me into the group. Both of us had one foot in the BSU and the other in the parachurch ministry through which I received the gospel. In the latter, discipleship largely meant Bible study, with an emphasis on apologetics and evangelism. In the former, however, discipleship meant more of an interpersonal process of exploration.

Del was the first person I had met who was both an ordained minister and a marital therapist. He brought both ministerial and therapeutic sensibilities to the ways in which he shepherded us. As a new Christian still learning the basics, there were times when I bristled against Del's teaching. I wanted the kind of straightforward certainties that spilled from the pages of my parachurch workbooks. And yet, Del sketched for us a Jesus that was more dangerous and more unpredictable than I was comfortable with. But Del was a patient, transparent and non-anxious teacher and pastor—just the thing for college students still learning who we were. When Suha and I married a few years later, it was Del who performed the ceremony.

My primary mentor during my graduate school years and during my early years of teaching was the late Dennis Guernsey, who was director of the Marriage and Family Ministry program when I began at Fuller. I first met Dennis during a social that was designed to welcome new students. I was standing in line for dessert, a little shell-shocked. Standing behind me, Dennis introduced himself and then asked my name. When I told him, a light of recognition flashed across his face: "You graduated from Berkeley, right?" He would later explain that he had remembered my application because of my GRE scores. At the time, however, the reason did not matter. He knew my name, and that made me feel welcomed.

Dennis was the one most responsible for getting my career on track.

Though we never discussed it directly, I felt as if he had taken me on as a protégé—seeing things in me that I could not yet see in myself. From the beginning, Dennis entrusted me with leadership opportunities that I would never have sought on my own. Later, when a faculty position opened up at Fuller, he was instrumental in advocating for my candidacy. Moreover, after I was hired, he supervised my clinical work.

Dennis modeled for me a first-rate clinician with a passion for the things of God. His love for the church and heart for ministry infused the ethos that still characterizes the program. Year after year, he and his wife Lucy opened their home to students for orientation and graduation celebrations. These gatherings were always times for us all to share and marvel at the stories of God's providential care in students' lives.

I did not have much contact with Dennis after he left Fuller for Seattle Pacific University. We soon received the news that he had been diagnosed with a rapidly advancing brain tumor that eventually took his life. I went up to visit him the week before he died. The tumor made it impossible for Dennis to speak in coherent sentences. He seemed frustrated, as if he knew what he wanted to say but could not. Clearly, however, he had not lost his sense of mission to families. With what words and gestures he could muster, he was still encouraging me to continue with that work. Dennis was the one dying, yet his concern was to give *me* a last word of counsel. I only hope that I have done some small honor to the trust he so generously bestowed.

Two other men from the Fuller faculty have been formative in my development: Jack Balswick and Ray Anderson. First, Jack was my dissertation chair. He and his wife, Judy, joined the faculty after I had already completed my masters' level coursework, so I never had an actual class from either of them. But after Dennis and Lucy Guernsey left Fuller for Seattle Pacific, the Balswicks picked up the Guernseys' baton of hospitality and began hosting numerous student events in their home.

What Jack Balswick modeled was a respected scholar who always went about his work with quiet humility and self-effacing humor. To paraphrase what Jesus said of Nathanael in John 1:47, of Jack it could be said: "Here is a true sociologist, in whom there is nothing false." It could have been awkward for me to make the transition from student to faculty member. But Jack treated me as a colleague from the start, even encouraging me to turn my dissertation into my first book. Together, both he and Dennis made it easy for this newly minted Ph.D. to become a full-fledged member of the team.

Finally, my approach to integration has been profoundly influenced by another Fuller faculty member, the late Ray Anderson. I arrived at Fuller as a relatively new Christian, with no theological training. In our very first quarter, my classmates and I had Ray's course on theological anthropology. The common experience of this course was that of being collectively thrown off the deep end of the theological pool. Ray had a penchant for long words (his favorite was "quintessential") and complex diagrams. He would start lectures innocently enough, with a textbox or stick figure drawn in the middle of the board. Soon, however, arrows would start sprouting like weeds, and it was all we could do just to keep up.

We did not remain lost, however. For each of us, the moment of insight would eventually come. You could see understanding dawning on the face of one student, then another. Each of us would finally grasp the essential relationality of human existence, as beings created in God's image. But one other thing came through clearly in all of Ray's courses: his pastoral concern to put theology at the service of the church. It was in learning this lesson that all of us would learn to incarnate Christ in our various ministries to families. In other words, we learned from Ray that theology that was not lived out in the praxis of ministry did not deserve to be called *theology*.

It was also in Ray's courses that I was first exposed to narrative theology. We were assigned to read Stanley Hauerwas's (1981) *A Community of Character* the year it was published, well before narrative approaches began to populate the therapy literature (e.g., White & Epston, 1990). A few years later, Dennis introduced me to social constructionism (Berger & Luckmann, 1967). From these seminal works, an abiding interest was born. Throughout my career, I have continued to explore narrative and constructionist themes that cut across domains of study such as theology, ministry and psychotherapy.

More recently, I have begun to stress the importance of having a biblically formed narrative imagination. The idea is found repeatedly in the work of those whom I consider mentors through their writings, such as Eugene Peterson and N. T. Wright (e.g., Peterson, 2008; Wright, 1999, 2008). For example, one excerpt from Peterson on the kingdom of God will suffice:

> Kingdom is what is going on all the time, whether we are aware of it or not. . . . Kingdom requires a total renovation of our imagination, so that we are able to see what our eyes do not see. . . . [Jesus] is training our imaginations so that we will be able to participate appropriately in the great salvation drama that is taking place right now. (pp. 129-30)

*Imagination* does not refer to *flights of fancy* any more than *story* must of necessity be opposed to *fact*. In speaking of the imagination, Peterson is referring to the only way in which we can take hold of a reality that cannot be reached by reason alone. Christian imagination dwells in the world that is revealed by Scripture—and imagination is as crucial to integration as is integrity. I count myself blessed to have been formed in personal ways by others who have each shown me how such imagination might operate in a Christian's life and work.

## STRUGGLES

Years ago, one of our graduating students came to see me in my office. She was bubbling enthusiastically about the skills she had developed in practicum. It is, after all, a heady experience to watch people's lives change for the better as a result of your intervention.

Then came her rhetorical question, which stunned me to silence: "If I can help people that way, then why do I need to be a Christian?" I honestly do not remember what I said in response. Hopefully, I would be better able to keep my pastoral bearings now. But the conversation still haunts me. I remember that I could not help feeling that somehow we had failed her.

Was this student merely saying that she did not need to be a Christian in order to offer people psychological assistance? That would certainly be true, if a bit obvious. But there was more to it than that.

Health, conceived in psychological terms, had become the *telos* of human existence. Against that implicit metanarrative, the Christian faith itself seemed quaint at best and irrelevant at worst.

Being trained as a therapist shapes us in ways that we sometimes do not recognize, ushering us into patterns of thinking and speaking that take on the quality of self-evident truth. Over and over again, I have heard students proclaim, with the flush of newfound professional insight, that a client would be better off if she would just realize her problem was psychological and not spiritual. I know that for some students, psychological narratives represent liberation from oppressive church backgrounds. But the solution for such a dilemma may be to reexamine our theology rather than to assume that clinical diagnosis should trump spiritual language.

An integrated, narrative coherence requires both a coherent theological worldview as well as a coherent psychological one. Neither worldview should be taken for granted, but the former one may be harder to come by. When dealing with human behavior, therapeutic narratives are frequently more coherent—and frankly often experienced as far more helpful—than the religious perspectives we have learned in church. And this is particularly the case if we come to our theological convictions piecemeal.

Moreover, for many, the faith has become what Christian Smith has called "moralistic therapeutic deism" (Smith & Denton, 2005, e.g., pp. 162-70): that is, God loves us and wants us to be happy and nice, and he is ready to help us if we have a problem. This religious metanarrative may be reasonably coherent, but it is dramatically out of step with the biblical story. Here one might say that the theological has been colonized (Habermas, 1981/1984) by the therapeutic (cf. also Lee, 1989; Rieff, 1987).

Colonization, of course, may also run in the other direction, as when the language of salvation simplistically trumps that of psychological health. Put bluntly, some students have wondered, if evangelism isn't appropriate in clinical settings, then what's the point of doing therapy with non-Christian clients? We may be able to reduce symptomatic behavior or help clients' relationships be a bit more harmonious—but this sort of "solution" seems somewhat like rearranging the deck chairs on the *Titanic*. Then again, if all that matters is going to heaven when you die, why do therapy with *anyone*?

These are not hypothetical scenarios. Sometimes our theological commitments neither compose nor derive from a coherent, habitable metanarrative. Confronted with human problems and compelling psychological explanations, we are therefore often left with a sense of the irrelevance of our theological commitments. We may staunchly defend them, or we may rigidly compartmentalize them, but in either case, our integrative efforts will be severely limited.

Sometimes, the problem is not internal coherence. Again, moralistic therapeutic deism is coherent in itself, but it is an insipid and inaccurate appropriation of the gospel, and it is itself shaped by a therapeutic culture. Similarly, to measure the value of therapy by evangelistic standards might stem from an internally consistent theological perspective, but it might be a constricted view of what the Bible means by salvation. In both cases, the main problem is one of external coherence; that is, the problem is the lack of coherence between our theological commitments and the full scope of the biblical metanarrative.

This is not the place to fully work out such a thesis. Suffice it to say that I believe that much (though not all) of our integrative struggles stem from the incoherence or incompleteness of our theological narratives. But I do not mean this in a merely academic sense, as if narrative coherence were solely a property of texts, independent of perceived and lived reality. Instead, I mean to say that this is the place where imagination comes in. To paraphrase the above-mentioned quote from Peterson (2008, pp. 129-30): the reign of God is a present reality; it is here, now, all around us—even in the clinic. Therefore, the real question for us becomes, do we have the theological imagination to perceive it?

I openly acknowledge that all I have spoken of in this section may be more reflective of my own theological struggles as opposed to my integrative struggles per se. But if my framing of integration as the integrity of narrative imagination makes any sense, then my claims here about incoherence may be reduced down to the following simple observation: In contemporary America, our imaginations need more help on the theological side than on the psychological one. At least mine does. It is one thing to say that I believe what the Bible says, but it is quite another for me to have a coherent grasp of the reality that the Bible reveals. Moreover, it is still another thing for me to learn to live within that reality. In my own writings (e.g., Lee, 2004) and in my own pulpit ministry, I have tried to find ways to make exposition serve the goal of reimagining the world in biblical terms. And yet I find myself regularly opting for simpler psychological truisms. Thus, one could say that my main integrative struggle is that I am still in the process of learning to consistently inhabit the narrative world of Scripture. For me, this struggle likely promises to be a lifelong pursuit.

## SPIRITUAL DISCIPLINES

At this point, a discussion of spiritual disciplines seems particularly apropos. I approach this section, however, with some hesitation. I had coffee with a Christian friend of mine recently, who was a little taken aback when I shared a personal prayer request with him. He told me, quite clearly, that I give the impression of "having it all together"; I assured him that I do not.

But those like myself, who are viewed by many as teacher, counselor or pastor, are faced with a double-edged occupational hazard. On the one hand, I am constantly tempted to win approval by playing the part of one who seems spiritually mature, or at least theologically sophisticated. On the other hand, even appropriate self-disclosure does not always make a difference. My admissions of fallibility either go unheard, or they are taken as further evidence of my spiritual depth. Apparently some people believe that humility from a Ph.D. is somehow more virtuous than humility from others.

So at the risk of sounding pedantic, I begin on a cautionary note. If it is true that many of us struggle to live out of a sound Christian metanarrative, then our understanding of spiritual disciplines will be shaped by the cultural or subcultural narratives we already inhabit.

For example, in the evangelical subculture into which I was socialized in college, I quickly learned to feel like a reprobate if I did not have an hour of "quiet time" each day. We all know it is important to read our Bibles and to pray. But do we ever just rush through a quick reading or spend a few hurried moments in prayer so that we can check it off our mental list and feel like we have done our due diligence? Add to this the self-help pragmatism of American popular culture. What do I do when my prayer life is not as meaningful as I think it should be? I march myself down to the bookstore. Surely, with all the books on prayer out there, someone has the right program to help me fix the problem.

My point here is that the spiritual disciplines must be means, not ends in themselves. And in the present context, if the desired end is integration via a coherent narrative imagination, then we must ask, what spiritual practices help foster such coherence?

Obviously, Bible reading and study are essential. The question, however, is not *whether* we should read the Bible—it is *how*. Short devotional readings that are shorn of their narrative and historical contexts will simply not do. Our historical distance means that we will probably need some help getting beyond the level of moral rules and principles to get at the symbolic world of the text (Hays, 1996).

It is not cheating to read scholarly commentaries alongside Scripture, as long as we do not have commentators do all our thinking for us. The historical introductions can be particularly valuable. Also helpful are books that attempt to bring a sense of narrative unity across the Old and New Testaments. Bartholomew and Goheen's (2004) *The Drama of Scripture* is useful in this regard; for a more theologically oriented starting point, I would recommend N. T. Wright's (2006) *Simply Christian*.

Similarly, the question is not whether we should pray but how. Paul's well-known admonition to "pray continually" (1 Thessalonians 5:17) suggests that prayer is more than a particular set of behaviors that can be put on a schedule. We do not just pray instrumentally, in order to ask God to do things; instead, we pray in order to continually immerse ourselves in the biblical story, as God gradually reshapes our imaginations by his Spirit.

To that end, I have found journaling to be particularly helpful. Reflecting on the past day or week can, of course, easily degenerate into either narcissistic navel-gazing or the parallel and distracting desire to produce something of literary merit (e.g., can I get publication credit for all of this articulated reflection?). Still, coupled with the attitude of prayer, journaling is a good way to practice what has provocatively been called a "not-knowing" stance (Anderson, 2005; Anderson & Goolishian, 1992). In other words, we need a place to step outside the utilitarian concerns that censor our imaginations, so that we can engage our curiosity about what God may be doing in and through us. Journals provide a medium for humbly noticing and reflecting on things we cannot fully grasp, as well as for challenging taken-for-granted meanings and for rehearsing new ones. Unfortunately, there are no explicit instructions to tell us what or how to write. However, anything that helps us to renovate a truly *Christian* imagination will serve the purposes of integration well.

## THERAPY

As mentioned in my opening disclaimer, I am not a therapist. Some people seem to think that is a good thing. At a banquet some years ago, at which several clinicians were in attendance, I had a conversation with the woman seated next to me. We exchanged small talk until the inevitable question arose about what each of us did for a living. She frowned slightly and asked: "You're not a therapist, are you?" When I confirmed that I was not, she replied: "I didn't think so. You seem so normal."

I did not ask, but this woman's comment made me wonder what her experience of therapists had been. And I suspect that it is not just about therapists, but professionals of any type—including professors and pastors—whose knowledge separates them from the rank and file of humanity. I had a similar conversation with a member of our church, who blurted out to me one time: "You mean you have a Ph.D.? You don't act like a Ph.D." Suddenly embarrassed, he quickly assured me that he meant that as a compliment.

Suffering and problems of living come in all shapes and sizes. When people seek our professional expertise, the first thing they want is often a solution, a "how-to." And sometimes we have workable solutions ready at hand. But it is a constant temptation to trust in the certainty of our answers and our expertise too much, even as we become puffed up with what we know and begin to lose the capacity for empathy. In other words, we become the kind of therapists and academics who fit the stereotype.

This brings us back to the so-called not-knowing stance. The very idea of not-knowing seems to fly in the face of our modernist constructions of professional expertise. Some misconstrue not-knowing as a therapeutic technique, or they fear that this stance is just another example of postmodern excess, a relativistic posture in which anything goes.

However, as Harlene Anderson (2005) has lamented, much of this criticism misses the point. For example, Anderson was not saying that therapists have no useful professional knowledge; instead, she was cautioning us against allowing our professional meanings to run roughshod over our clients' lived experience. In terms of moral character, what Anderson sought to encourage in therapists is a deep humility, along with a corresponding respect for clients' inside knowledge of their own stories.

The therapeutic conversation in such a model is not simply about gathering the information needed for a proper diagnosis; on the contrary, it is an imaginative immersion into the client's narrative world. This type of a commitment requires an other-directedness that is not always easy to maintain in actual practice. For instance, when someone seeks my counsel, I often find myself unable to focus on what they are saying. I might be lost in my own internal dialogue, searching what I know for an answer to their problem. Sometimes this search is out of genuine concern for the other. But sometimes—and perhaps to some extent, all the time—it is out of a concern to be the expert that the other person thinks I am.

To adopt a not-knowing stance is not to devalue knowledge but to recognize our need for humility in the face of mystery. At some level, paradoxically, we must adopt a not-knowing stance in order to know, in order to notice what we might otherwise miss. No psychology can exhaust the depth of human experience. To be a therapist is to be allowed the privilege of peering into darkened corners with what meager flashlights we have. In such situations, humble curiosity may be a greater virtue than confident certainty.

Similarly, no theology can circumscribe God. To be a Christian is to be alert to and to stand amazed in the presence of the miraculous. It is to live inside the kind of truth that is best appropriated through story-telling and story-listening. It is to recognize not just the *value* of an imagination trained by immersion in the narrative world of the Scriptures but also the *necessity*.

And that world is not separate from the one in which we do therapy. I recognize that the perspective being proposed here will not in itself answer many of the more specific questions encountered in the interface of psychological and theological imagination. But I offer these reflections simply as an encouragement to not miss the forest for the trees. We must continue to cultivate the kind of biblically trained narrative imagination that allows us to see all of creation as the sphere of God's redemptive work, therapy included. Even without that realization, we can still explore some interesting and relevant integrative questions. But ultimately, our integration will lack something in the way of integrity.

## LETTER

To my fellow companions on the journey:

It has been about thirty years since I began my graduate training in both psychology and theology. Each of these fields shapes my understanding of myself and others, as well as my understanding of the world we live in. Each field also informs my sense of vocation in ways that continue to develop over time.

Yet there is no escaping the fact that each field frames reality differently. It is that realization that not only made *integration* a buzzword before I began my graduate studies, but it makes a place for a book such as this one today. *Integration* suggests the hope that someday, somehow, it will all make sense—together.

What can I say to encourage that hope? It is hard to distill out a few choice words without sounding trite or feeling as if I should have more to show for three decades of work! So with the appropriate apologies, I offer you four thoughts, under the headings of humble realism, personal commitment, diligence and freedom.

First, realism. Excellent integrative work has been done in the past three decades, much of it by the contributors to this volume. But it is in the nature of academia to reward innovation over integration. The literature in psychology and in theology continues to expand and diversify, and the literature in integration simply cannot keep pace. To say, therefore, that we are about "integrating psychology and theology" (or whatever terms one wishes to insert on either side of the "and") seems a little grandiose, when neither discipline is really integrated within itself. Thus, supporting cross-disciplinary efforts *within* each field will support integration *across* the fields, and there are hopeful signs in this regard. As Christians who know our own finitude compared to God, we should readily be able to admit that our understandings are always partial. Any piece contributed to the integration puzzle should therefore be received as a gift.

Second, I do not want to leave the impression that integration is, for lack of a better term, an "academic" pursuit alone, however. Integration is motivated by more than mere intellectual satisfaction. As I have suggested, I believe that integration should be understood as a lifelong journey toward the kind of integrity that is characterized by narrative coherence. If this assertion is at all valid, then integration must be the personal commitment of every Christian. We must cultivate the imagination that allows us to inhabit the reality that is revealed to us in Scripture.

Here I do not mean to echo a pious platitude on the order of "We should all try to be better Christians." As Christian professionals, many of us know the experience of double-mindedness, of flipping back-and-forth between secular and spiritual ways of thinking and being. We might, for example, privilege Christian language on Sunday and secular clinical theory on the other days of the week. The commitment to integration is thus the commitment to personal integrity as a believer. It is *supported* by our academic pursuits, but it is not *reducible* to them.

Third, the pursuit of this kind of integrity will require diligence. My specific pastoral concern is that a coherent and theologically sound

Christian imagination may be harder to come by than we realize. Every culture poses its own challenges. For example, in America, we tend to interpret the gospel in ways that have already been heavily influenced by individualistic and therapeutic perspectives. The challenges, therefore, arise not only from outside the church but from inside as well.

Thus, the personal commitment to integration is active and not passive. As I have said to my students repeatedly over the years, integration is not a spectator sport. On the one hand, it includes reexamination of our theological beliefs and linguistic practices, even ones that we have long taken for granted. On the other hand, it also includes a reevaluation of our psychological beliefs and practices. We must push past the therapeutic pragmatism of "what works" and ask the hard questions about what metanarrative assumptions our favored theories rest upon.

Finally, my hope is that all our integrative endeavors can be done in the spirit of freedom rather than of compulsion. The Christian life is not something we labor at under the anxiety of having to get it just right. The good news is that God himself is in the process of restoring creation, of remaking a world that has been spoiled by sin. And I believe that the work of therapy participates in God's redemptive work, even when it is not about saving our clients' souls.

To put it in terms I have used elsewhere (Lee, 2004), Christian therapists can act conscientiously as agents of God's shalom, moving people toward the wholeness for which humans were created. This does not require the development and practice of a specific "Christian psychology" per se, but it does call for the desire to participate in God's work of putting things right in whatever way he makes possible.

In other words, there is freedom in realizing that healing is God's work before it is our own. We cannot save the world—that is God's job; and the project is already under way. But by his grace, God has chosen to give us an advanced peek at the fullness of redemption, by allowing us to have a share in his kingdom work. To some, God has given the gifts that are needed to be good therapists, along with the privilege of serving as his peacemakers—that is, his agents of shalom—through their professional efforts. Imagine that.

## REFERENCES

Anderson, H. (2005). Myths about "not-knowing." *Family Process, 44,* 497-504.

Anderson, H., & Goolishian, H. (1992). The client is the expert: A not-knowing approach to therapy. In S. McNamee & K. Gergen (Eds.), *Social construction and the therapeutic process* (pp. 25-39). Newbury Park, CA: Sage.

Bartholomew, C. G., & Goheen, M. W. (2004). *The drama of Scripture: Finding our place in the biblical story.* Grand Rapids, MI: Baker.

Berger, P., & Luckmann, T. (1967). *The social construction of reality: A treatise in the sociology of knowledge.* Garden City, NY: Doubleday.

Habermas, J. (1984). *The theory of communicative action. Vol. 1. Reason and the rationalization of society* (T. McCarthy, Trans.). Boston: Beacon Press. (Original work published 1981)

Hauerwas, S. (1981). *A community of character: Toward a constructive Christian social ethic.* Notre Dame, IN: University of Notre Dame Press.

Hays, R. B. (1996). *The moral vision of the New Testament: Community, cross, new creation; A contemporary introduction to New Testament ethics.* San Francisco: HarperSanFrancisco.

Lee, C. (1989). *Beyond family values: A call to Christian virtue.* Downers Grove, IL: InterVarsity Press.

Lee, C. (2004). *Unexpected blessing: Living the countercultural reality of the Beatitudes.* Downers Grove, IL: InterVarsity Press.

Peterson, E. H. (2008). *Tell it slant: A conversation on the language of Jesus in his stories and prayers.* Grand Rapids, MI: Eerdmans.

Rieff, P. (1987). *The triumph of the therapeutic: Uses of faith after Freud.* Chicago: University of Chicago. (Original work published 1966)

Smith, C., & Denton, M. L. (2005). *Soul searching.* New York: Oxford University Press.

White, M., & Epston, D. (1990). *Narrative means to therapeutic ends.* New York: Norton.

Wright, N. T. (1999). *The challenge of Jesus: Rediscovering who Jesus was and is.* Downers Grove, IL: InterVarsity Press.

Wright, N. T. (2006). *Simply Christian: Why Christianity makes sense.* New York: Harper.

Wright, N. T. (2008). *Surprised by hope: Rethinking heaven, the resurrection, and the mission of the church.* New York: Harper.

# Contributors

**Alvin C. Dueck, Ph.D.,** Fuller Seminary, is the Evelyn and Frank Freed Professor of the Integration of Psychology and Theology at Fuller. In addition to teaching courses that focus on the dialogue between theology and psychology, he is engaged in research on the role of religion in therapy, congregational health, and conflict resolution between Christians and Muslims. He is the principal investigator in a research project on the spiritual experience of Christians, Muslims and Jews funded by the Templeton Foundation. He also participates in the Center for Research on Religion and Psychotherapy. Dueck is a licensed psychologist with a long history of teaching in the seminary setting. Prior to joining Fuller's faculty in 1998, Dueck was director of the Marriage and Family Counseling program at the Mennonite Brethren Biblical Seminary. He presented the Integration Lectures at Fuller in 1986, which have since been published in a book titled *Between Jerusalem and Athens: Ethical Perspectives on Culture, Religion and Psychotherapy.* Together with Cameron Lee, he has edited a volume of essays titled *Why Psychology Needs Theology: A Radical-Reformation Perspective* (2005). He also edited and contributed an article titled "Modern and Postmodern Approaches to Integration" to a special issue of the *Journal of Psychology and Theology.* Dueck serves as manuscript reviewer for the *Journal of Psychology and Theology.* His professional affiliations have included the American Psychological Association, the California Psychological Association, the Christian Association of Psychological Studies, the American Academy of Religion and the Association of Mennonite Psychologists. He was a board member and chair of the board of directors of the Kings View Mental Health Corporation. Dueck has also served as a consultant to international mission agencies since 1984 and is actively involved in encouraging indigenous mental health awareness and services in Guatemala, Africa and China. He was a participant in a mental health tour to the Soviet Union in 1989. His areas of expertise include systems/symbolic/object relations psychotherapy, postmodernity and psychological theory, healing structures in congregations and communities, spirituality and psychotherapy, ethics and therapy, Jung and Christianity, and integrative research.

**Elizabeth Lewis Hall, Ph.D.**, is Associate Professor at Rosemead School of Psychology, where she teaches clinical and integration courses. In addition to teaching, she maintains a small clinical practice at the Biola Counseling Center in La Mirada, California. Her empirical research focuses on women's issues in the evangelical subculture and on the application of clinical psychology in the context of missions. She is also committed to the practice and teaching of the integration of psychology and theology, and most recently has been integratively examining the meaning of having bodies. In addition to publications in evangelical journals such as the *Journal of Psychology and Theology*, the *Journal of Psychology and Christianity* and *Christian Scholar's Review*, she has contributed a Christian voice in secular venues such as *Mental Health, Religion and Culture, Sex Roles,* and *Psychology of Women Quarterly*. Dr. Hall serves as council representative for division 36 (Psychology of Religion) of the American Psychological Association. Dr. Hall lives in Whittier, California, with her husband, Todd, who also teaches psychology at Biola. She has two sons, Brennan and Aiden, and her experiences as a wife, mother and professional are a continuing source of inspiration for her research in women's issues.

**William L. Hathaway, Ph.D.**, is the acting dean in the School of Psychology & Counseling at Regent University. Dr. Hathaway has a diverse background, having been employed as a full-time clinician for several years, participating in federally-funded research studies, teaching extensively as an adjunct faculty member in the United States and

Europe, and serving as an Air Force officer. He is a licensed clinical psychologist in Virginia where he has served as gubernatorial appointee to the state licensing board in psychology. He has a broad clinical background but specializes in child and adult attention-deficit/hyperactivity disorder (ADHD). He has served in leadership roles in his profession and is currently past president of the Psychology of Religion division of the American Psychological Association. He has authored and coauthored numerous publications and journal articles, and presented at national conferences. He is currently cowriting a text on the integration of psychology and Christianity for InterVarsity Press.

**Cameron Lee, Ph.D., M.Div.**, is a professor of family studies at Fuller Seminary. He has been a member of the Marriage and Family program faculty since 1986, and was part of the program's move from the School of Theology to the School of Psychology in 1987. While teaching family studies courses on the Fuller campus, he also speaks off-campus as a family wellness instructor and trainer, a certified family life educator, and a licensed minister in the American Baptist congregation where he is a member. He teaches and preaches regularly in church settings. Lee has been published in a variety of journals, including *Family Process, Family Relations*, the *Journal of Psychology and Theology*, and the *Journal for the Scientific Study of Religion*. He has written two books and several articles on the lives of clergy families. His current research with the Fuller Youth Institute involves a longitudinal study of high school youth group participants transitioning to college. His most recent books are *Why Psychology Needs Theology: A Radical-Reformation Perspective* (2005), coedited with Al Dueck, *Unexpected Blessing: Living the Countercultural Reality of the Beatitudes* (2004), and *Beyond Family Values: A Call to Christian Virtue* (1998). Lee is a member of the National Council on Family Relations. His areas of expertise include family systems theory, college transition and identity, dynamics of clergy families, and family life education.

**Mark R. McMinn, Ph.D.**, is a professor at George Fox University. He received his undergraduate degree from Lewis and Clark College and a

Ph.D. in clinical psychology from Vanderbilt University. McMinn taught at George Fox from 1984 to 1993 before leaving to help start the Psy.D. program at Wheaton College, where he later assumed an endowed chair position. He has been a licensed psychologist since 1985 and board certified (ABPP) since 1995. He especially enjoys working with clergy, both in his clinical work and through a data-based method of church-based consultation. McMinn is a past president of APA's Division 36 (Psychology of Religion), and the author of various trade books, professional books and journal articles. Primary areas of research interest include clergy-psychology collaboration, clergy health, and the integration of psychology and Christianity. Dr. McMinn's hobbies include tending honeybees, growing a small organic apple orchard, home construction, computer programming and sports. During his free time he also enjoys reading, landscaping and playing basketball.

**J. Derek McNeil, Ph.D., M.Div.**, is an associate professor in the graduate school of psychology at Wheaton College. He received a bachelor of science degree in psychology from Eastern University in St. Davids, Pennsylvania. He also earned a master of divinity degree from Fuller Theological Seminary and holds a Ph.D. in counseling psychology from Northwestern University in Evanston, Illinois. Dr. McNeil has authored chapters in several books, including *The Black Family: Past, Present and Future, Men to Men: Voices of African American Males* and *This Side of Heaven: Race, Ethnicity and Christian Faith*, published by Oxford University Press in 2007. Dr. McNeil is a national leader in the field of psychology, focusing his research on the identity development of African American males, marital and family therapy, and group dynamics. He has traveled nationally and internationally, presenting workshops and seminars on these topics. He has worked as a clinician in private practice, a diversity advisor and coordinator, an organizational consultant, and an administrator. McNeil also serves as a consultant and faculty specialist for Salter McNeil & Associates. As an organizational consultant he uses his psychological expertise and vast knowledge to provide in-depth analysis of group dynamics issues, identify organizational readiness and barriers to the reconciliation process.

In addition, Dr. McNeil works with faculty and administrators regarding diversity-related recruitment and retention issues. He also provides executive coaching to develop and implement targeted strategies to increase the intercultural competency of faculty and staff at Christian colleges and universities.

**Glendon L. Moriarty, Psy.D.**, is a licensed psychologist and an associate professor in the School of Psychology and Counseling at Regent University. Dr. Moriarty is the author of the *Pastoral Care of Depression: Helping Clients Heal Their Relationship with God* (Routledge/Haworth Press, 2006). He is also lead editor on the *God Image Handbook for Spiritual Counseling and Psychotherapy* (Routledge/Haworth Press 2007). He has received multiple awards for his contributions, receiving the Leadership Award, Fellowship Award, Distinguished Young Alumni Award, and being named among Who's Who of Universities and Colleges. He is a member of the American Psychological Association, the Society for the Scientific Study of Religion and the Christian Association for Psychological Studies.

**L. Rebecca Propst, Ph.D.**, is a psychoanalyst and psychologist in private practice in Portland, Oregon. She received her undergraduate degree from West Virginia University, and her Ph.D. in clinical psychology from Vanderbilt University in 1975. She was assistant professor of clinical psychology at Ohio University from 1975 until 1980, and then assistant and associate professor in the counseling graduate program at Lewis and Clark college from 1980 until 1995. She also obtained an M.A. in theology from the University of Portland in 1991. She began training in psychoanalysis at the Northwest Center for Psychoanalysis in Seattle in 1996, and graduated and became certified as a relational psychoanalyst in 2003. She served in various capacities in Division 36 of the APA while an academic, and has been a licensed psychologist since 1977. She is the author of several empirical research studies in mainstream psychology journals and a book on the subject of treating clinical depression using Christian religious faith, as well as publications on other topics. She is also an enthusiastic fan of the great Pacific

Northwest outdoors, and includes hiking, camping, cross-country skiing, fishing and canoeing in her life whenever possible.

**Jennifer S. Ripley, Ph.D.**, is professor of psychology and director of the MMATE Center at Regent University. Her research is primarily in religion and marriage, with focus on the hope-focused approach to couples counseling. Her research has produced dozens of articles, book chapters and almost 100 professional presentations at conferences. Her professional leadership has primarily been with APA Division 36 or CAPS, where she is a former national board member and the associate editor for case studies for the *Journal of Psychology and Christianity*.

**Siang-Yang Tan, Ph.D.**, is a professor of psychology at Fuller Seminary and has been an active member of the faculty since 1985. He has previously served as director of the Psy.D. program and director of training at Fuller's Psychological Center. Of Tan's many publications, he is best known for his book *Lay Counseling* (1991) and more recently for *Full Service: Moving from Self-Serve Christianity to Total Servanthood* (2006); *Coping with Depression* (2004, rev. and expanded ed.), with John Ortberg; *Rest* (2000); and *Disciplines of the Holy Spirit* (1997), with D. Gregg. He also coauthored, with W. Brad Johnson, a chapter titled "Spiritually Oriented Cognitive-Behavioral Therapy" in *Spiritually Oriented Psychotherapy* (2005). More recently, he authored "Use of Prayer and Scripture in Cognitive-Behavioral Therapy" (2007) and "Using Spiritual Disciplines in Clinical Supervision" (2007) in the *Journal of Psychology and Christianity*. He is associate editor of the *Journal of Psychology and Christianity*, contributing editor of the *Journal of Psychology and Theology*, and editorial consultant for the *Journal of Spiritual Formation and Soul Care*. Tan is an active member in the American Psychological Association (APA), where he is also a fellow; the Canadian Psychological Association; the Christian Association for Psychological Studies; and the American Association of Christian Counselors. He served as president of Division 36 (Psychology of Religion) of the APA from 1998 to 1999. He is also a recipient of the Distinguished Member Award from the Christian Association for Psychological

Studies (CAPS), the Gary R. Collins Award for Excellence in Christian Counseling from the American Association of Christian Counselors, and the William C. Bier Award for Outstanding and Sustained Contributions to the Applied Psychology of Religion from Division 36 of the APA. Tan is senior pastor of First Evangelical Church Glendale in Glendale, California. His areas of expertise include cognitive-behavioral therapy of anxiety, anger and depression, behavioral medicine/health psychology, paraprofessional/lay counseling, cross-cultural psychology and counseling, integration of psychology and the Christian faith, spiritual disciplines and mental health, the Holy Spirit and counseling, religious psychotherapy, and Christian psychology.

**Everett L. Worthington, Ph.D.**, is professor of psychology at Virginia Commonwealth University. He is also a licensed clinical psychologist in Virginia. He has published over 25 books and over 250 articles and scholarly chapters, mostly on forgiveness, marriage and family topics. He frequently discusses forgiveness, marriage and family in media. He is the current president of the American Psychological Association Division 36 (Psychology of Religion and Spirituality), and a fellow of the American Psychological Society.

**Linda M. Wagener, Ph.D.**, Fuller Seminary, is the associate dean for the School of Psychology at Fuller Theological Seminary. She also teaches courses on clinical work with youth. Wagener is committed to exploring the relationship of moral and spiritual development to adolescent well-being and the study and practice of human flourishing. Wagener's work on adolescent well-being has been published in various scholarly journals, including *Applied Developmental Science,* the *Journal of Psychology and Christianity,* and *Christian Counseling Today.* She is coeditor of the recently published *Handbook of Spiritual Development in Childhood and Adolescence.* She is a member of the American Psychological Association, the Society for Research in Child Development, and the Society for Research in Adolescence, and has presented research findings at their meetings. Wagener also serves as a delegate of the National Council of Schools and Programs of Professional Psychology. As codirector for the Center for Research and Child and Adolescent Development at Fuller, Wagener gives leadership to various research projects that center particularly on positive youth development. One of these is the Fuller Youth Initiative (FYI), a major project that seeks to identify critical intervention strategies for youth at risk of violence and other destructive behaviors. The FYI research was funded by a grant of nearly $2.8 million from the U.S. Department of Justice's Office of Juvenile Justice and Delinquency Prevention. Her areas of expertise include spiritual and moral development, positive youth development and human flourishing.

**Mark A. Yarhouse, Psy.D.**, is the Hughes Endowed Chair of Christian Thought in Mental Health Practice and Professor of Psychology at Regent University in Virginia Beach, Virginia, where he is a core faculty member in the doctoral program in clinical psychology. Yarhouse has spent several years promoting dialogue between people who view the topic of sexual identity differently. In 2000 he chaired a groundbreaking symposium at the American Psychological Association's annual convention that brought together gay psychologists and conventionally religious psychologists to discuss common ground in treatment options for persons sorting out sexual and religious identity conflicts. He chaired similar symposia (dialogues between professionals who represent different communities) at the APA on the many meanings of marriage (among different religions and among various groups within the gay community), services for adolescents experiencing sexual identity confusion, and a recently proposed sexual identity therapy framework.